Designing and Managing Urban Railways

Designing and Managing Urban Railways

Editors:

Piers Connor, Nigel G. Harris and Felix Schmid

First published 2015

ISBN 978-0-952-9997-5-1

Published by

The University of Birmingham

Edgbaston, Birmingham B15 3TT, UK

and

A & N Harris

43a Palace Square, London SE19 2LT, UK

Printer

Hobbs the Printers Ltd. Registered Office: Brunel Road, Totton,
Hampshire SO40 3WX, UK

RESEARCH LED EDUCATION AT THE UNIVERSITY OF BIRMINGHAM

The interdisciplinary Birmingham Centre for Railway Research and Education (BCRRE) has brought together researchers of the Schools of Civil Engineering, of Electronic, Electrical and Computer Engineering, of Metallurgy and Materials and of Geography, united by an interest in improving the performance and sustainability of railways. They are engaged on research into: wheel-rail interactions, aerodynamics, meteorology, railway capacity modelling, data mining and remote conditioning monitoring systems that use advanced algorithms to achieve lower maintenance cost.

Programmes of postgraduate studies in Railway Systems Engineering and in Railway Risk and Safety Management allow participants to acquire the skills and know-how to become recognised experts in the railway domain. The Master of Research (MRes) programme in Railway Systems Integration prepares participants for research careers. Taught blocks are available as part of Continuous Professional Development.

The education and research connections are complemented by relationships with private companies, government bodies and regulatory authorities.

Please contact Mrs. Joy Grey (j.grey@bham.ac.uk, 0121 414 4342) for further information about postgraduate courses and Prof. Felix Schmid (f.schmid@bham.ac.uk) to enquire about research.
RSEI, BCRRE, Gisbert Kapp, University of Birmingham, B15 2TT.

The University of Birmingham encourages equality of opportunity for all and offers railway engineering studies as part of its provision of higher education in a research-led environment.

UNIVERSITY^OF BIRMINGHAM

Contents

CONTENTS

List of Figures

List of Tables

Preface

Rail transportation is widely recognised as the most ecologically efficient and cost effective system for mass transit in the urban and suburban environment. This book has been prepared to provide transport planners, students, engineers, operators, city authorities and administrators with a textbook that offers a wide coverage of the requirements for the development, design, building, operation, staffing and maintenance of suburban and urban railway systems.

The work has its origins in an earlier book, 'Planning Passenger Railways', by Nigel G. Harris and E. W. Godward (Editors), Transport Publishing Company, Glossop, 1992, that is now out of print. This new book has been written by a wide range of experts from many different areas of the transport business. The different structures and systems used for the railway are covered and how these systems fit and operate together are discussed in various chapters. The need for good design and maintenance is emphasised and separate chapters show how aesthetics and engineering can be integrated, as is the need for good communications systems. Overall, the systems nature of the railway requires a holistic view, which this book aims to provide.

Glossary

A

AC	Alternating Current
AEIF	Association Europénne pour l'Interopéabilité Ferroviaire
AGT	Automated Guided Transit
AGV	Automotrice Grande Vitesse
AT	Auto Transformer (AC electrification scheme)
ATC	Automatic Train Control
ATP	Automatic Train Protection
AWS	Automatic Warning System

B

BCRRE	Birmingham Centre for Railway Research and Education
BT	Booster Transformer (AC electrification scheme)

C

CENELEC	European Committee for Electrotechnical Standardisation
CIS	Customer Information System
CSS	Customer Satisfaction Survey

D

DC	Direct Current
DMU	Diesel Multiple Unit

DSD	Driver's Safety Device

E

EIA	Environmental Impact Assessment
EIRENE	European Integrated Railway Radio Enhanced Network
EMC	Electro-Magnetic Compatibility
EMU	Electric Multiple Unit
ERTMS	European Railway Train Management System
ESPOO	Informal name for Convention on Environmental Impact Assessment in a Transboundary Context
ETCS	European Train Control System

G

GIS	Geographical Information Systems
GSM-R	Global System for Mobile Communications - Railway
GTO	Gate Turn Off thyristor

H

HS1	High Speed One - British high speed rail route between London and the Channel Tunnel.
HS2	High Speed Two - Proposed British high speed rail route between London and the Midlands and North.

I

IGBT	Integrated Gated Bi-polar Transistor

L

LC (filter)	An inductor-capacitor (LC) filter
LCH	Lost Customer Hours
LGV	Lignes à Grande Vitesse (High Speed Lines)
LIS	Line Information Specialist

| LMA | Limit of Movement Authority |
| LU | London Underground |

M

MCDM	Multi Criteria Decision Making
MM	Midland Metro (Birmingham, UK, tramway system)
MSS	Mystery Shopper Survey

N

| NET | Nottingham Express Transit |
| NSE | Network South East (Former railway management area for London and suburbs) |

O

| OHLE | OverHead Line Equipment |
| ORR | Office of Rail & Road (UK government appointed regulatory body) |

P

PHP	Passenger Help Points
PPHPD	Passengers Per Hour Per Direction
POM	Passenger Operated [ticket] Machine
PSR	Permanent Speed Restriction
PTI	Platform Train Interface
PWM	Pulse Width Modulation

R

RAMS	Reliability, Availability, Maintainability and Safety
RP	Revealed Preference
RTI	Real Time Information

S

SCR	Station Control Room
SCWP	Stray Current Working Party (for electric tramways and railways)
SIS	Staff Information Survey
SP	Stated Preference
SPA	Swept Path Analysis
SPAD	Signal Passed At Danger

T

TfL	Transport for London
TGV	Train à Grande Vitesse
TPWS	Train Protection & Warning System
TRB	Transportation Research Board (of the United States)
TSI	Technical Standards for Interoperability

U

UIC	International Union of Railways (Translated from French)

V

VCS	Vehicle Control Systems
VDE	Vehicle Dynamic Envelope
VoIP	Voice over Internet Protocol
VoT	Value of Time
VVVF	Variable Voltage Variable Frequency

Chapter 1 Railway Systems Engineering and Operations

by Felix Schmid & Piers Connor

1.1 Modes of Transport and their Performance

Before we consider urban and suburban railways in detail, it is essential to understand the basics of the rail mode of transport and the relationships between the various systems that make up the railway. A major requirement of a successful railway operation is a properly structured and integrated system approach to its design, construction, operation and maintenance. Without these ingredients, the railway cannot function effectively and cannot offer its customers an efficient service. In this chapter, the authors examine the components of a railway system and show how these components must be integrated to provide a successful operation.

The transport of people and goods is generally perceived as a negative but necessary economic activity. It is, in effect, a distress purchase. Passengers have to buy travel in order to complete another activity. All modes and forms of transport play essential roles in logistics, commuting and long distance business travel. Only in some sectors of the tourist industry does the journey itself form an objective.

In contrast to road transport, the rail mode is generally suited to medium- and large-scale flows of goods and people since the life cycle cost of even a basic railway system is high. Only water borne transport and pipelines can handle larger flows than railways.

1

Another important feature is the difference in first cost: users of private transport, whether for passengers or goods, tend to make a big initial investment while the cost of maintenance and fuel is relatively low. The marginal price is therefore low. Providers of public transport services, on the other hand, have to recover their initial investment through fares and charges. The user of public transport thus tends to perceive a high unit cost. The effect of this on railways' competitiveness is pronounced since they are responsible, in an all-encompassing manner, for the quality of the interfaces between their infrastructure, the power supply and the means of carriage, that is, the rolling stock.

A railway operator pays for the initial construction of the infrastructure as well as its maintenance, renewal and later upgrades. There is rarely any possibility for sharing the cost with other users and mandatory standards for safety result in additional charges on the infrastructure, which are largely independent of usage. This has a particularly damaging effect during periods of economic downturn. Such a situation does not generally apply to operators of road, water and air traffic.

The infrastructure of a railway includes the structures, permanent way, power supply, stations, control systems, signalling and level crossings. The rolling stock includes locomotives, multiple units, coaches and freight vehicles, including their propulsion subsystems. The management of the interfaces provides a substantial degree of control over the quality of the assets but it also involves risk: railway infrastructures, for example, were largely built during a period when individual railways were inward looking and thus only a minimum level of standardisation or commonality was enforced. As a result, rail transport has to cope with many barriers inhibiting free movement and has thus lost market share to more flexible road transport. The investment required for updating the large railway asset base Europe-wide can only be justified in situations where long-term traffic growth is guaranteed.

Today, following the implementation of European Community Directive 91/440, many railway operators no longer have direct control over the infrastructure they use. All the same, they are entirely dependent on its specification, quality and availability. Instead of direct control over this essential resource, railway undertakings now have to rely on contractual arrangements. In this situation, only modern approaches to systems design and management allow railways to be successful in the long term, particularly since competing modes are striving to be as environmentally friendly as the railways.

1.2 A Brief History of Railways

Railways were not 'invented' but evolved out of wagon-ways built of tram-plates (L-shaped plates on stone blocks) linking mines and quarries to canals. Even the 'standard gauge' of railways predates the first stone, wooden and pig-iron rails: 1435mm (4ft 8^1/$_2$ins) corresponds to the distance between the ruts of Roman roads, which were a consequence of the standardisation of the distance between wheels throughout the Roman empire.

Most railways existing today were built on a private basis in the 19th century, when labour and other resources were relatively cheap, to satisfy particular traffic flows. In many countries, the railways acted both as catalysts for industrialisation and for technological education. Throughout Europe, the private railways were regulated to avoid exploitation of monopoly power. With the exception of Britain, railways in Europe were nationalised in the early 1900s, either to increase state control of transport provision or to prevent wholesale abandonment of socially necessary services. In Britain, the railways were nationalised in 1948 to allow the rehabilitation of a railway network ravaged by the effects of the Second World War.

Unlike the United States, where railways are now largely freight dominated, Europe is the domain of the mixed traffic railway, where there are many potential conflicts between different train types. From the 1960s onwards, the desire to create faster journey times in order to enable rail to compete with the rapidly developing car and air modes, created capacity and compatibility problems on the mixed traffic railway. National railways addressed these problems through investment in major new railway lines (TGV-SudEst in France, Direttissima in Italy) and multi-tracking to separate traffic types.

Sweden satisfied the requirements of European Union Directive 91/440 by creating a state-owned infrastructure manager, Banverket, and by awarding operating contracts to its State Railway (SJ) and to other organisations. In Britain, the infrastructure was privatised as a separate company,

Railtrack (now known as Network Rail), while train operations were franchised on a line by line basis. Other governments have chosen less radical approaches to reorganisation but the need to reduce operating subsidies to railways has resulted in staff reductions and outsourcing almost everywhere. Cost reduction has also resulted in abandoned and simplified infrastructures throughout the European Union and in the Eastern European countries preparing for membership of the Union.

During this process, corporate knowledge and skills have been lost or transferred to much smaller private sector entities. In one form or another, this pattern of privatisation has now spread world wide. In parallel with it, but not necessarily because of it, there has been an increase in traffic that has, in some countries, put stress on the available capacity.

The safe, dependable and economic operation of railways can thus no longer be reliant on the excess capacity that was available in the system in the 1970s and 1980s but must be based on the optimum use of people, technologies and organisational methods. In systems engineering terms this can be seen as the creation of dependability, that is a combination of reliability and availability. Dependable operations enhance the predictability of the train service and thus increase the attractiveness of the rail mode of transport. Dependability also reduces the need for standby resources, in terms of both staff and equipment, and thus leads to major economies.

1.3 Characteristic Features of the Rail Mode of Transport

The interface between vehicles and infrastructure for road transport is basic and flexible, thanks to the freedom to steer in two dimensions. Pneumatic tyres offer low stiffness, good damping performance and high levels of adhesion under normal operating conditions. Government regulations are limited to the minimum: length, width, height, axle-load and tyre tread depth. The physical interfaces between infrastructure and planes in air transport are even less constraining although, in most countries, there are demanding government regulations for airlines and the management of air traffic. Other standards, such as pollution limits, apply to all modes of transport.

Drivers of cars, lorries and buses create a speed dependent virtual space around their vehicle and may adapt their speed according to the characteristics of the invisible boundary of the space and of the speeds and expected behaviours of other traffic partners. Air traffic controllers allocate slots in corridors to commercial aircraft operating in congested areas, that is, individual volumes of air space. Like ships they maintain a distance from other planes using radar—in effect an extension of line-of-sight operation. Private planes use non-controlled air space by line-of-sight, if necessary extending the visible horizon using radar.

In contrast to these modes of transport, railways rely on the operation of infrastructure based equipment to set up the correct path at junctions between origin and destination. At a macroscopic level, trains are essentially single degree of freedom devices that can move in three dimensions along an alignment fixed by an infrastructure or track. Infrastructure elements of time-variable geometry are required to choose the appropriate route for a train. In legal terms, all forms of transport requiring guidance are regulated by government agencies; in the UK this is Her Majesty's Railway Inspectorate (HMRI), a part of the Office of Rail Regulation (ORR). In their definition, guided transport includes railways using the conventional steel wheel/steel rail arrangement, metro-systems using tyres on steel or concrete beams, monorails and any magnetic levitation system. The present chapter though, is generally focused on traditional suburban and suburban railways.

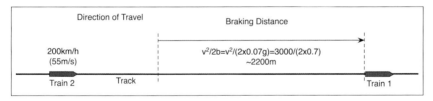

Figure 1.1: *Typical Braking Characteristic of a Main Line Train. F. Schmid.*

1.4 The Interface between Vehicle and Infrastructure

A narrowly defined interface between infrastructure and rolling stock differentiates the rail mode of transport from other modes. This close 'steel on steel' relationship provides accurate guidance and low friction. However, it is not only the source of the main strengths but also one of the main weaknesses of the mode as the following list shows:

1. The accurate guidance by the rails minimises the space requirement and eliminates steering but it reduces flexibility when compared with cars, heavy goods vehicles, aircraft and shipping.

2. Changing direction and overtaking are only possible in places where the infrastructure is equipped with variable shape elements, points, which require special control methods and maintenance.

3. Because of the limited flexibility of the infrastructure, train operation must be based on a conflict free timetable, agreed between all parties in advance, with adequate recovery time.

4. The two steel surfaces of the wheel-rail interface not only provide low friction and thus good efficiency but they also create low adhesion, a major problem in climbing hills and accelerating and braking trains. A typical braking situation is shown in Figure 1.1. Values for the coefficient of friction used in braking calculations range from $\mu=0.03$ to 0.15, resulting in deceleration rates of 0.03g to 0.15g for steel on steel while it is possible to achieve 0.25g for rubber on steel.

5. Long braking distances caused by the limited adhesion available result in a need for extensive space separation, headway constraints and the need for complex control systems.

6. In the case of a component failure, the guidance characteristic of the track can make an accident with severe consequences unavoidable.

7. The physical interface exhibits high stiffness and low damping and the two surfaces must thus be maintained to a very good standard. Rubber-tyred metros have a less demanding relationship between track and vehicle, thanks to the inherently resilient wheels.

8. The high pressure, longitudinal forces and lateral forces existing in the contact patch between rail and wheel create wear and fatigue. As a consequence, an elaborate standards framework has evolved for all aspects of rail transport.

9. The accurate guidance of the trajectory of trains allows the use of electricity for propulsion since it makes current collection arrange-

6

ments relatively straightforward. Electro-magnetic compatibility issues (EMC) must not be neglected though.

As demonstrated in *'Wheel-Rail Best Practice Handbook'* (ed. F. Schmid, 2010), managing the wheel-rail interface and the railway itself requires good co-operation between all the partners in the system, from rolling stock designers through to infrastructure maintainers. The parties must understand exactly the factors that determine the performance of the system as a whole and must contribute to its safe and efficient operation.

The railway requires real time control of the whole system because it relies on variable geometry track elements (points or turnouts) for route selection. As a result, since stopping distances are normally longer than the line of sight, means of signalling the current limit of movement authority (LMA) to the train must be provided. Again, this requires intense co-operation between technical personnel and, in this case, train operators, dispatchers and signalling staff. Operating decisions are usually highly constrained by the availability of infrastructure, rolling stock and staff and should only be taken by people with a thorough understanding of the system as a whole.

Unlike road transport, railways and air transport are highly regulated industries, throughout Europe. Safety and reliability issues and the associated government regulations impact strongly on the relationships between the people involved in designing, financing, building, operating and maintaining railways. Interoperability between railways, both within a country and across national borders, requires far higher degrees of co-ordination than cross border traffic using cars and trucks. In Europe also, freight traffic frequently mixes with passenger traffic and this must be carefully managed to maintain the punctuality of the passenger services.

The Association Europénne pour l'Interopéabilité Ferroviaire (AEIF—translates as European Association for Railway Interoperability), for example, has drawn up a number of standards for the interoperability of high speed services that deal with issues like supply voltages and the station to train interface. More detailed standards are provided by CENELEC (the European Committee for Electrotechnical Standardisation).

Type of Railway	Passengers / h & direction	Passengers per Vehicle	Right of Way Ownership	Commercial Speed	Performance in Traffic	Other Issues
Main Line Railways	5-25,000	80	100%	60-200	Good	
RER and S-Bahn (regional rail)	8-35,000	140-210	100%	40-70	Excellent	Separate from Freight
Heavy Rapid Transit	10-40,000	140-280	100%	25-60	Good	Level Access
Automated light transit	8-15,000	50-150	100%	20-50	Very Good	
Light Metro / Pre-Metro	6-20,000	110-250	30-100%	20-45	Good	Cost
Light Rail	6-20,000	110-250	40-80%	18-40	Fair to Good	Signalling
Tramways	4-12,000	100-200	0-40%	12-20	Unreliable	Track Brakes
High tech bus, trolleybus and bus	3-7000	30-100	0-30%	10-15	Poor, Unreliable	Flexibility of Routing
People Movers and Ultra Light Rail	1-3000	25-70	0-20%	10-15	Unreliable	Battery, Fly-wheel, etc.

Figure 1.2: *A table showing types of typical passenger railways. F. Schmid.*

8

1.5 Types of Passenger and Freight Railways

There are many approaches to the classification of passenger railways, but the most commonly used categorisation differentiates between light rail, metros and heavy rail, as shown in Figure 1.2. This division is independent of track gauge, methods of electrification and train control but relates to capacity and method of operation. Commercial speed, headway, vehicle capacity and train lengths determine the system capacity and figures given in the table are indicative only and vary widely throughout the world. The Tuen Mun Light Rail System in Hong Kong, for example, shares many characteristics of tramways but offers the capacity of a heavy metro system due to the high levels of loading of the wide vehicles. Similarly, the Sneltram in the Amsterdam suburbs operates at RER/s-bahn type speeds thanks to its exclusive high speed right of way.

1.6 The Systems Approach to Designing Railways

When designing new lines or new services, railway managers have traditionally started out with the definition of a demand-based or a resource (operationally) based timetable. Either approach results in less than optimal operations since transport demand and resource configuration are both multi-parameter factors.

Demand for transport is a function of economic activity and the performance of competing modes. Passengers and shippers evaluate their options using a number of criteria, including access, waiting and travel time, fare paid, comfort etc. Operators must therefore undertake an extensive user-requirements capture, which can then be translated into the specification for the new railway or the new services. Conflicting requirements may result in the need to operate more than one service between an origin and a destination, potentially bringing an economic advantage. In general though, a purely demand-based timetable is not affordable since it requires resources that are only used for a small proportion of the time.

In general, resources such as infrastructure and rolling stock will have been designed or acquired as a consequence of the railway's history or to cope with operational requirements rather than passengers' and shippers' needs. The availability of resources therefore determines the ability to operate services and indirectly affects their cost. A resource-based timetable will only ever be able to satisfy a proportion of the market requirements. Regardless of its genesis or the design methods used, the timetable becomes the objective function that must be satisfied by the operation of the railway. This contrasts with the on-demand nature of operation of the private car and of systems such as the Rockwell Industries personal people movers.

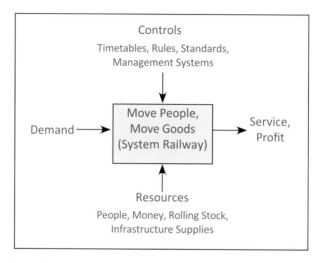

Figure 1.3: *A diagram demonstrating the concept of the system railway. F. Schmid.*

The conventional approach to the design of railway services neglects many relationships and is thus not suited to today's complex transport markets where many different players compete to satisfy a limited demand. The level 0 IDEFØ diagram (Figure 1.3) presents a view of the railway as an activity or process that has inputs, outputs, controls and resources or mechanisms. Based on the available transport demand (input) and the required characteristics of the output (the quality of the transport product and the profit level) it is possible to define the level of resources required and to identify the appropriate methods of control. The diagram in Figure 1.4, expands this general overview to include the context of the transport system as a whole and the way in which a particular subsystem affects its own demand level.

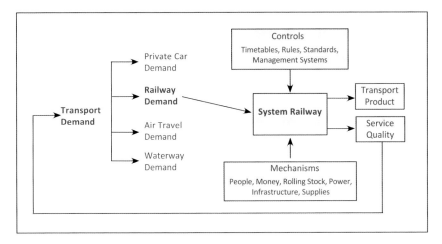

Figure 1.4: *A diagram demonstrating the creation of demand for the system railway. F. Schmid.*

The need for transport is a derived demand and does not necessarily favour a particular mode. Service improvements yield additional demand for the railways only if the service satisfies customers' needs while profits can only be generated if the cost of providing the appropriate service level is in line with the potential revenue streams. The quality level of the system output, shown separately in the diagram, may be assessed against one or several criteria. These include the comfort and ride quality offered, the fares charged by other modes, and, perhaps most importantly, the promise made in the timetable that provides the control function for the system.

As shown in Figure 1.4 a railway organisation can thus be viewed as a system that creates a transport product in response to a demand. To create the transport product, railways require both staff and physical resources, such as an infrastructure, rolling stock and power. In this quality control loop, many parameters vary rapidly, often as result of environmental changes.

Economic change may influence transport volumes while societal change can affect customers' perception of journey quality. All suppliers in the transport market place must therefore adapt their products continuously to the new demands. This in itself changes the competitive environment

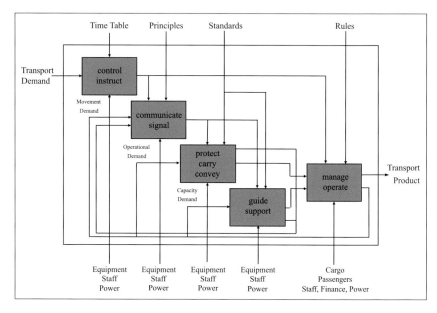

Figure 1.5: *A graphic showing the second level relationships of the system railway. F. Schmid.*

for each player and increases the pressure to adapt to new situations. Railways are inherently disadvantaged in this respect due to their high fixed costs and the long planning horizons required by large organisations. In many European countries, this realisation has led to the privatisation or regionalisation of railways, with most progress in Germany and Sweden.

Figure 1.5 offers a more detailed view of the system railway, showing the different subsystems with their inputs and outputs. Subsystems must interact in order to produce the desired output of the system as a whole. The diagram does not show the feedback loops necessary for successful operation; however, these will typically result in actions taken at the level of the control function. Cargo and passengers, as well as finance, are shown as resources in this diagram since they must be available in a timely fashion if the operations function is to be able to produce the final output, passenger and tonne/km.

1.7 Elements of the System Railway

Figure 1.5 shows how the system railway includes a number of subsystems, each with a specific function. A function can be provided in a number of different ways and the choice of technology or methods largely determines the first cost and whole life cost. All the functions are closely linked and must be selected in line with the overall system specification so as to provide the correct quality of service at an appropriate cost. The grouping of functions into subsystems as described below reflects a modern approach to systems engineering for railways.

1.8 Control: Safety, Scheduling & Timing

The system railway must be controlled to operate in accordance with the timetable. This provides the yardstick against which its performance is measured. The most basic performance measures for a railway are punctuality, that is, the percentage of trains arriving within a given limit after the scheduled time and reliability, that is, the percentage of trains in the timetable that ran. However, the system railway must also be measured against the standard criteria applicable to any business, that is, staff productivity in unit-km/person, resource utilisation, incident rate per unit-km, return on capital employed, return on assets etc.

At the highest level, the control function defines the safety requirements of the system and of its component parts or subsystems. These are implemented largely during the system design stage and controlled through the management processes in the operations function. The safety demands placed on a railway are high because of the inevitability of an accident in the case of a system failure.

At the next level, the control function translates the timetable into resource demands for rolling stock and track. Based on the reliability of the equipment, this leads to both short-term and long-term availability requirements for motive power, vehicles and carriages, as well as for tracks, passing loops and sidings, to deliver the service to the right standard. Availability and maintainability together then determine the detailed resource requirements, that is, the number of trains etc. needed to cover the services to be run, taking into account additional trains retained for maintenance purposes.

The top two levels of the control function are thus related to the RAMS (reliability, availability, maintainability, safety) requirement of the system as a whole. The third level of the control function deals with the translation of the timetable into control actions for rolling stock and infrastructure elements. Depending on the level of intelligence vested in these subsystems, the control actions will need to be more or less detailed and may cover substantial periods of time ahead. Most of the control processes require substantial databases and appropriate management tools.

1.9   Communicate: Radio, Telephone & Signalling

The operation of a railway requires the transfer of large amounts of information including safety-critical instructions and commercial data. Traditionally, these were separated into digital and analogue signals of different levels of criticality. Even the cable links to semaphore signals could be considered as early data transmission systems.

As the requirements of railways became more demanding, more and more transmission systems were provided. These included secure voice communications links between drivers and signal box or control centre staff (by radio and telephone), safety critical links to signals, track circuits and points, data links for ticketing and performance management systems. Information could be transmitted electrically in an analogue or digital format or as visual indications for drivers and signallers.

Today, such divisions are no longer appropriate since most communications are based on complex protocols such as the ISO seven-layer model where the physical transmission process is of no concern to the user. There are standard arrangements to cover any communications needs including the GSM-R standard developed by International Union of Railways (UIC) with the European Integrated Railway Radio Enhanced Network (EIRENE).

1.10   Guide and Carry: Alignment, Tracks, Sidings & Points

The construction of the track and its substructure determines the permissible axle-loads and all-up weights of trains. Track gauge, curvature

Figure 1.6: *A High Speed Train on a long distance suburban service in the countryside of England near Didcot. Infrastructure improvements and train designs for higher speeds over the last 30 years have allowed some commuting distances in Britain to increase to over 100 miles. P. Connor*

and super-elevation (or cant) determine the speed of trains on plain line while the form of construction and radii of points (or turnouts) determine the speed at which trains can change tracks. Since civil works often represent more than 50% of the cost of a project there is a clear benefit of studying carefully all possible tradeoffs. An example is the loading gauge, which not only affects the size of tunnels but can also act as a barrier to inter-modal freight operations or double-deck trains. In Great Britain, for example, the loading gauge is very restricted and the idea of double-deck passenger trains is often put forward as a solution to line capacity issues but is impractical because of the limited space available.

1.11 Design Choices

The alignment and, to a lesser extent, the track gauge of a railway determine both its capacity and performance. Traditionally, narrow gauge track has been chosen for low cost railway solutions to allow the choice of small radii of curvature. Such a choice minimises the cost of civil engineering works but reduces the ride quality and the maximum stable speed of operation. Gradients and curvature define the maximum mass and length of trains and influence the acceleration and deceleration rates, thus affecting headways and journey times. Travel times between centres and major agglomerations form one of the important factors in determining the attractiveness of a railway service. However, an increase in top speed over part or all of the distance is not necessarily the best approach to reducing journey times. In most situations it is more effective to reduce the spectrum of speeds, that is, to eliminate as many stretches of low speed operation as possible. Customers perceive reductions in the number of speed restrictions very positively. Infrastructure improvement has been the orthodox way of achieving better performance.

1.12 Ownership Arrangements

Any change to the physical infrastructure of the railway incurs large costs and cannot generally be financed from operating revenue, because so many of the benefits (e.g. reductions in travelling time and environmental improvements) are unpriced. Some European governments therefore treat railway infrastructures in the same way as roads and canals, that is, as national economic assets. In Sweden, the track and structures of the railways were transferred to the state-owned company Banverket, which receives direct government funding to improve the railway assets. Operators pay access charges to the government.

In Britain, the infrastructure of the national railway company, British Rail, was sold to the private sector company Railtrack in order to attract private funding and to establish a commercial approach to the provision of railway services. When Railtrack collapsed following the Hatfield accident of October 2000, Railtrack was replaced by Network Rail, an organisation subsequently retaken as a government asset. Any funding for socially or environmentally beneficial schemes is channelled through an access charge regime where the operator obtains a subsidy from the government if a service is not conventionally profitable.

1.13 Convey: Carriages, Vehicles & Motive Power

The optimal choice of rolling stock is a function of the customer needs and the constraints imposed by the infrastructure and funds. It is the objective of the customer and of the railway to maximise the payload. However, this may conflict with the track gauge and the loading gauge. There is also a trade-off between volume and mass. A further consideration is the convenience of users, both of passengers and shippers. On some passenger railways, level access to vehicles is assured by means of high platforms while tramways and light railways are moving towards low floor sections suitable for low platforms or kerb entrances. Although the latter approach minimises infrastructure cost it leads to space constraints for suspension systems and to complex running gear.

Complex suspension systems may also be required to achieve a given ride quality on poor quality track. It will be necessary to use a life cycle costing technique to test whether lightweight construction can save energy overall. Crashworthiness of vehicles may be an important issue for railways where there is no Automatic Train Protection.

A steeply graded infrastructure reduces land-take and the cost of civil works but results in a need for high power/weight ratios in terms of motive power and in the requirement for high peak rating of the power supply arrangements. The decision on the choice of traction system though, must not be based simply on a route specific comparison of diesel and electric power options but on economic, technical, environmental and ergonomic issues. Reliability and availability considerations must also be taken into account when making engineering decisions about such systems.

1.14 Supply of Traction Power

The choice of power supply is critical when designing a new railway or re-equipping an existing system since it influences infrastructure cost, system flexibility and environmental impact. Electric power can be generated away from the point of use, essential in the case of nuclear, combined cycle (gas and coal) and hydro-electric power plants. Thermal generation of electricity in power stations however, is not necessarily environmentally sound because the overall efficiency, including transmission losses, is generally less than 40%.

There is also no need to compromise between the amount of fuel carried and the operating range. The overload capability of electric motors (expressed as the one hour rating) is very high and therefore reduces the overall size of the power conversion equipment. Better use can be made of this capability by managing overload control by on-board computers. In general, electric traction is the preferred choice for urban and suburban railways.

Traditionally, the choice of electric power for new passenger services has been automatic in situations where overhead electrification already existed or where a small amount of add-on electrification provided the possibility of a fully electric service. Recent worries about the economic and environmental benefits of new electrification and of replacing life expired electricity supply systems have opened up the debate about the best choice of motive power and have moved the discussion from the policy and strategy level to a service by service decision.

The use of diesel power for services running mostly or wholly on electrified lines is no longer viewed as heresy. Norwegian State Railways have demonstrated for many years that is possible to mix diesel operation with electric operation. Diesel Multiple Units (DMUs) are electrically hauled, by Electric Multiple Units (EMUs) or locos, as far as a junction where a non electrified branch line leaves the main line.

1.15   Operate: Managing Personnel and Resources

The management of rail transport is a complex activity that relies on many inputs and that interacts with all the subsystems of the railway. Essentially, the operations function ensures the timely provision of the necessary resources in terms of staff, rolling stock, train paths, the selling of the services and finance. It also deals with partners in multimodal operations and it negotiates with regulatory authorities. The management of railway operations is thus concerned with the management of the interfaces within the limitations set by the physical, regulatory and financial constraints.

1.16   Resource Provision

Assuring the timely provision of resources requires the establishment of a maintenance organisation that satisfies a defined set of RAMS requirements. Reliability is generally measured as the mean time to failure of a system. In the case of railways, failures are normally defined in terms of minutes of delay. Reliability can be improved by using better quality components, introducing redundancy and the application of reliability-centred maintenance techniques.

Availability is measured as the proportion of time a system is ready for service or is being used, against the theoretically possible service period. Availability can be enhanced by extending maintenance intervals, better scheduling and through improved maintainability. Modular subsystems with clearly defined interfaces facilitate fault-finding and allow unit exchanges with minimal downtime, key features of maintainability. However, RAMS issues can only be managed successfully if they are considered as part of the original specification and the design of equipment. It is thus essential that the maintenance organisation be consulted during the procurement stages.

Routine maintenance of rolling stock is generally carried out at night or during off-peak periods. Balanced exams minimise the time vehicles are out of service for the regular inspection of critical subsystems and thus allow better use of maintenance resources. Fewer spare vehicles are needed to cover for equipment being serviced and management effort is reduced thanks to more standardised procedures. Availabilities of 95% are no longer unusual for new locomotives in Britain and lead to dramatic reductions in the first cost of providing the rolling stock for a particular service pattern. To be successful, operators must invest physical resources in depots and management effort in optimising the use of rolling stock.

The desired train paths can be used fully only if the infrastructure is reliable and available. The operations function of an infrastructure provider is responsible for the maintenance and improvement of track and structures. While rolling stock can be maintained away from the operating railway, using spare vehicles, track and infrastructures tend to be too expensive for duplication. Any intervention therefore tends to result in disruption of normal service. Maintenance strategies vary between different operators, e.g., French National Railways arrange maintenance 'windows' lasting several hours as part of the normal timetable, particularly on high speed lines. Other railways, including the Swiss and German administrations, use temporary speed restrictions to work on the infrastructure while trains are passing. They rely on the recovery time built into the schedules of trains to ensure timetable stability.

Keeping the maintenance of rolling stock or infrastructure assets as a core operating skill in-house or relying on contractors with more experience is an important decision for the operator since it affects both the cost and capability of the organisation. Once a decision has been taken to out-source maintenance activities it becomes very difficult to rebuild an in-house strength.

1.17   Managing Staff and Contracts

Historically, the hierarchy of railway staff was modelled on military organisations. On the negative side, each employee had his or her highly specific job description with a rule-book laying down the procedures for carrying out all tasks. On the positive side though, promotion was not limited by paper qualifications. This approach to operations is no longer viable since most railway staff now must be multi-skilled and multifunctional. Much routine work has been automated and staff roles therefore tend to be concerned with the management of non-standard situations and customer care. Staff qualifications are therefore changing rapidly.

Adopting the British model, for example, where the ownership of infrastructure and rolling stock are separate from the train operations function, has brought about much smaller organisations with flatter hierarchies. Under this model, companies buy in most services and the focus on managing large numbers of staff has moved to the management of a complex legal framework. Specialists must often be hired from outside the industry, thus reducing the scope for promotion of existing staff. For example, a train operator's staff can no longer gain experience of infrastructure management or the installation of track.

References

Estournet, G. and H.-D. Pöhls, (1998) SYFERAD - ein neues Konzept für FunkFahrBetrieb auf Nebenstrecken, Signal+Draht, Vol.90, No.4, April 1998.

Ford, R. and D. Haydock, (1992) 'Signalling and Timetabling', in 'Planning Passenger Railways', NG Harris and EW Godward (Editors), Transport Publishing Company, Glossop, 1992.

Harris, N.G. and E.W. Godward (Editors) (1992), Planning Passenger Railways, Transport Publishing Company, Glossop, 1992.

Harris N.G. and E.W. Godward (1997), The Privatisation of British Rail, Railway Consultancy Press, London, 1997.

Jackson, C. and Osman, A.R. (1996), Tilting Trains Spearhead KTM Modernisation, Railway Gazette International, May 1996, pp 269-272.

Meyer, N.(1992), Pendolino-Marketing: Mit Takt und Tempo in neue Märkte, Die Deutsche Bahn, 8/92, August 1992, Hestra Verlag.

Netchen (1998), Digest of UK Energy Statistics, 1997 and NETCEN, 1998, Figures refers to 1996.

Ripley, D., (1989), The Peak Forest Tramway, Locomotion Papers No. 38, The Oakwood Press, Oxford, 1989.

Wegenstein, P, Signaltechnik auf Regionalbahnen der ÖBB, Signal+Draht, Vol.90, No.12, December 1998.

Chapter 2   Defining the Urban Railway

by Felix Schmid & Piers Connor

2.1   What is an urban railway?

The earliest railways were developed as a means of moving coal from mines to ports or factories. Later, they moved into the passenger business, taking people from city to city. By the late 19th Century, cities had become so large in themselves that they were capable of supporting railway systems within their own boundaries and, as a result, urban railways appeared. In many cases they started as tramways, horse-drawn at first and integrated with surface roads, the precursor of what we know today as light rail systems. From the late 1880s, electric tramways were introduced and quickly began to spread to many cities in the developed world. Soon, as surface congestion increased, new routes had to be pushed below ground to become variously known as 'metros' or 'subways'.

In spite of the perception that they are different from 'real' railways, urban lines or metros are very much the same sort of beast. Indeed, in many countries, main line suburban services have moved towards metro style operations with multiple-unit trains, even interval services, reduced seating in favour of large standing areas and peak frequencies of up to 20 trains per hour (tph).

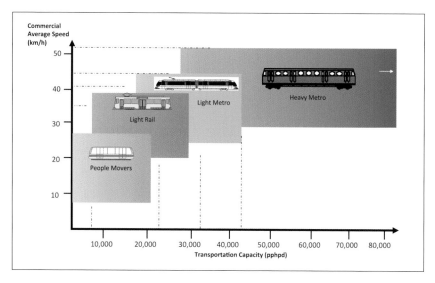

Figure 2.1: *Chart showing the range of urban railway systems. Note the wide range of capacities and speeds covered by the various descriptions used around the world. Capacity is defined as passengers per hour per direction (pphpd) and refers to the peak hour in one direction. Chart after Adtranz.*

Most metro operators work in a high frequency, densely trafficked, high cost, highly politicised atmosphere with expensive equipment, a restrictively maintained infrastructure and, when they occur, service-destroying failure modes. With the consequences of system failures invoking safety degradation, health risks and overcrowding even leading to civil unrest in some countries, operators and engineers must provide cost effective, operable and reliable equipment. For the public, perhaps the only real difference between a metro and a main line operation is in perception. For the operator, they are very similar, just varying in scale (Figure 2.1).

A simple definition of an urban railway might be 'a system that runs a frequency such that the passenger does not require a timetable', which could be described as one that operates at a regular 10 minute headway or less. For the engineer, they are also very similar, but urban railways usually require more equipment because of the denser traffic and have more difficult maintenance and access conditions because of long tunnels and intensive train operations. In this chapter, the urban railway, the suburban route and light rail system are defined, as far as it can be, with some examples.

2.2   Variations on a Theme

There has long been a debate over the meaning of 'light rail', 'heavy metro' and their various derivations. In the authors' view, it is whatever you want to call it. Around the world there are many examples of urban rail systems that use a wide variety of titles, usually politically imposed, but that all have the same objective—the movement of large numbers of people with frequent, regular services offering a 'turn up and go' service. To offer a flavour of the range of systems, Figure 2.1 shows a view of the types of systems available, common names, and ranges of commercial speeds and passenger levels. In reality, London with a maximum of 30,000 passengers per hour per direction (pphpd) and Hong Kong with 80,000 pphpd, both said to operate 'heavy metro' systems, are a long way apart on the passenger capacity scale.

Perhaps the defining descriptions offered here can be summarised by suggesting that 'metro' systems are wholly segregated, whether referred to as light metro or heavy metro, while light rail systems are either partly or wholly integrated with road traffic. There are also mixed route systems known as 'tram-train' where main line and light rail systems use the same tracks.

At the other end of the scale, suburban or commuter networks are invariably run as part of a main line or national railway system. They fall into the urban rail system description as they form an essential part of the economic and social structure of cities as much as any other type of urban rail system and they are often operated under similar frequencies to those of metros and with high passenger loads. Many commuter routes extend into the country areas and small towns that surround major cities, where passengers may be experiencing journeys of over an hour and who will require more on-board services such as catering and lavatory facilities.

25

Figure 2.2: *An example of a people mover system at Changi Airport, Singapore. Such systems are low capacity and usually fully automated and driverless. Many operate on rubber tyred guidance systems with special ground-based electrical power and control lines. They are popular as inter-terminal transport for airports. Photo: Adtranz.*

2.3 People Movers

At the bottom end of the capacity and speed scale are people movers, sometimes referred to as AGTs (Automated Guided Transit) now marketed by the main North American-based manufacturer, Bombardier (Figure 2.2) and others. These systems are popular for connections between airport terminals (Gatwick, Singapore, Frankfurt, Dallas-Fort Worth etc.) and are additionally used in Singapore for local transport around several government-built housing developments to connect them to local metro stations. They are normally constructed on elevated viaducts. The Bombardier type uses a centrally-positioned guidance system, which also carries the 600-volt AC traction supply and the ATC vehicle command transmission system. People movers are invariably rubber-tyred and fully automated, without an on-board attendant. In the absence of on-board attendants, stations are usually equipped with platform edge doors for safety reasons. Similar systems have been supplied by Japanese manufacturers.

26

Figure 2.3: *An example of an integrated light rail system in Nottingham. Here the tramway shares the road with street traffic. Stopping places are built with raised platforms to provide level boarding. Photo: P. Connor.*

2.4 Light Rail

Here we move into the name game, with the liberal interpretation of the word 'light' in the phrase light rail. Perhaps a happier expression would be 'tram' but it is not universally acceptable since, in the US, this refers to a suspended cable-car system and they use the term 'streetcar' for tram. So, it might be concluded that 'light rail' is the modern, international expression for an urban system with medium capacity, using either integrated routes with street traffic (Figure 2.3) or segregated railway formations, sometimes both on the same route. Traction is generally supplied by overhead wire at between 600 and 750v DC and driving is manual. Emergency braking of a high order (2.5m/s^2 compared with 1.4m/s^2 on a totally segregated system) is required to match road traffic conditions.

Maximum line speeds of light rail systems in Britain are between 60 and 100 km/h, with acceleration rates of 1.2 m/s^2 and braking rates of up to 2.2 m/s^2. On integrated routes, trams must adhere to road traffic speed limits where they share the public highway with cars, lorries and other traffic. Average speeds (including stops) are sometimes as low as 20 km/h when operating on alignments shared with cars but can be as high as 40 km/h when running on segregated tracks.

Railway type signalling is usually confined to the segregated sections but some priority signalling is provided with road traffic signals. Light rail systems are popular in German-speaking and eastern European areas and have been re-introduced in the UK and France over the last 15 years. More are planned or hoped for, being seen as a means of reducing traffic conges-

Figure 2.4: *STAR light metro system in Kuala Lumpur, Malaysia. Routes are fully segregated. Traction supply is through a bottom contact third rail. Photo: Adtranz*

tion by providing an environmentally acceptable and attractive alternative. Nottingham has been particularly successful in this respect.

2.5 Light Metro

The light metro form of urban railway has become popular in the last 20 years or so. One of the first examples in the world was the Newcastle-based Tyne & Wear Metro, opened in 1980. Docklands Light Rail (DLR) in London is really a light metro, although its expansion and increasing train lengths are realistically moving it into a heavier category. Another such system is the STAR light metro system in Kuala Lumpur, Malaysia (Figure 2.4). Such systems operate on segregated routes, under normal railway regulation with fixed signalling and some form of train protection. They may be regarded as a cheap metro solution, where rolling stock and infrastructure is not necessarily built to main line railway standards. Structures can be lighter and curves sharper than on main line railways or heavy metro systems. Routes can be underground, at grade or elevated, although the expense of lengthy underground construction will normally only be economic if the traffic levels are in the heavy metro category.

Traction supply can be overhead (Figure 2.5) or third rail (Figure 2.4). Trains are generally of light construction and some are little more than adapted street tram designs. Indeed, some of the older DLR vehicles have been converted into light rail street vehicles for use in Germany.

28

A few light rail systems have been expanded into new areas by being integrated with mainline railway systems. In Germany and the US, route sharing between light rail and main line systems has been introduced on a small scale. For some heavy metro systems this is not new, having been part of the London Underground operation since inception but for the newer systems, with modern train protection provided, the idea has been seen to work and their success has led to proposals being developed in the UK. They have become known as tram-train systems.

2.6 Tram-Train Systems

The tram-train system is, effectively, a mix of tram and mainline railway, a concept borrowing features of both modes. Tram-trains have attracted some interest in Britain, having been pioneered in Karlsruhe and Saarbrücken in Germany. The rolling stock of tram-train systems is largely modelled on trams but the vehicles are equipped to run on suitable sections of mainline railway, sharing tracks with both passenger and freight trains as necessary.

First generation tram-trains in Germany were standard high-floor trams with a transformer and rectifier installed under the floor, allowing current collection at 600 or 750 V DC on street running sections and 15 kV, 16.7 Hz on mainline railway routes. More modern tram-trains, such as those of the Saarbrücken network, have low floor areas, a feature that is suited to both the low pavement platforms on the street-running sections and the low platforms on the Deutsche Bahn/RFF routes to Saarlouis. Kassel tram-trains have a different, hybrid propulsion system, allowing 600 V DC overhead line operation in town centres and diesel operation on the mainline system.

Generally, tram-train vehicles have lower levels of crashworthiness than main line trains but are equipped with train protection systems that interface with the infrastructure on the shared sections. The better braking performance (up to 2 m/s^2) compensates to some extent for the reduced strength of the vehicles. In Germany, some undertakings use double-block operation to reduce the risk to tram-trains. This reduces line capacity to a limited extent because, normally, there are very few main line services on the routes affected. Tram-trains are particularly effective where a mainline station is some way away from the town centre or where an

Figure 2.5: *Example of a heavy metro line in Hong Kong. The first lines were opened in 1979 and the system has been expanded in stages ever since. These trains have a planning capacity of 2500 passengers and use a 1500v DC overhead traction supply. Photo: Author's collection*

under-used mainline railway is available for part of a route between two urban centres, with a conventional tramway already in existence in one of the centres.

2.7 Heavy Metro

This is the top end of the urban railway market and many systems are built to rigorous standards, often more onerous than main line railway standards, because of their heavy traffic and long sections in tunnel. Many major capital cities have extensive metro systems and some have become iconic, being elevated to a selling point for visitors and prospective businesses, some even becoming tourist attractions. London, Paris, New York, Tokyo and Moscow could be taken to represent the 'big five' of the older systems, while Hong Kong, Singapore, Mexico City and Sao Paulo are representative of the newer systems. All of them employ some form of Automatic Train Protection (ATP) and many have Automatic Train Control (ATC) as standard. Traction supply is mostly 3rd rail with some overhead systems. Operationally, overhead is preferable, allowing evacuation without it being necessary to switch off traction power to the trains but some cities regard the visual aspects along open sections as unacceptable.

The New York City subway provides an example of traditional heavy metro writ large. An extensive and complex network covers the city and its suburbs making it one of the largest in the world. Driving is manual (two-person operation) with fixed block signalling and trainstop protection.

Traction supply is 3rd rail. Trains are long (up to 11 cars) and are of two types, large profile and small profile.

Most lines operate with local (stopping) and express (limited stop) services. Some lines like the No 7 (Flushing) Line have a central, reversible track for peak hour directional express operation. Technology development has been slow due to previous bad experiences with suppliers and budget limitations. In recent years AC traction has been introduced on new trains and, after a lengthy, experimental ATC programme, equipping a second line is in progress.

Hong Kong MTR (Figure 2.5) represents a more recent version of the heavy metro model (first section opened in 1979) and is at the top end of the capacity scale with regular periods of 85,000 pphpd capacity in peak hours. Traction supply is overhead. Trains are large and long with a capacity of 2500 persons (London is generally less than 1000). All lines are equipped with ATC and there is an on-board attendant in the leading cab. A continuous programme of re-equipment of trains and signalling, line extensions and political backing has kept the system in the top segment of the international performance scale for many years.

2.8   Suburban Railways

In this book, the editors have included suburban railways, since they are often operated using the same techniques as urban railways. However, suburban railways invariably use main line routes and main line railway standards and will therefore vary from the specifics used by purpose-built urban systems. Suburban railways were developed for large conurbations, connecting the outlying suburbs with the central areas of the city. Generally, train frequencies are lower than those expected on metros and the passenger will usually require a timetable to aid travel plans.

Some metro systems are combinations of metro and suburban services. The Metropolitan Line of London Underground is a good example where the inner area of the route has a metro type frequency but there are a variety of destinations to outer suburbs at lower frequencies. Regulation of such a service is complex and recovery from service delays difficult to manage. New metro systems should strive to avoid such arrangements.

Maximum line speeds of mainline railways in Britain are between 110 and 200 km/h, with acceleration rates of 0.6 m/s^2 and full service braking rates of up to 1 m/s^2. Average speeds (including stops) can be from 50 km/h on suburban routes to 160 km/h on intercity lines. Trains are designed for high levels of crashworthiness and are protected by sophisticated train control systems. Multiple unit passenger trains have axle loads of up to 15t (metric), while freight wagons and locomotives often have axle loads between 22.5 and 25t.

In Britain, passenger trains normally require platforms that are at a similar level to that of the floor of the vehicle, i.e. about 1m above the top of the rail. This is in contrast to continental European mainline railway practice where platform heights are generally between 20 and 50cm above the top of the rail. Mainline railways are normally built to a standard that allows any train to run on any line, subject to electrification systems being compatible with the traction system on the train. Alignments must be chosen carefully to limit gradients to 25‰ or less and with curve radii that allow running at line speed without causing discomfort to passengers.

2.9 Guided Bus Systems

Guided bus is an intermediate capacity and mid-quality mode of transport. Guided bus systems are advocated as a lower cost alternative to trams and other forms of rail based rapid transit. They use slightly adapted 'standard' buses and their requirement for a special infrastructure, the guide-way, is limited to core sections of a route or network. The concept allows the modified buses to run on ordinary roads in the suburbs and in the city centre, so as to collect and distribute passengers, while running at high speed on a segregated route between distant suburbs and the boundary of the commercial centre of a city. Most such systems have physical guidance by means of guide-wheels running along specially positioned kerbs (kerb guidance) or, in the case of Guided Light Transit (GLT), by means of a central rail in the middle of the dedicated lane.[1]

Guided buses operate by line of sight but junctions with roads are normally protected by standard road traffic signals. Guide-way construction

---

[1]The two commonly known GLT systems are Translohr and TVR

Figure 2.6: *Cambridge guided busway. This is the longest such system in the world at 25km. There is still much controversy over the value of such systems compared with trams. Photo: Scania*

generally requires utility diversions and the scale of work may be compared to that required for the construction of a tramway.

Although Adelaide (1989, 12.1km) in South Australia and Essen (1980, 6.5km) in Germany have successfully operated guided buses for between 20 and 30 years, the mode has not been adopted widely. In Britain, there are guide-way sections for suitably equipped buses in Bradford (2001, 2.3km), Crawley (2004, 1.5km), Ipswich (1995, 0.2km) and Leeds (2001, 2.5km). All these systems are still in operation today whereas the one in Birmingham, for example, has been abandoned. The Cambridgeshire Busway (Figure 2.6) opened in August 2011 and is 25km long. It is the longest such installation in the world and is used by both single and double deck buses run by two different operators.

Chapter 3   Demand-Based Railway Planning

by Nigel G. Harris

3.1   Objectives

This is the first of two chapters providing a summary of railway planning issues and techniques. They concentrate on the transport planning part of this process and therefore exclude the contribution made by estimating engineers required to produce capital and operating costs, or that made by accountants as part of the standard budgeting process.

The purpose of this chapter is to define the three key concepts underlying railway planning, viz. Generalised Cost, Value of Time and Elasticities. It demonstrates the different approaches in demand-based planning (i.e. qualitative or quantitative, aggregate or disaggregate, and Revealed Preference or Stated Preference) and shows how planning fits into the overall business of running a railway. A fuller text giving examples of all methods and the underlying theory is Ortuza & Williemsen (2011).

3.2   The Planning Process

Planning is an iterative process that should be an integral part of running any business, railway or any other organisation(see Figure 3.1). This chapter concentrates on transport planning, which is that part of the process designed to improve the customer interface of a railway. It does not include other business-led decisions regarding purely engineering or administrative elements e.g. whether to source widgets from a different supplier, or to contract out the canteen.

Demand-based planning starts from the premise that the most successful railways run the services that their customers require. Operational considerations are treated separately in the following chapter. Although it is possible to plan a railway solely on demand criteria, or on operational criteria, trade-offs between these extremes inevitably occur. Moreover, as we shall see, there are also trade-offs required within each of these approaches—not all passengers have the same needs, and these may be mutually incompatible.

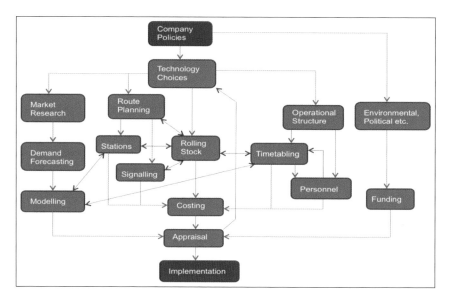

Figure 3.1: *Railway Planning Organisation Chart. Typical linkages and feedbacks shown in red. Source: N G Harris*

The demand-based planning process of a railway includes a number of key areas, including:

- Market research

- Market analysis

- Demand estimation

- Scheme testing and evaluation

Significant management effort in other areas is required to underpin large changes in demand expected to result from demand-based planning improvements (Andersen & Pedersen, 1991).

3.3 Key Concepts

Generalised Cost

Travel is a means to an end. Economically, it is considered to be a disutility—a necessary evil of wanting or needing to do other things such as going to work, shopping, or visiting friends and relatives. There are usually two main elements to this disutility—time and money. Economists have brought these together in the concept of Generalised Cost (GC), which may be understood as an 'index of hassle'. It relates to perceived, not real, time. Algebraically, with GC calculated as a time,

$$GC = f/VOT + b_1 \times A + b_2 \times W + b_3 \times R + n \times I + b_0,$$

where

f:	fare (in money terms)
VOT:	value of time (money per time Ð see below)
b_1, b_2 and b_3:	are parameters or weightings; b_1 and b_2 are normally about 2
A:	access (and egress) time
W:	waiting time
R:	running time (in-vehicle time)
I:	interchange penalty (time—note that this relates solely to the perceived effort on top of the real extra walking and waiting)
n:	number of interchanges undertaken
b_0:	error term, including other elements whose impact is either measured, understood or simply guessed (e.g., train interior decor).

As generalised cost is a negative expression, the importance of this theory is its corollary that the key to stimulating demand is to minimise total generalised cost. Resources should therefore be committed to this end and should not necessarily merely be applied to the situations with the largest current number of passengers.

Value Of Time (VOT)

If Generalised Cost includes both time and monetary elements, then customers can trade them off against each other. The Value Of Time (VOT) is simply the relationship between the two elements, and is usually expressed in £/hour or pence/minute. It varies significantly by journey purpose, and was extensively originally researched by MVA et al (1987).

Elasticities

Customers (whether passenger or freight) respond to different attributes of the service in different ways. Elasticities measure the responsiveness of customers to service attributes. Commonly used is the fares elasticity (e_f), described as:

$$e_f = \frac{proportionate\ change\ in\ demand}{proportionate\ change\ in\ fares}$$

Note that values are negative—ncreases in fares lead to decreases in demand. As fares elasticities differ significantly by journey purpose (and hence by time of day and route), considerable improvements in fares revenue can be had by careful targeting of fares increases (Harris, 1988; Hensher, 1998). Application of across-the-board increases is very unlikely to be the best policy.

Other elasticities are similarly derived. Examples are the generalised cost elasticity (e_{gc}) and the journey time elasticity (e_{jt}), which tends to be more important for longer-distance rail traffic. Also note that elasticities refer to proportionate changes, and are often understood relative to a percentage change in the independent variable. Note that elasticities of parts of generalised cost are merely proportionate to the generalised cost elasticity, i.e.:

$$e_f = e_g \times f/GC$$

Variations in elasticities are driven by three main factors:

- different passengers have different weightings for the different attributes;

- they are also likely to have different values of time, dependent upon their journey purpose;

- the attributes are of differing proportions in different journeys (e.g. Inter-city v metro).

3.4   Market Analysis

Market Research

Details of one's customers are important for any business, but particularly so in transport where demand is time-dependent and cannot be stored. Quantitative data is required in order to drive the relevant level of service provision, and how this varies by time of day, day of week, and time of year. Information is also needed on passengers' characteristics, in order that marketing can be directed appropriately. Qualitative data is essential if passengers' preferences are to be understood; this enables limited funds to be applied to those parts of the service to which passengers are likely to be most appreciative. Other research is also needed; indeed Sheldon (1992) noted seven main purposes for market research for railways, including pricing research, demand forecasting, and design research. Geographical Information System (GIS) data is increasingly being used to understand market segments (Miller & Carlson, 2005).

Econometric Analysis

Because travel is a derived demand, the level of economic activity is important in determining the demand for rail travel. Regression or more sophisticated econometric techniques are a statistical approach used within the railway industry to attempt to find which indicators of economic activity drive railway demand, and exactly what the relationship is. GDP, employment in Central London and personal disposable income are all relevant variables but the analysis is less straightforward. For instance, there is often a 'lag' in passenger responses to changes in services. However, the advantage of these types of variables is that they are forecast independently (e.g. by the Treasury), so future trends in overall railway demand (and the resulting impact on the business) can be estimated (e.g. Wardman, 2006). However, structural changes such as the impacts of the use of IT devices and higher insurance premiums on car use may not be picked up in advance (TEG, 2014).

Different Types of Service Attributes

There are a large number of service attributes, but it is often convenient to consider quantitative and qualitative ones separately. This is because data collection and analytical techniques can be different for each. Quantitative aspects of the service are attributes such as speed, fare, waiting time and so on, whereas qualitative aspects include decor, the provision of at-seat facilities etc. Many recent advances in techniques have been associated with attempts to quantify the qualitative variables.

Aggregate and Disaggregate Methods
Methods of transport planning can also be split into their level of aggregation. Aggregate methods are those which look at the transport market as a whole, whereas disaggregate methods look at individual users. For instance, on the freight side, the estimation of demand for cross-Channel services could either be estimated from economic forecasts about Britain's trade with the rest of Europe, or by speaking to individual shippers. With their level of capital expenditure, Eurotunnel clearly needed to do both (Roberts & Vougioukas, 1994).

Aggregate methods are useful as a first step in understanding the market, and also where the actual number of journeys is very high. For instance, aggregate analysis is appropriate on the London Underground, where 1250 million passengers use a discrete part of the network every year.

However, disaggregate methods are to be preferred behaviourally, as the average values used in aggregate analysis may overlook significant variation between users. For instance, an average interchange penalty might be given as ten minutes, but this might disguise two passenger groups, with penalties of five minutes and half an hour, respectively. The existence of the latter could warrant a special through service if they were concentrated at one particular time of day.

3.5   Demand-Based Planning Techniques

Revealed Preference and Stated Preference
Some possible changes to railway services are easily assessed using data derived from previous experience e.g. recent fares changes, or the pattern of existing demand. This is termed the Revealed Preference (RP) approach, and can be used for either passenger or freight (e.g. Pitfield & Whiteing, 1985). However, it is not always possible to use RP data. First, some aspects of the service are so small that it is statistically very difficult to get parameter values for them; nevertheless, in a large railway, substantial investment might be considered for these service aspects. This

would particularly be the case for qualitative service elements (Copley et al, 1993). Secondly, some proposed changes are outside the experience of current passengers, and it is therefore difficult for them to visualise and give meaningful responses to questionnaires. Estimating the demand for light rail systems epitomises this. In both of these cases, Stated Preference (SP) techniques are useful.

The essence of SP is to give respondents a choice between a small number of service packages, which include one variable that is well understood (e.g. fares) and others that are not (e.g. the desire for a window seat). The packages are carefully chosen according to a complex statistical technique, which enables passengers' valuations of the variables to be estimated from the order of preference of the packages. SP was developed in the 1980s and the method is now mature and has widespread agreement on technical issues such as required sample sizes and the optimal choice of attribute values. Respondents' rankings generate coefficients that enable researchers to determine the exact trade-off between the different variables—this is the boundary line if drawn graphically. The use of different attribute values is essential in order to develop accurate results.

Because passengers are normally considered in groups, however, estimates of preference are normally quoted in terms of probabilities. (It cannot merely be assumed that because one alternative apparently has a GC 10% less than the other, that all passengers will use the 'better' alternative.) Given a valuation of the worth of the attribute under consideration, the proportion of passengers preferring it can be estimated (either using RP or SP data), and logit analysis is often used for this purpose. The logit model can be summarised as:

$$P(a) = \frac{e^{k \cdot GC_a}}{e^{k \cdot GC_a} + e^{k \cdot GC_b}}$$

Note that modelling using algebraic relationships may be based on RP data, SP data, or both; it is just that SP data can be developed for a wider range of data types and variables e.g. rolling stock type as noted above.

Estimating the Demand for New Stations and Services

The estimation of the impact of changes to existing patterns of service, or service frequency improvements, is well within the capability of aggregate techniques such as network modelling. For instance, changing the origins and destinations of individual train services on LU's District line is a problem ideally suited to network modelling. Improving service levels to a standard hourly pattern might also appear to be soluble using aggregate techniques, but the existence of a standard hourly pattern might itself bring additional benefits of 'rememberability', in which case SP methods might be needed to estimate the worth of this extra benefit. Classically, a 'sparks effect' has been found upon electrification, as passengers even react to additional attention being focussed on a service.

Estimating the demand for new stations and services is therefore an area in which disaggregate techniques are likely to be useful. However, such techniques can be expensive, and so there is a hierarchy of methods:

Trip Rate methods: apply a factor to the resident population of the area.

Direct Demand methods: use a gravity model to estimate the likely demand between a suburban area i with a population P_i and a nearby city j with P_j jobs or shops. The gravity model suggests that the number of trips between i and j will be:

$$T_{ij} = \frac{k \times P_i \times P_j}{D_{ij}^2}$$

where d is the distance between i and j, and k is a constant.

Generalised cost comparisons: For each major traffic flow, examine the generalised cost of travel by the various modes available (e.g. car, bus, train) and assign the traffic to the mode with the lowest generalised cost. A more sophisticated version of this uses the logit model to allocate traffic on a probabilistic basis, rather than all to one mode, for each Origin:Destination pair.

Network Modelling
Effectively an automation of generalised cost comparisons, network modelling is a classical aggregate technique used by highway, as well as public transport planners in urban areas. Two types of modelling occur: in station-to-station models, data relates solely to the journey on the railway, whilst in zone-to-zone models, examination occurs of the entire trip between origin (e.g. home) and destination (e.g. work). In both cases, however, data is assembled on the time taken to traverse parts of the network, service frequencies and patterns, a trip matrix of existing pas-

senger movements, and parameters such as interchange penalties and the VOT. Estimates are then made of the probability of users choosing one route through the system; these estimates are then summed to produce forecasts of loadings on individual links and services. In this way, options can be tested before their implementation.

Considerable development of network modelling techniques has occurred, as these aggregate methods have attempted to incorporate as many behavioural variables as possible, in order to maximise their accuracy (Shires, 2006). Models are available for many major urban areas (e.g. London (Vorraa et al, 2012)) and entire countries (e.g. the PLANET model used for modelling rail demand across Britain, especially for the HS2 scheme). The technique can also be used to evaluate the disbenefits arising from temporary closures of parts of the rail network, whether planned or unplanned (McKenna et al, 1996).

Simplified techniques can be used for those parts of the railway where geographical options are not available. The MOIRA revenue allocation system, for instance, is an aggregate line-based method of estimating the impact of service changes on Britain's main line railways. However, these methods run into difficulties when extensions into new areas are considered, and external estimates of demand are required in order to continue the method (Harris, 1994). Technically, these problems are non-marginal.

SP and Logit Modelling: Stated Preference questionnaires are used to interview local residents, from which parameters can be estimated. These parameters are then input into a logit model comparing the modal alternatives (e.g. train vs car) and probabilities of rail use assigned to different categories of trips. From these probabilities, the total demand and revenue for the service can be estimated.

The simpler methods noted above are RP methods, and are useful when screening options, since they are cheap and quick. However, given the expense involved in capital railway works, a full SP/logit analysis will be required for most schemes, and certainly for those involving line re-openings where there is no local experience of using train services. A comparison of methods was undertaken by Preston (1991), but easier methods can be required in Third World countries, where data is simply not available (Wirsanghe & Kumerage, 1998). Note that the provision of new stations often disbenefits through passengers, whose journey is lengthened; the impact of this is, however, readily estimated using generalised cost theory (Harris & Callaghan, 1997).

In complex conditions, for instance where Government funding is being sought for a major light rail scheme, a logit model would commonly be used to determine the likely preference of passengers between public and private transport. The input data for the logit model would be GC 'skim' matrices for all relevant modes, summarising the total GC between every origin and destination; the skims for all modes (including the new rail mode) would have been derived from network models (e.g. see Gregory & Sansom, 1995).

3.6 Appraisal Techniques

Schemes need to be analysed in order to provide sufficient information for management to make a decision as to their business value. In the commercial sector, monetary NPV and IRR calculations may be sufficient. These compare the financial benefits from increased demand and reduced operating costs with the capital expenditure from the works proposed; both are discounted to provide equality of treatment.

Some railway planning models provide revenue outputs as a matter of course, but others require assumptions to be made. For instance, some models estimate changes in passenger miles, and require fare rates to be applied; these, however, may be inaccurate if new traffic does not have the same characteristics as current traffic, or if it crosses fare zone boundaries. Secondly, most planning models are calibrated to peak conditions, and these need to be grossed up (or annualised) to provide yearly estimates. This grossing-up is dependent upon the amount of off-peak traffic, which can vary considerably (Fearon & Harris, 1994). Thirdly, traffic does not accrue immediately from service changes, but takes up to five years to build up, during which time the revised operating costs have been applicable (Preston, 1992).

Even when a scheme has been analysed, a prioritisation exercise may occur if funds are limited (e.g. Anderson & Smith, 1994). This may be on the basis of strict financial value, or on other criteria fulfilling management objectives for the railway business as a whole. For instance, there can be capital cost savings from conducting several schemes together, whilst there can also be synergistic effect on demand—several minor improvements made simultaneously can be marketed more effectively as they are more noticeable than isolated changes.

In some cases (typically in urban areas where road congestion relief may be an important result of a rail project) cost:benefit analysis may be used. This permits the railway to include time, accident and environmental savings as benefits to the scheme. Scheme worth is therefore measured by

$$B : C\ Ratio = \frac{revenue + other\ benefits}{capital + operating\ costs}$$

Schemes are unlikely to be considered if the benefits are less than 1.3 times the costs, or if ongoing revenues do not exceed operating costs.

However, various formulae are used, depending upon circumstances and the desired impact. For instance, the appraisal of light rail schemes in the UK has followed the 'Section 56' rules, in which the aim is to minimise public sector contributions whilst ensuring that the largest possible burden of the scheme falls to users and is paid for through the farebox. In large projects, a separate environmental assessment is required, in order to detail the various (often unquantifiable) impacts on the environment that may accrue from a scheme (Carpenter, 1994).

References

Andersen, P B & Pedersen, J (1991) 'How to Manage a 100% Increase in Rail Travel', Transpn. Res. 25A pp 173-180.

Anderson, J & Smith, J (1994) 'Optimised Planning of Railway Investment', vol 1 pp 93-100 in COMPRAIL Conference Proceedings, Wessex Institute of Technology.

Carpenter, T G (1994) 'The Environmental Impact of Railways', Wiley, Chichester.

de Cea, J, Ortuzar, J de D, Willumsen, L G (1986) 'Evaluating Marginal Improvements to a Transport Network', Transpn. pp 211-233.

Copley, G et al. (1993) 'Use of Stated Preference Methods to Determine London Underground Passenger Priorities', PTRC Summer Annual Meeting.

Fox, J., Patruni, B., & Daly, A. (2012), 'Comparison of the Long-Distance Model and PLANET Long-Distance Phase II Demand Model'. Rand Corporation.

Glaister, S (1998) 'Some Characteristics of Rail Commuter Demand', Jnl. Transp. Econ. & Pol. pp 115-132.

Gregory, D & Sansom, T (1995) 'Modelling of Metrolink Extensions and the Experience Gained from Line One', Transp. Plng. Systs. 2 (4) pp 31-40.

Harris, N G (1988) 'A Study of Demand in a Two-Tier Fares Environment', Jnl. Transp. Plng. & Tech. pp 231-237.

Harris, N G (1994) 'Computer-Based Planning Techniques and the Appraisal of an Underground Railway Extension', vol 1 pp 65-74 in COMPRAIL Conference Proceedings, Wessex Institute of Technology, Southampton.

Harris, N G & Callaghan, M J (1997) 'Railway Profitability and Station Closures', Trans. Pol. 4 pp. 41-47.

Hensher, D A (1998) 'Establishing a Fare Elasticity Regime for Urban Passenger Transport', Jnl. Trans. Econ. & Pol. 32 pp.221-246.

Jingxua, C., Xuewua, C, Weia, W, Baolb, F. 'The Demand Analysis of Bike-and-ride in Rail Transit Stations based on Revealed and Stated Preference Survey'. Procedia - Social and Behavioral Sciences Volume 96, 6 November 2013, Pages 1260-1268, Intelligent and Integrated Sustainable Multimodal Transportation Systems Proceedings from the 13th COTA International Conference of Transportation Professionals (CICTP2013).

McKenna, J. P., Dowton, A P & Harris, N G (1996) 'Estimating the Disbenefits of Railway Service Disruption', vol 1 pp 297-303 in COMPRAIL Conference Proceedings, Wessex Institute of Technology, Southampton.

Miller, S. G. & Carlson, M (2005) 'Transport Accessibility Analysis with ENIF and Railplan', Intnl. ENIF Users' Meeting, INRO, California. www.inro.ca/en/pres_pap/international/ieug05/Railplan.pdf

MVA Consultancy, ITS Leeds University & TSU Oxford University (1987) 'The Value Of Travel Time Savings', Policy Journals, Newbury.

Ortuzar, J. D., Willumsen, L.G., (2011) 'Modelling Transport', 4th Edition, March 2011, Wiley.

Pitfield, D. E. & Whiteing, A E (1985) 'Forecasting Rail Freight Flows in Britain', ch. 9 pp 209-236 in Button, K J & Pitfield, D E (eds) International Railway Economics, Gower.

Preston, J. (1991) 'Comparing Alternative Demand Forecasting Techniques for New Railway Stations and Services', Jnl. Transp. Econ. & Pol. pp 183-202.

Preston, J. (1992) 'Estimating the Demand for New Stations and Lines', ch 7 pp 71-86 in Harris, N G & Godward, E W (eds) 'Planning Passenger Railways', TPC, Glossop.

Roberts, D. & Vougioukas, E. M. (1994) 'Forecasting Short-Term Demand for the Channel Tunnel', Transp. Plng. Systs. 2 (1) pp 61-73.

Sheldon, R. (1992) 'Market Research for Passenger Railways', ch 6 pp 62-70 in Harris, N. G. & Godward, E. W. (eds) 'Planning Passenger Railways', TPC, Glossop.

Shires J. D., (2006) 'Review of Public Transport Models', http://www.its.leeds.ac.uk/projects/distillate/outputs/Deliverable F Appendix B.pdf.

Tanriverdia, S.C., Shakibaeib, S .& Tezcan, H.O. (2012), 'A Stated Preference (SP) Study on Individuals' Transportation Decisions, Focused on

Marmaray Project in Istanbul', Procedings - Social and Behavioural Sciences, Volume 54, Pages 1-1396 (4 October 2012) Proceedings of EWGT2012 - 15th Meeting of the EURO Working Group on Transportation, September 2012, Paris.

The Transport Economists' Group (TEG) (2014) Changing factors that affect transport demand. Trans. Econ. 41 (4).

Vorraa, T. (2012) 'Progress Report on the New Advanced London Transport Model', Citilabs http://www.citilabs.com/sites/default/files/files/1_TV_Progress_new LTS Model.pdf

Wardman, M. (2006) 'Demand for Rail Travel and the Effects of External Factors', Trans. Res. E 42 pp. 129-148.

Wirasinghe S. C. & Kumarage A. S. (1998), 'An aggregate demand model for intercity passenger travel in Sri Lanka', Transportation, February 1998, Volume 25, Issue 1, pp 77-98.

Chapter 4 Operations Based Planning

by Nigel G. Harris & Piers Connor

4.1 Operational Planning Issues

Visitors from foreign railways sometimes comment on how much more productive Britain's railways are than theirs. This is often because planning a railway solely on demand-led criteria can lead to an inefficient use of resources, including rolling stock. energy, staff and infrastructure. However, the danger is that an operationally-led railway (as British Rail was in the past) is a customer-unfriendly one. Even if an operationally-based approach is used, there may be a range of alternatives, as outlined by Pettitt (1998).

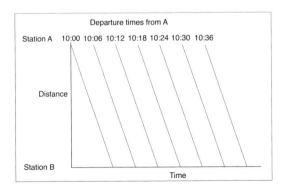

Figure 4.1: *Simple train graph for trains of equal performance running at 6-minute intervals. Source: N G Harris.*

4.2 Train Graphs

Ways are needed of presenting information regarding the running of trains. One simple approach is the train graph (Figure 4.1). Rising diagonal lines can also be drawn to show services in the opposite direction, which enables the impact of single-line sections to be shown easily (Rey, 1994). Stationary trains are represented by horizontal lines; where trains pass at loops, both services need to be shown as horizontal and overlapping. More advanced analysis (e.g. Hansen & Pachl, 2008) is based on the principle of 'blocking times' (the times during which track sections are occupied), which highlights the longer times that trains effectively occupy track circuits and conflict with each other.

Figure 4.2: *Train graph for trains of differing performance showing how paths are lost compared with train all running at the same speed. Source: N G Harris.*

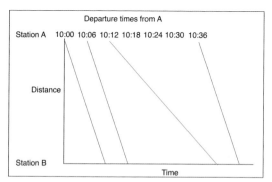

4.3 Fast and Slow Services: Their Impact on Capacity

On a standard double-track railway signalled with absolute block signalling, capacity is reduced if a mixture of fast and slow trains is to be operated without delays occurring. This is simply because the time taken for a slower train to pass through each section of line must be longer than that required by a faster moving train. The same occurs with a train that stops at more stations than another. This can be seen on the train graph of Figure 4.2, where 'white space' shows up the unused capacity caused by the difference in train performance. Careful timetabling is required to make the most of infrastructure that is used by both fast and slow trains.

4.4 Segregating Traffic: Number of Tracks Available

If traffic is substantial and varied, additional tracks may be considered. By grouping fast trains on one track and slow trains on the other, capacity can be increased to more than double the capacity of the original line. Often, it is necessary to segregate urban traffic from other types, such as freight and long distance services.

Conversely, if traffic is sparse, single line operation may be all that is required. This, however, limits traffic to a level below half what a double track line could offer, since overlaps must be provided at each end of any single-track section, and time is required for points and signals to be changed.

4.5 Passing Loops

If traffic warrants more than two tracks, but less than four, additional passing loop tracks may be considered. At such points, slow trains are diverted onto a short section of additional track, whilst they are overtaken by faster services. Slower trains are inevitably delayed unless the loop is 5km or more in length; whilst this can be acceptable for engineers' or ballast trains, it is less acceptable for revenue-earning traffic, whether passenger or freight.

Often the solution can be adopted at stations, where the passing loop is used for stopping trains but this requires precise timetabling and tightly controlled stopping times. In some operations, skip stopping has been tried, where successive trains call at alternate stations in order to speed up throughput. Again, this requires a very tightly controlled operation if delays to non-stopping trains is to be avoided. The inability to perform under such conditions has led to it being abandoned by many urban operators.

4.6 Junction Working

The design and operation of junctions must be carefully considered if both the operator and the maintainer are to get the most effective performance out of the system. In a standard, flat (at grade) arrangement is adopted, inevitably there will be conflicts in train movements, so grade separation should be the optimum solution wherever possible. If the cost cannot be justified, the standard double track junction (Figure 4.3) is operationally preferable to the 'ladder' junction (Figure 4.4). Parallel working of several

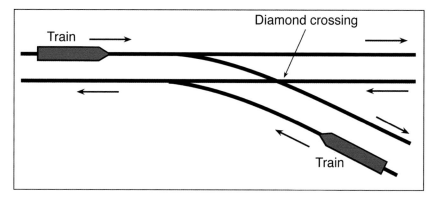

Figure 4.3: *Schematic of parallel working over a double track junction to maximise capacity. It involves the use of a diamond crossing. Drawing: P. Connor.*

trains at once permits much greater capacity (and also flexibility (in times of disruption) and safety) than if all traffic is routed across one pair of points (as the single-lead junction). However, a trade-off is needed, since more turnouts mean increased capital and maintenance costs.

4.7   Train Frequency and Regular Interval Services

A simplistic way of planning a railway is to find the passenger volume wishing to travel between A and B, and to determine the service frequency simply by dividing the volume by the capacity of the trains to be used. This, however, is certainly not the optimum solution against any criterion for a network. Most importantly, theory shows that demand is generated by reductions in generalised cost. This implies that extra resources should be committed where they can maximise the total reduction in generalised cost (not necessarily where there are the greatest number of passengers). Secondly, it ignores the time when passengers wish to travel, and travel demand is usually peaky.

However, on a long inter-city route operated independently of others (perhaps because of different traction arrangements), a regular-interval service is attractive. Its memorability means that even infrequent travellers are unlikely to turn up at random, whilst signal staff will also get used to the pattern of service, and are likely to regulate other train services accordingly. If the offset is chosen carefully, the service can be run efficiently, with a number of out-and-back diagrams. This is the basis of the basic-interval timetable or Taktfahrplan, pioneered by the Swiss, but also used in the Netherlands and on parts of Britain's railways. However, it may require investment for track speeds and in additional platforms to enable connection to be made at key hubs.

The number of trains required for service is:

$$round - triptime(hours) \times frequency(trainsperhour)$$

rounded up. The round-trip time depends upon the journey time and the layover or turnround time allowed at the end of the line, as well as time for passenger alighting and boarding and driver changes. This also needs to include some slack in order to permit recovery from delays en route. Turnround time is a function of journey length and should not be less than about 8 minutes for suburban services but can legitimately be as long as an hour for long-distance services arriving in urban areas, which need re-supplying with food, drink, water and toiletries. This has implications for the number of platforms needed.

4.8   Short-Turning

Inevitably, some trains will be less used than others, particularly at the ends of their journeys. Operators of regular-interval services therefore often consider turning some services short of their final destination. This means that they can pick up the path of an earlier return service, thereby reducing the number of trainsets requiredF. There are disadvantages, however, first in terms of crowding; there is a greater demand for the 'through' services, and the short-turning ones can be relatively empty. Secondly, there is a reduced service frequency on any extremities beyond the point(s) where short-turning has occurred; worse, it may be difficult to maintain a regular service of through trains, thereby exacerbating the increased waiting time.

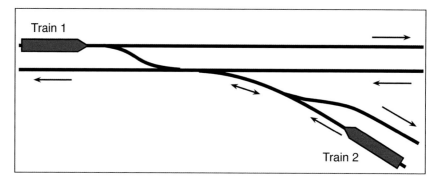

Figure 4.4: *A schematic of a ladder junction, where crossovers between each track are used to allow trains to reach a branch line. Note how Train 2 must be held until Train 1 has completed the movement through the route across the junction. Drawing: P. Connor*

4.9   Cross-Forming, Through Running and Shuttles

Trains only earn money when they are moving. It may be that two services from A and C both terminate at point B, and have long layovers (Figure 4.5). By combining the two, however, with trains from A to B then going to C (rather than back to A) (and vice versa), the overall requirement for trains may be reduced. Unfortunately, this has impacts on reliability; if a problem arises on the route between A and B, the service to C is also likely to be disrupted. It can, however, make sense to combine a service from A to B with one from B to D if overall layover time can be reduced. Although this has attractions in reducing the requirement for interchange at B (thereby increasing demand as generalised cost falls), care has to be taken with recovery time.

It can be shown that lateness is a function of journey distance; additional recovery time is needed if services are to be linked and unreliability is to be avoided. If reliability is crucial, then operating separate shuttle services can be worthwhile, especially if the service involved is frequent and therefore its layovers relatively short. However, this has the disadvantage that proportionately higher levels of spare trains are required to maintain a given level of reliability, the smaller the pool of trains. Glover (2013) provides some useful case studies of timetabling problems in the British context.

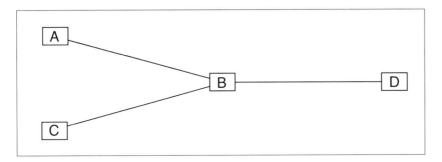

Figure 4.5: *A diagram to assist in demonstrating how cross forming of train services, as described in the text, may be used on branch lines. Diagram: N. Harris.*

4.10   Locomotive Hauled Trains

In operations planning, understanding the types of train available and their limitations is essential. The traditional train comprises a collection of coaches (or freight wagons) with suitable motive power attached, usually at the front, in the form of a locomotive. The train is made up of sufficient vehicles to carry the traffic offering and provided with enough power for the job. For passenger operations, one locomotive is usually sufficient.

A good deal of flexibility is possible with locomotive haulage. As long as the train weight remains within the capacity of the locomotive(s), any number of vehicles can be attached, although limits will be imposed by platform or siding lengths. Locomotives themselves can also be flexible, many being designed to cover a range of duties.

The advantages for locomotive hauled trains mean they are the best option for many railway operators around the world, particularly for freight but, where traffic is dense, i.e. where a large number of trains are required, a more rational approach is necessary, particularly at terminals. In addition, in very predictable operations like commuter services or metro lines, fixed formation trains will be the most efficient.

4.11 Terminal Operations

One disadvantage of traditional locomotive haulage shows up at the end of the line. When a train arrives at a dead end terminal, the locomotive is trapped between the train and the buffer stops. The only way to release the locomotive is to remove the train and for that, a second locomotive is required. This second loco is attached to the other end of the train and will be used to provide power for the return trip. When the train has been removed, the first locomotive is released, moved away from the platform to a 'loco siding' near the terminus and stored until used for the return trip of another train.

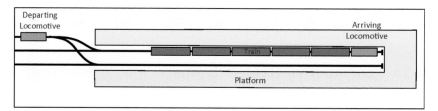

Figure 4.6: *A diagram showing how locomotive changes are carried out at a terminus. Once the departing locomotive has taken the train out of the platform for its next trip the arriving locomotive will move out of the platform to take over the position of the departing locomotive. Diagram: P. Connor.*

Of course, the arrangement would not nowadays be suitable for a major city terminus where space is at a premium and land is very expensive, so efforts are made to use tracks to the optimum. So, although locomotive changing operations at terminals were, and still are commonplace, where there is intense traffic, additional movements for loco changing can restrict the terminal capacity. Also, at least two additional locomotives are required to cover these terminal operations for each service. To overcome these limitations, the Multiple Unit was introduced.

4.12 Multiple Unit Operation

Locomotive operation of intensive services was rapidly phased out when electric traction, using 'multiple unit' operation, was introduced late in the 19th century for US urban railway lines. Within ten years the idea had spread to Europe. The facility for the electric traction system to be spread out along the train, compared with cramming it all together into a bulky locomotive, allowed a number of small power units to be distributed underneath the floors of several vehicles in the train. They were all simultaneously controlled by the driver in the leading car through wires running the length of the train. Thus was born the electric multiple unit or EMU. In later years, DMUs (diesel multiple units) were developed using the same principles.

A modern passenger multiple unit train (Figure 4.7) is now made up of a number of inter-dependent vehicles that cannot operate unless all the vehicles are of the right type and are coupled in the correct position in the train. Power and auxiliary equipment is usually distributed under more than one vehicle and is all controlled from the driving position. Vehicles in multiple units are usually referred to as 'cars' and are known as 'motor cars' if powered and 'trailer cars' if not.

Figure 4.7: *Multiple unit trains in a depot on the Rotterdam Metro. All these are built as 2-car fixed units but units may be coupled to make longer trains of 4-car or 6-car formation. Photo: F. Schmid.*

Multiple unit trains are formed into 'units' or 'sets' of two or more cars. They are often semi-permanently coupled together, only being uncoupled inside a workshop for heavy maintenance. Units can operate singly - providing driver's cabs are provided at both ends - or coupled to form longer trains. Some operations require two (or more) multiple units to be coupled together to provide sufficient capacity for a particular service.

This also allows trains to be lengthened or shortened whilst in service by adding or cutting units.

Multiple unit trains are mainly used for high density suburban operations where traffic levels are easily predicted and form constant patterns that allows fixed train formations . In recent years, long distance traffics have shown the same tendency and many railways are now adopting the multiple unit formation for these routes - e.g. the French TGV, the UK HST, the Japanese Shinkansen.

The multiple unit is simple to reverse at terminals. All you have to do is provide driver's controls at both ends of the train, connect them to the train wires and give the driver a key to switch in the controls at the end he wants to use. Locomotive changing is instantly eliminated, terminal space is released and trains can be turned round more quickly. All the driver has to do now is change ends. Another form of multiple unit operation was adopted in the early 1960s when a new concept appeared called push-pull.

4.13   Push-Pull Operation

Push-pull operation was really only an adaption of the multiple unit principle but applied to a locomotive powered train. Assuming a regular level of traffic and an even interval service was required, trains could be formed with a locomotive at one end and a driving cab on the coach at the other end. If you could find a way of doing it cheaply by converting existing coaches, it could represent a big step forward.

The idea has now been adopted world-wide in two forms. One, as stated above, uses a locomotive at one end and a coach equipped with a driver's cab at the other end. The number of vehicles in between them may be varied seasonally if required but the formation is not normally varied on a train by train basis. In the UK, the coach at the rear has become designated a Driving Van Trailer (DVT). It is used to carry luggage and passengers are not permitted to ride in it facing forwards when it is at the front of the train at speeds over 160 km/h.

The second push-pull form uses two locomotives, one at each end of the train. This first appeared in 1959 with the UK's Blue Pullman series of trains. A diesel power car was provided at each end of a six- or eight-coach set. The concept was further developed in the 1970s with the UK High Speed Train (known as the HST) and in France with the TGV (Train à Grande Vitesse). The former is diesel powered, the latter electric but the concept is the same. Both these trains employ a power unit at each end with a set of passenger carrying coaches in-between. The two locomotives are necessary in these cases to provide sufficient power.

4.14   Timetabling and Crew Scheduling

Traincrew also need to be timetabled as well as the trains themselves. However, traincrew need Personal Needs Breaks (PNBs), are limited to the number of hours they can work per day, and generally need to finish their day at the same place from they started it; these are all requirements not applicable to trains. Whilst they can cause difficulties of problem size if examined manually, a number of systems are in place worldwide that do these processes automatically, even through to producing timetable posters for the public (Kwan et al, 1996; Kataoaka & Komaya, 1994).

For frequent passenger services, crew scheduling is not a limiting criteria. However, for passenger trains running only a few times per day, and for freight trains that may run only weekly, crew scheduling can make an operation profitable or not. Particular problems arise with services that run an odd number of times per day. Here, crews cannot operate 'out and back' along the entire route length, and it may be necessary to arrange for crews to swop trains where they pass, even if this causes delay to passengers. Even this is relatively inefficient and the marginal crew cost of an additional daily service may be zero.

For infrequent services, route knowledge also needs to be taken into account. Drivers are only passed to drive over particular routes, so that they know signalling and line speed details. If, in a roster of 100 drivers, only one duty takes them on a particular stretch of line, then some drivers will never traverse this line within a year, and specific route training will be required, which adds to the cost of running the service.

4.15   Interaction with Different Types of Capacity

Train services cannot be planned alone; in busy systems, station capacity may also be relevant. As we have already seen, station stops add time to block sections, and reduce capacity. If station stops are prolonged through heavy traffic flows, capacity is further reduced. Unfortunately, this leads to an increased demand per train, which further reduces capacity as station stops become ever longer. 'Blocking back' can occur, in which case trains queue up behind a busy station, waiting for an opportunity to enter the platform. This causes further delay (as trains have to slow down and wait at signals that they should pass at line speed), and the whole system degrades. There are several ways out of this vicious cycle and, given its importance for urban rail, this issue is explored in detail in later chapters.

4.16   Planning for Reliability

Some timetables are robust (i.e. they continue to function when problems occur), whilst others degrade completely (once one train is late, the whole service disintegrates). There are various techniques to avoid the latter.

First, it is inadvisable to use all available capacity. For instance, one recent timetable on LU's Northern line used all the inner area reversing capacity completely. However, when the service was disrupted, it was not possible to reduce delays by turning trains short, since the sidings concerned were already in use. Consequently, the service deteriorated, and often could not be restored before the end of the traffic day.

Secondly, recovery time and pathing allowances can be included in the timetable as a matter of judgment. Better still, the characteristics of the service can be examined to ascertain what is an appropriate amount of recovery time. Train delays are a function of distance, train type and other known variables, so some indication of likely punctuality should be available (e.g. Rodley & Harris, 1988).

However, it is not possible to guarantee correct time arrival 100% of the time. Rather, it is more sensible to plan for (say) 95%, which is easily achieved by using the second technique. As 95% of occurrences in the normal distribution arise within two standard deviations of the mean, then this can be calculated from analysis of train running. The train path might be widened to protect this amount of capacity.

In congested conditions, this luxury is not available (which is why congested railways are less reliable than relatively empty ones). In these cases, services should be standardised as much as possible, so that as many passengers as possible can board an alternative service if theirs is running late.

4.17 Contingency Planning

Because railways are, by their nature, fixed track affairs, train breakdowns can be critical in disrupting services, and the impacts of these need to be minimised. Staff training is crucial as to what arrangements should be made. In particular, accurate information needs to be promulgated as widely and quickly as possible. However, planning can have a role here. Since there are only fixed points at which trains can cross from one track to another, the number of possible places of disruption is not as limitless as it may seem at first sight. Secondly, the relative frequency of failure can be guessed at through knowledge of the relative train frequency at that point, or other factors (e.g. steep inclines forcing motive power to overheat). If reliability is critical to service image (as on Eurostar services), it might even be considered worthwhile to provide standby motive power at strategic locations. The demand impacts of failures can, in fact, be assessed using standard techniques such as network modelling (Harris & Ramsey, 1994).

4.18 Operational Simulations

For anything beyond the simplest of railways, manual methods of timetable construction and analysis are tedious if not impossible. Recent advances in IT have, however permitted the development of operational simulations (and even signalbox duplicates such as Control Centre for the Future (CCF)) contained in standard PCs. VISION (McGuire & Linder, 1994) and LU's Train Service Model (TSM) (Weston & McKenna, 1990) both enable the adequacy of infrastructure to be tested against proposed services, which can be disrupted through both specified and random delays. The TSM, however, also contains data on passenger movements, so that the interactions between passenger movements and train services can be examined - issues such as blocking back, and cross-platform interchange.

Station service models, such as PEDROUTE (Ash, 1993; Turner et al, 1991), enabled similar analyses of station environments to be carried out and have more recently been replaced with simulations using artificial intelligence and better visualisation. Both types of model enable proposed changes to be analysed in the office before operating practices are changed or expensive capital works implemented. Such detailed work can pay dividends even if only seconds can be taken off a sufficiently large number of journeys, since passengers are sensitive to reliability.

References

Ash, N (1993) 'New Modelling Techniques for Assessing Alternative Railway Station Designs', PTRC Summer Annual Meeting.

Glover, J, (2013), 'Principles of Railway Operation', Ian Allan, Horsham, 160pp.

Hansen, I. A. & Pachl, J. (eds.) (2008), 'Railway Timetable & Traffic', Eurail Press, Hamburg, 228pp.

Harris, N G & Ramsey, J B H (1994) 'Assessing the Effects of Railway Infrastructure Failure', Jnl. Ops. Res. Soc. 635-640.

Kataoaka, K & Komaya, K (1994)'Computer-aided Railway Scheduling Systems for High-Density Train Operations', vol 2 pp 43-50 in COMPRAIL Conference Proceedings, Wessex Institute of Technology.

Kwan, A S K et al. (1996) 'Producing Train Driver Shifts by Computer', vol 1 pp 421-435 in COMPRAIL Conference Proceedings, Wessex Institute of Technology.

McGuire, M & Linder, D (1994) 'Train Simulation on British Rail', vol 1 pp 437-444 in COMPRAIL Conference Proceedings, Wessex Institute of Technology.

Pettitt, G (1998) 'Making Better Use of our Rail Infrastructure', Mod. Rlys. 246-248, May.

Preston, J (1992) 'Estimating the Demand for New Stations and Lines', ch 7 pp 71-86 in Harris, N G & Godward, E W (eds) 'Planning Passenger Railways', TPC, Glossop.

Rey, G (1994) 'A Study on the Capacity of the Gotthard Base Tunnel', vol 1 pp 49-56 in COMPRAIL Conference Proceedings, Wessex Institute of Technology.

Rodley, J W E & Harris, N G (1988) 'Why are Trains Late'?, Mod. Rlys. 634-636.

Turner, R P, Jones, M A & Weston, J G (1991) 'Modelling Pedestrian Movement', Transp. Plng. Systs. 1 (2) pp 35-44.

Weston, J G & McKenna, J P (1990) 'London Underground's Train Service Model: a Description of the Model and its Uses' pp 133-147 in COMPRAIL Conference Proceedings, Wessex Institute of Technology.

Chapter 5   A Stations Primer

by Felix Schmid and Piers Connor

5.1   Introduction

Airport, harbours and stations form interfaces within modes and between multiple modes, providing both intermodal and intramodal connectivity. However, a more in depth analysis reveals that such facilities have functions that go beyond their role of links in a transport chain. The authors discuss some of the issues that arise from the need to satisfy a multitude of requirements, focusing on passenger transport[1].

5.2   A Beacon for the Area

Stations in city environments, with other major structures in close proximity and often surrounded by large, visually and commercially attractive corporate buildings, have to stand out as beacons for the community and the city. They must be eye-catching, built to high standards and they must attract passengers to the railway. Good examples are Berlin Hauptbahnhof in Germany, Lille Europe in France, Liège-Guillemins in Belgium (Figure 5.1), Bejing South Station in China and the future Canary Wharf station of Crossrail and the renovated St. Pancras in London. However, while a station might have an important function as a beacon, it must still be designed to meet the needs of the railway, of the people using it and

---

[1]This chapter was developed from a presentation made to the delegates attending the Intelligent City Forum held in Birmingham on 26 May 2011, sponsored by Rail Champions and published in 'Rail Technology Magazine', July 2011.

Figure 5.1: *Rebuilt station at Liège-Guillemins, Belgium, designed by the Spanish architect Santiago Calatrava in 2008 and demonstrating the beacon effect. Photo: by Le Cointois.*

of the staff running it. A station is a transport hub, by definition. Even the most humble stop in a tramway network allows interchange between movement on foot and travel by tram. Railway stations thus represent focal points for journey mode changes, places that travellers require for business, commuting and leisure travel. They arrive on foot, by bicycle, car, taxi, bus, coach, tram and metro, and they carry luggage ranging from a small computer bag to a pair of cases each the size of a steamer trunk, so they must be able to find the station easily and they must have good access to the facilities and the trains. The station must be designed to allow easy modal changes and to provide a simple approach from within the cityscape.

5.3   Circulation

One of the most important requirements of any station is that of accommodating circulation. This relates to movements of trains as well as those of passengers with their luggage and other people such as 'meeters and greeters'. The station also must create a safe interface between the two types of traffic. It is essential that the people movement flows in a station are designed carefully, both during normal operation and during emergencies like security alerts and evacuation. Signage and sightlines form an important part of maintaining efficient flows for passengers, while ef-

Figure 5.2: *Passenger circulating area at Waterloo station, London with train service destination display. Retail units are provided at both ground floor and first floor levels. Photo: P. Connor.*

fective railway control allows trains to arrive in and depart from stations with minimum delay (Figure 5.2). Intermodal changes also need careful evaluation, so that passengers arriving by road can access the station facilities easily and without obstructing waiting areas, or exits. Equally, ticket offices and machines need to be positioned and provided in sufficient numbers so that users can queue and access the facility without obstruction and without resulting in shuffling lines of stressed travellers blocking the station's pedestrian and vehicle routes.

Mixing types of passengers can cause congestion and frustration. At St Pancras International station in London, arriving international train passengers merge into the local commuter crowds flowing towards the Underground station interchange. At peak times, this creates a mix of slow and fast moving pedestrians in a narrow space obstructed with pillars, lifts and greeters.

Private car access is often an issue at stations. Drivers meeting trains can cause congestion if a suitable short term parking area is not provided. People do not want to pay exorbitant parking charges just to meet relatives and friends who have chosen to come by train. Such charges can discourage train travel.

Figure 5.3: *Dutch station cycle point with secure, automated, smart card storage, CCTV and a cycle shop. The system is provided at over 40 stations in the Netherlands. Photo: F. Schmid.*

5.4 Interchange Role

Passengers arrive and leave by train but almost universally, they change their mode of transportation at the station[2]. It may be from train to train, or from train to any other movement mode, from foot to bus, taxi, car, bicycle or metro. The Kings Cross and St Pancras stations complex gives a good example of the variety of modal changes possible and the good and bad features of all of them.

First, we should realise that the area covered by the combination of the stations of St. Pancras and Kings Cross is vast. It takes ten minutes to walk directly from one side to the other. Clearly thought out routes are essential for arriving and departing passengers. Secondly, the whole complex has been rebuilt and updated, as far as is possible within the considerable restrictions imposed by English Heritage, a body that has been described as a willful inhibitor of the modernisation of Britain's infrastructure. Despite its rebuilding, the area still suffers from poor interchange facilities because passengers gravitate towards the rebuilt St Pancras International station. So, what is wrong with the facilities provided? Looking at facilities for cyclists first, these are provided but they are a long way from the station, sharing space with a car park north of

---

[2]Saglians in the Grisons area of Switzerland is a rare example of a station where only intramodal connectivity is provided since there is no road access.

the St Pancras station complex. The premises are secure but a casual user would be pushed to find the cycle storage area unless they had done their research first. Other countries do it better (Figure 5.3)

Car and taxi pick up and drop off points are provided, of course, but it is not always clear where taxis are supposed to stop and there are different locations around the complex. There is nowhere for cars to wait to ease picking up duties. Confusingly, the Network Rail description of the available facilities does not align with what is on the ground.

Buses have a total of nine different locations for access around King's Cross and St. Pancras, scattered across the roads around the complex, some of which are best accessed by using the subways intended for users of the Underground station. The access route for the Underground is split, with two connections from the St Pancras side and one from Kings Cross.

5.5 Cost of Time

As we have seen in Chapter 3, Section 3.3, passengers value the time spent on different parts of a journey differently, within the overall aggregate 'generalised cost' of the journey. In a station, the whole activity of changing between trains can have a perceived generalised cost of up to 30 minutes (especially if people are forced to climb stairs), even if the real time taken is much shorter. It just depends on how efficient and convenient it is and how the situation is perceived by passengers. However, the existence of places to eat and shop can enable passengers to use potentially-wasted time usefully, thereby effectively reducing generalised cost.

5.6 Facilities at Stations

Passenger and other users' facilities must be an integral part of station design, aligned with the size and importance of the hub as a whole. Apart from pedestrian routes designed to separate incoming and outgoing flows and areas for general circulation and waiting, there must be a structured approach to establishing the correct location of station facilities and the routes leading to these. Aside from the ticketing facilities mentioned above, there is normally a need for information enquiry points, toilets and waiting rooms—or at least decently sheltered open areas—or departing passengers awaiting trains. Nowadays, in the UK, the tendency is to limit well provided waiting lounges to premium passengers paying first class fares, while other passengers are expected to remain in the general circulating areas or to use the coffee shops scattered around larger stations.

5.7   Retail Outlets

Station owners and architects are always looking for ways to develop the commercial possibilities of the station and its environs. Good retail outlets of the right type can add a useful source of income for the station owners or operators and they help to provide a sense of community and interest within the station and its surroundings. They also provide an extra presence within the station that reduces the opportunities for crime and vandalism and instills in passengers a better sense of security.

Care must be taken to choose the right kinds of shops and to ensure that the sales and services are appropriate for the station context. Thus, on a railway that suffers from alcohol related excesses, it may not be sensible to allow alcohol to be sold and it might be unwise, from a security standpoint, to accept a lease offer from a retailer selling military memorabilia in a gift shop. Fast food shops may also not be desirable because they create the potential for vast quantities of litter.

The usual outlets seen on stations are cafes, sandwich shops, newspaper stalls, bookshops, florists and gift shops. Dry cleaners and shoe repairers are also popular. Larger stations often have room for fashion outlets. In almost all cases, it is important that the shop fronts are obvious to customers but, at the same time, they must not restrict walkways through the station or obstruct exits, escalators and lifts. Leases must also include a requirement for retailers to meet the railway's fire and safety protection requirements and that staff are properly trained for alarms, evacuation and emergencies. It is essential that station managers regularly inspect retail premises to ensure that they comply with their lease obligations.

The location of retail premises and their proportion in relation to the station size and shape must be designed in at the very earliest stages of the

Figure 5.4: *Bank of five escalators at Canary Wharf Underground station in London. Photo: K. Rennie.*

station planning process. They must not be allowed to fill space that is needed for passenger movement or waiting. Until 2012, Waterloo Station in London had some large retail units spread along the main concourse area. These provided a very good utility for the shoppers but they prevented passengers from moving around freely, obstructed the view of the large train describer systems and caused serious overcrowding problems whenever services were disrupted. As a consequence of ever increasing passenger numbers, the retail units had to be removed to recreate the necessary circulating space. Happily, the visual impact and station sightlines of the whole concourse area have been hugely improved as a result.

5.8 Lifts and Escalators

Escalators (Figure 5.4) have a number of advantages over lifts. As well as having greater capacity, they enable changes of height to accommodate changes in location so that, for instance, entrances on street corners can directly be linked to lower-level locations where a lack of building foundations enables wide, straight and level platforms to be provided. However, lifts are essential to accommodate the mobility-impaired and are preferred for passengers encumbered with heavy luggage, who tend to be their major users.

Figure 5.5: *Example of poor and confusing signage at station exit. Safe and clear signage is essential for good passenger circulation. Photo: P. Connor's collection.*

5.9 Communications

We must not forget that a large station involves a wide and complex communications network, including telephone, radio, CCTV, public address, train arrival and departure displays, news media, WiFi and both fixed and variable direction signs. In performance terms, reliable communications are an essential feature of a station, under both normal and emergency conditions (Figure 5.5). Large steel structures, such as station roofs can form a considerable obstruction to a communications network if the propagation of electromagnetic waves has not been allowed for in the design. The use of specialist communications systems by emergency services must also be addressed in the design of the facilities. Power supplies for all these systems must be secure and reliable.

5.10 Maintenance

Maintenance of both the fabric and equipment of the station must not be neglected at the design stage. Apart from the usual requirements for waste disposal and the provision of robust surfaces that make for easy cleaning, pity such visitors as the window cleaner, who may be required to reach large and very tall structures. Safe access for cleaning and glazing replacement must be built into the design. Remember too, that escalators and lifts may have to be withdrawn from service for maintenance or renewal, so additional facilities must be available under these conditions.

5.11   Operations

We should not forget that a station has to have trains in it. Careful planning is essential to get the right layout to accommodate the type and volume of trains expected. With a design life of at least 60 years, the layout must be flexible and must allow for future expansion. The folly of providing only four platforms for the Midland Main Line at St Pancras is already apparent and the restriction on the capacity here will become worse when the line is eventually electrified throughout.

The type of service provided will affect capacity at stations. At a through station with a mix of local and commuter services, combined with long distance trains, the layout of the station needs to combine efficient train movements and the shortest unconstrained passenger flows possible through the facilities and to and from the modal change areas.

At a terminus, turnround time is important and, as discussed in Chapter 4, this depends upon the type of train service (e.g. commuter v long-distance). It should also be remembered that the time taken for each train to clear the platform and access route plus the time for the next train to occupy the platform (platform re-occupation time) must be allowed for.

5.12   Faregates

Many stations now incorporate gated barriers, dividing the station into 'paid' and 'unpaid' areas. The whole question of gates is emotionally charged: passengers who pay their fare regard barriers as an obstruction and an unwritten accusation that they cannot be trusted. Less frequent travellers see them as difficult and many do not understand how to use them. Gate design in general leaves much to be desired, with sluggish operation, unreliable performance, non-universal ticket recognition and too few units to cope with peak hour traffic. Railway operators regard

Figure 5.6: *Example of paddle type faregates at Waterloo station in London. The paddles are at a height to prevent persons jumping over the top. Photo: P. Connor.*

them as hugely beneficial, since it has been shown that, after they have been installed, fraud is reduced and income increased, with additional benefits experienced in terms of station security (Figure 5.6). More needs to be done to encourage acceptance by users.

5.13   Do not Forget the Staff

A station forming a part of a city hub is a major employer and most major stations are open 24 hours a day. As a rule, each job that must be staffed 24 hours requires the employment of five persons, to ensure sufficient cover for shift patterns, holidays etc. Some jobs will involve temporary or part time attendance at the station and staff movements and changes will be frequent. There will be permanently employed staff for the station operation and, probably, contract staff for maintenance and cleaning, personnel of the operating companies, retail staff and separate units for policing and security and they all have different needs in terms of the station environment. Emergency services must also be considered when designing access to the site and any special facilities provided for them.

Train crews, for example, will require accommodation at large stations, some being permanently based there but some requiring only facilities for personal needs breaks or as waiting areas. Their facilities should be as close to platforms as possible to remove excessive walking time from their duty periods.

Managing and providing facilities for the large permanent and transient staff population forms an essential part of a station's operation. The station will need full and complete facilities for them, including control rooms, rest areas, offices, bathrooms, storage, training equipment and conference rooms. All these facilities must designed to be secure and easily inspected, if the station is to work effectively and safety.

5.14   A brief summary

For a station to function as part of a significant city hub, good architecture and design are essential but the choice of structure and facilities must be founded on the underlying principles of how passengers, staff and third parties behave. Providing simple free-flowing circulatory areas is a key element in assuring the main function of a station: boarding, alighting and transferring within and between nodes. Today, these basic principles are becoming ever more important as the sheer volume of users is threatening the performance of many stations.

Chapter 6 Platform Protection

by Piers Connor

6.1 Background

From the very earliest years of railway operation, a problematic relationship has existed between the moving train and the fixed structure of the railway station. The need for a safe and reliable means of loading and unloading passengers has vexed the minds of railway managers for the last 150 years. Many railways around the world simply provided a smooth, ground level area and steps attached to the train to allow passengers to climb up into the coaches to board while others, notably the British, used a built-up that reached almost to the level of the vehicle floor.

The raised platform offered a somewhat easier access to the train but it tended to isolate the passengers from the track, a situation reinforced by the British tradition of fencing off all railway property and restricting access across railway tracks to fixed level crossing points. Many other railway administrations around the world left lines unfenced for the most part and passengers and the general public were expected to treat the railway much as they would a roadway, looking after themselves and crossing under their own judgement.

For the platform/train interface, the traditional arrangements described above have generally sufficed for conventional railways, with little change up to the present time, but for fully automated systems like airport people movers and heavily used urban routes, a more protective approach has been considered necessary. This led to the development of various forms of platform edge doors.

Figure 6.1: *Fixed barriers provided on metro platform edge of Sangwangsimni Station of Line 2 Seoul Metro. These are simple to erect and provide a degree of protection but cannot prevent falls and have a large gap between train and barriers where a person could be trapped. Photo: Marc Daouani, Wikipedia 19th December 2007.*

6.2   Origins

In the case of airport people movers, the desire to use trains under unattended automatic operation, suggested that some form of protection was required for passengers waiting on a station platform, so the idea of installing powered doors along the platform edge was born. In the more recent past, driven by increasing crowding and a more pro-active approach towards safety, together with concerns about climate control within stations and air conditioning energy costs, metro designs have moved towards systems to physically separate passengers on platforms from the track and its moving trains. These systems have included both fixed barriers and various designs of powered doors, generally described as Platform Screen Doors or Platform Edge Doors.

In one case, in St. Petersburg, Russia, platform doors were installed as part of the engineering requirements. The track tunnels were bored separately from the station tunnels and the two were joined by transverse openings at the train doorway positions. The openings were sealed by unglazed, elevator-type doors once train loading/unloading was completed. The design was known as the 'horizontal elevator'.

The design was restricted to 10 stations on one line constructed in the early 1960s. The reasons for the design were said to be because it was cheaper to bore tunnels with rotary machines and to construct station tunnels separately (Metrobits 2008). The retention of walls between platform and track assisted with the spreading of ground loads in the very

Figure 6.2: *Enclosed platform structure showing platform screen doors at a station on the Taipei Metro. Here the screen doors provide both safety enhancement and climate control. Photo: Wikipedia, 6th November 2010.*

deep tunnels required by the poor ground conditions in the city. The plain steel doors were found to be unpopular with passengers and were not repeated for subsequent construction in St Petersburg.

6.3 Definitions

The simplest form of platform/train protection is a fixed barrier (Figure 6.1). These provide a degree of protection but cannot prevent falls onto the track and they really do little more than provide an indication of the location the train doors. The term 'Platform Screen Doors' (PSDs) is used here and elsewhere to describe the provision of full height door systems (Figure 6.2) including additional panels to provide a complete seal between the platform and the track area of a station. Such systems are normally required where climate control is the principal purpose of the system but they also provide a safety improvement as an additional benefit.

Another type of system is known as 'Platform Edge Doors' (PEDs), so-called because they do not form a complete division between platform and track. Rather, the design forms a full- or half-height barrier along the platform edge (Figure 6.3) but does not provide the air seal required for full climate control. In some cases, like the Jubilee Line extension in London opened in 1999, the full height PEDs (Figure 6.5)were installed partly to provide additional ventilation control and partly as an anti-suicide measure and partly to convince Londoners that they were getting a modern

Figure 6.3: *Half-height doors on Paris Metro station showing several typical features. Glazing is used for main part of the screen; doors open are indicated by lights on the structure; additional pillars are provided on the train side of the doors to reduce risk of passengers being caught between doors and train; tactile band provided on platform surface inside the door structures. Photo: Pline photo personnelle; Wikipedia, June 2006.*

metro (Mitchell, 2003). Strangely, the stations were also equipped with anti-suicide pits, like all other deep level tube stations in London.

6.4   Reasons for PSDs

There are three basic reasons for the installation of platform screen doors (PSDs) as follows:

- Safety—prevention of conflicts between passengers and moving trains at stations;

- Climate Control—maintaining comfortable temperatures within platform zones;

- Reduction of costs for station heating and cooling;

- Reduction of rubbish on track;

- Ventilation Control—Reduction of discomfort generated by underground station draughts.

In Japan, some stations, where high speed trains pass through without stopping, have fences fitted along the platforms at about 2m distance from the edge (Muraki et al, 2010) to prevent passengers being sucked off the platform by the vortices created by the fast moving trains. The fences have gates at suitable locations to allow access to stopping trains (Figure 6.4). PSDs will also have additional benefits. They can reduce the level of train noise, create a cleaner platform environment and, if designed carefully and sympathetically, improve the visual aspects of the platform area. They can also be used to reduce risks caused by fire and smoke.

6.5   The Case for PSDs

Justification for the installation of PSDs originated in the early 1970s as a result of the decision to operate unattended automatic trains, such as airport people movers, and then later for the French designed VAL (Véhicule Automatique Léger) system built in such cities as Lille, Toulouse and Rennes, and at Airports like Chicago O'Hare and Paris Orly and de Gaulle. More recent installations have been derived from issues such as high ambient temperatures in underground stations or safety for heavily crowded platforms.

Many modern systems have been built with PSDs in the tunnel sections but not at open stations, the logic being that the underground stations, with higher passenger loads than open stations, present a better business case in terms of both safety and climate control. However, this logic has more recently been overcome in some cities, where selected stations have been provided with half-height gates in place of full height doors at both open and tunnel stations.

In Tokyo, large scale retrofitting of half-height gates has been carried out on a number of metro lines, in addition to provision on any new builds. Half-height gates are simply added as a safety measure, since they cannot realistically affect ambient temperature in the station. Hong Kong has also started retrofitting half-height gates at some stations. There, the cost of the installation is around £6.6k per metre (The Standard, 2008). They also installed them from new on the MTRC line to Disneyland.

Figure 6.4: *Japanese high speed platform at Shin Kobe with safety fence and gates provided to reduce the risk of people being dragged off platforms by the pressure waves generated by passing trains. Other stations, where all trains stop, have the fence closer to the platform edge. Photo: Jason Kaechler, Wikipedia 1st April 2008.*

6.6 Benefits

Although the installation of PSDs is expensive—in the range of £6k - £10k per metre[1] for a full-height screen and doors, depending on location—there are considerable and quantified benefits. In one study carried out on the Hong Kong Mass Transit organisation (Law et al, 2011), where PSDs were retrofitted along platforms in tunnel stations between 2002 and 2006, it was determined that, after installation, death and injuries due to suicides and accidental falls onto the track fell by 75% across the system and the service disruptions from such incidents fell by 69.4%. The original reason for the installation was to improve climate control within platform areas and to save energy used in station air conditioning and tunnel ventilation.

Interestingly, one of the arguments against the fitting PSDs as a means of preventing suicides was that the potential suicidees would merely seek an open station to commit the act. In the Hong Kong study, this proved to be largely unfounded, since the recorded incidents at open stations rose by only 12% during the post installation period. Climate control and energy savings form a large part of any business case for platform screen doors but cannot be counted for platform edge doors and half-height systems. In these cases, safety will be the primary factor, with the additional benefits of easier crowd control at peak times.

---

[1]Calculated using known prices in London and Hong Kong and uplifted to 2014 values.

Figure 6.5: *Platform Edge Doors installed at Southwark station on the Jubilee Line in London. The equipment has full height doors but does not have the enclosed screening needed to allow for climate control. Photo: P. Connor.*

6.7 Design Issues

The installation of PSDs in any form is necessarily a complex project, particularly if a retrofit is involved. In the case of new build, matters can be made easier by ensuring that the design parameters are understood at an early stage and that all the necessary interfaces with rolling stock, train control, communications, power supplies, emergency procedures, maintenance systems and the infrastructure are included. System engineering is an important part of the process, especially since train control must be linked with door control.

The door structure and glazing must be designed to allow emergency break-in to permit passengers to escape from the trackside. There must also be the facility to allow controlled evacuation from the train tunnel walkway to the platform. This is usually achieved by the provision of a separate end door.

The station control room will be equipped with a remote alarm system to alert staff to door failures or intrusions. A local control panel will be provided for each platform face, usually at the end of the platform where the train or platform staff can reach it quickly and have sight of the door line. Doors will be fitted with open indicator lights and with means to bypass local interlocking with train systems in case of failure. One feature of the design that must not be forgotten is the necessity for a proper electrical bonding and earthing system.

6.8 Case Study: Hong Kong

The Hong Kong Mass Transit Railway Corporation (MTRC) was the first railway in the world to undertake the complex task of retrofitting platform screen doors under a live passenger railway operation environment —(The Standard, 2008). The project was the largest of its kind in the world covering 74 platforms, three MTRC lines; namely the Tsuen Wan Line, the Kwun Tong Line and the Island Line. A total of 2,960 sets of PSDs were installed in 30 air-conditioned underground stations.

To ensure minimal disruption to the millions of passengers carried per day by MTRC, retrofitting works were carried out only during non-passenger service hours—between 2 am and 5 am every day. The primary objective of the retrofit was to improve the air-conditioning performance to get an ambient temperature to 24 degrees.

The scope of works consisted of Environmental Control System (ECS) modifications at 30 underground stations and Platform Screen Doors installations at 74 platforms. The works included:

- Modification of air-conditioning and tunnel ventilation equipment in 94 plant rooms

- Modification of some 27 km of air ducts

- Replacement of 170 air handling units of capacities from 400 kW to 1.5 MW

- Installation of an over-track PSD support structure and environmental seal

- Installation of 13.5 km of PSDs

For each platform, they had to install:

- 40 bi-parting doors-sets

- Controls and power supplies

- 10 emergency doorways

- Head and tail wall driver's and tunnel access doors

- Platform lighting & signage integrated into PSD header

The project cost HK\$2.3bn by 2008, equivalent to £12k per metre, including some additional air conditioning works.

References

'The Standard' Newspaper, Hong Kong, January 08, 2008.

Law, C K, Yip, P S F (2011); 'An economic evaluation of setting up physical barriers in railway stations for preventing railway injury: evidence from Hong Kong', Journal of Epidemiol Community Health, 2011.

Metrobits.org (accessed 30th June 2011) http://mic-ro.com/metro/platform-screen-doors.html

Mitchell, B (2003), 'Jubilee Line Extension', Thomas Telford, London, p 250.

Muraki et al (2010), 'Effect of Train Draft [sic] on Platforms and in Station Houses', JR EAST Technical Review-No.16, Spring 2010, Tokyo, Japan.

Chapter 7 Managing Station Stops

by Nigel G Harris

7.1 Introduction

For normal mainline railways, line capacity is determined by the signalling system, in particular, the number of aspects, and the spacing of signals. However, for urban railways, station stops may be the crucial feature, both for timetabling and operation. This is because the Run-Out/Run-In (platform reoccupation) time element of the headway is relatively fixed, but what happens at a station platform is potentially variable. Fortunately, that means that management can affect what happens across the four main areas of train service, station design, station management and rolling stock design. Each of these is considered separately below, but successful railways must manage these holistically, taking into account some basic principles of passenger flow, which are explained first.

7.2 Passenger Flow

Most understanding of transport passenger flow is based on the seminal work undertaken by J. J. Fruin in Canadian shopping malls in 40 years ago (Fruin, 1971). He identified a range of 'Levels of Service', corresponding to differing walk speeds and capacities. Level A represents free flow and Level F total congestion. On public safety grounds, most planning authorities will not accept station designs that could lead to conditions E and F and the key aim of station pedestrian planning is to ensure a smooth

Figure 7.1:
Wide stairway with greater provision for egress from platform above. Stairways also need to be sized for evacuation standards. Photo: N.G. Harris

(ideally continuous) stream of passengers between street and train (and vice versa).

Over the years, greater understanding has enabled the better application of the principles first outlined by Fruin. First of all, pedestrian movement is not equally fast in different physical situations, for instance being slower on stairs than on the level. This leads to the implication that passageways should be widened where there are stairs, although common practice is for stairs to be narrower, thereby creating an unnecessarily severe bottleneck.

Secondly, it must be recognised that passenger flow into stations may be reasonably even, but that leading out of stations is very 'lumpy', as large cohorts of passengers alight from trains and make straight for the exits. This leads to the conclusion that (even aside from considerations of egress during emergencies) facilities for exiting platforms and stations should be built larger than those for entering; although this is rarely done, examples do exist (see Figure 7.1).

Observations have also shown that people do not walk immediately next to walls or platform edges: so-called 'edge effects' apply to the edge 30 cms or so, which therefore remains relatively unused and does not contribute to the pedestrian flow capacity. On the outside corner of passageways, even more space may remain unused by pedestrians seeking to minimise their walking distance.

7.3 Train Service Impacts

Timetables for suburban services need to provide frequent even interval services. However, where mixed-traffic operation is required on the same tracks (e.g., the DART Northern corridor in Dublin has to retain some slots for inter-city services to/from Belfast), this may not be possible. As a consequence, more people inevitably turn up for trains on a longer headway (especially in the evening, when returning passengers have less control over their time of travel), leading to longer dwell times.

Where some trains turn short of the end terminus at an intermediate station, all passengers can board those trains that call at all stations to the end of the line, but only some find the shorter train workings valuable. The former services become more heavily-loaded (which means that it is more difficult for passengers to board) but more of them want to do so, so stop times tend to rise.

Figure 7.2: *Narrow platform, Shepherd's Bush, London. Photo: N.G. Harris*

Where services are branched, even if the branches have relatively even demand (e.g. the West Ruislip and Ealing Broadway branches of London's Central line), not all passengers board the first train, so platform capacity is at a premium. Those waiting for subsequent departures may interfere with passenger flow, again putting pressure on station dwell times.

Figure 7.3:
New train stopping marker posts at Oslo. Here they use the train length while in the UK the number of vehicles is used. Photo: N.G. Harris

7.4 Individual Station Design Impacts

In urban areas, individual stations really need to have platforms that are long enough to accommodate all trains, because train frequencies and loads make the consequences of service irregularity or selective door opening (SDO) too onerous. But platforms also need to be wide enough to handle the expected passenger flows: Network Rail width standards for 3m (side platform) and 5m (island platforms) also need to be tempered by the expected numbers of passengers. The Northbound platform at the new station at Shepherd's Bush (London) (Figure 7.2) had to be widened before opening in 2008, to ensure adequate space. Problems both with platform width and inadequate stair widths to avoid queuing on egress are also apparent in Paris' automated line 13.

Because trains may not be the same length as platforms, arrangements need to be put in place to ensure that passengers and trains alike use the same part of the platform. Appropriate signage is therefore needed both for train drivers and passengers (see Figure 7.3). A failure to do so leads to two problems: (i) an excess number of passengers may try to use the same door of the train, and (ii) any late-running passengers may have further (distance, hence time) to run to access the train. Both of these lead to train delays.

7.5 Station Impacts Along a Line

Problems with design at particular stations may be alleviated or exacerbated by the design of other stations on the same route. For instance, suburban stations on the route from London Victoria to Crystal Palace are well-spread between the front, middle and rear of the train, so evening peak trains leaving London are relatively equally-loaded, as passengers seek seats near to the exit at their particular station.

On the other hand, despite its excellent cross-platform interchanges and huge connectional value to London, LU's Victoria line suffers from having all the major entrances/exits to 14 of its 15 platforms right at the Southern end. This means that the southernmost vehicles are almost always crowded, even grossly so, whilst seats may be available at the other end of the train. Longer station stops caused by delays in the southernmost vehicle at Victoria were a key catalyst for station construction costing £500m but providing a new Northern entrance.

7.6 Station Management Impacts

A wide range of actions are available to train operators to reduce station stop times on urban railways to manageable levels. Perhaps the most widely known is that of actually pushing passengers on, in order to ensure quick door closure but this is relatively rare and increasingly unpopular with passengers. However, the wider issue of platform staffing can bring significant benefits, provided that they are pro-active.

Platform staff are rarely justified solely on the basis of their impact on punctual departures although, where train operators are penalised for poor punctuality, there can be a commercial case for doing so. Even then, the role of staff must include the pro-active distribution of passengers along the platform (which may mean temporarily keeping the areas at the entrance to platforms clear, quick attendance to any 'sticky' doors and an encouragement for passengers to stand clear when the doors are closing. However, a wider role also covering:

- information to passengers;
- assistance to the mobility impaired or any passengers taken ill;

Figure 7.4: *Platform Markings, Metro Rio. These are designed to encourage passengers waiting to board a train to stand either side of the doorway while others are alighting. Photo: N.G. Harris*

- minor cleaning; and

- security checks.

can make for a multi-purpose!cost-effective and satisfying job. The quantity of staff needed per platform should vary according to need and cost of labour, with some platforms needing only one person, part-time for an hour in each peak period, whilst at the other end of the spectrum, Sé station in Sao Paulo and Mong Kok in Hong Kong have one member of staff per train door during the peak.

Automated systems are also available to ensure the key principles of despatch (safety, consistency and process simplicity) but balancing punctuality and customer service can be difficult: doors that close on the basis of safe clearance authorised by laser may nevertheless shut in a passengers' face.

However, there are a range of cheaper and/or more subtle solutions that can also assist platform management. There is some debate about the effectiveness of markings on the platform (e.g., see Figure 7.4), since they inevitably attract the attention of boarders, who may then stand precisely in the way of alighters; use of an appropriate offset from the expected door position might perhaps be effective.

Other forms of information, both audible (whether pre-planned and/or ad-hoc) or visual (either fixed or variable (see Figures 7.5a and 7.6a) can also have a significant influence on the distribution of passengers. In

(a) *Fixed signage on London Underground station encouraging better passenger distribution at Vauxhall, London. Photo: N.G. Harris*

(b) *Train door sticker encouraging alighting before boarding, DSB, Copenhagen. Photo: N.G. Harris*

Figure 7.5: Information Signs to Encourage Efficient Passenger Behaviour.

addition, more subtle policies, such as the use of lighting, or the siting of attractive features such as suitably sited seating and shelter, also tend to draw people away from platform entrances.

Information should not be limited to the platform. In-train announcements and visual displays can encourage passengers to be ready to alight from the correct side of the train, and to know where to go upon alighting, thereby avoiding congestion on the platform. Again, displays can contain fixed information, such as the location of egress escalators (see Figure 7.6b) and real-time information (giving details of disruption on connecting lines).

Lastly, simple information on train doors can reduce one of the 'bugbears' of both passengers and operators alike—people trying to board before everyone has finished alighting. Stickers like that shown in Figure 7.5b have, in Copenhagen, been accompanied to good effect by humorous television advertising, emphasising the holistic approach needed in this area.

(a) *Real-time information on plat-form train describer at Danshøj sta-tion,Copenhagen. Photo: N.G. Harris*

(b) *Interior train display advis-ing of platform characteristics, JRE, Tokyo. Photo: N.G. Harris*

Figure 7.6: Information Provided on Trains for Passengers.

7.7   Rolling Stock Design

Although trains are built to carry people from A to B, their detailed design has a considerable impact on station stops and hence line capacity. Improving alighting and boarding rates means that cars with doors only at the ends are inadequate in urban areas, even though the vestibules split up the interior of the vehicle. Trade-offs need to be made between carrying capacity and throughput at stations: trains with up to 6 doors per car are known from the Far East.

However, the distribution of passengers along the train is also important and, for all intents and purposes, station stop times are determined by the busiest or critical door. Reducing the impact of the critical door can occur by reducing the number of passenger movements at it, which can be achieved either by increasing the number of doors or by spreading passenger demand in the train and on the platform more evenly.

Trains are commonly designed with capacity as a key output, but care must be taken with this, as maximising the number of seats will not maximise the capacity of the train as a whole; a seated passenger typi-cally takes up $0.3m^2$ whereas passengers are often required to stand at 4 passengers/m^2, 6/m^2 is a typical crush load in Western countries, and val-ues of up to 10/m^2 are known (e.g. from India, Brazil). However, seating

Figure 7.7: *Longitudinal seating and through gangways on Milan metro with wide aisles and a large number of handrails designed for maximum standing capacity. Photo: N.G. Harris*

quantity and configuration also have important impacts on passengers' ability to alight from, and board trains.

Having seats arranged longitudinally along the train eases the flow of boarders into the train, with grab-poles in the seated area encouraging them to stay there. However, the provision of wide through gangways can merely encourage more alighters and boarders to use the nearest door, which may become the critical one. Standback space behind the doors (i.e. in that part of the vestibule between the doors and any partition separating the vestibule from the seated area—see Figure 7.8) is particularly helpful in enabling a person (or luggage) to be kept out of the way and therefore not interfere with subsequent boarders.

In fact, door width is not always a direct influence on passenger movement rates, because it is dependent upon a key threshold being reached. As pedestrians are typically 60cms wide, any door less than about 1.3m does not permit the simultaneous movement of two people although Heinz (2003) did note that shoulder-to-shoulder flow enabled more than one person to move at once through smaller doors. Increasing door width beyond 1.3m has relatively little impact, because it is difficult to prevent passengers from either standing in the doorway or on the platform and constricting flow to about this width.

The positioning of grabpoles in vestibules also needs to be undertaken with care. If placed in the doorframe (as may occur with wide doors), they can obstruct multiple passenger flow, whilst the need for this can usually be catered for by adequate handholds on each side of the doorframe.

95

Grabpoles in the vestibule need to be located in such a way that passenger flow is not restricted when a group of passengers is holding on to the pole; even if centrally-located, this can be a problem in narrower trains.

Double-deck stock imposes serious increases in station stop times, for two main reasons: first, the steps from the upper and lower decks reduce average movement speeds, and secondly, in order to avoid loss of space, there tend to be fewer vestibules, so that the number of potential passenger movements at the critical door increases.

As well as impacting on passenger flows, door opening and closing processes, plus the operational rules for despatch, are also important in determining overall station stop times—it is rare for passenger movement time to constitute as much as half the time a train spends stationary at a stop. Modern safety systems often require more onerous interlockings to ensure full door closure of centrally-controlled doors, so that door opening and closing times are creeping up towards 5s and 10s respectively (see Buchmüller et al, 2008).

Figure 7.8: *Standback space provided next to doorway to reduce obstruction during boarding and alighting, Tyne & Wear Metro. Photo: N.G. Harris*

With legislation governing the provision of audible warnings before door closure commences, and staff reaction time (both to last passenger boarding, and to full door closure) also needed, achieving dwell times of as little as 20s is now increasingly difficult. However, train operators can make matters easier by moving to one-person operation, since this removes from the equation the need for the conductor's door to be closed after all the passenger doors, and for the extra despatch step of communication between the two members of staff.

7.8 Quantification

As managing station stops is particularly important for busy metros, a number of them have undertaken research in this area over the years. London Underground has perhaps been at the forefront of this, given the many constrictions of its old stations and the small loading gauge it inherited from being the world's first underground railway.

However, relationships postulated in 1988 have been found to break down at the highest passenger loads (Harris, 2006) whilst the metro and urban rail benchmarking programmes managed by Imperial College London have facilitated the collection of data internationally (Harris & Anderson, 2007). Following earlier research by Weidmann (1994), analysis of updated research undertaken for London Underground has now been published (Harris et al, 2014), which sets out for the latest relationships between many of the key potential variables and the rates of passenger boarding and alighting. These are summarised in Table 7.1 and 7.2.

7.9 Summary

Managing station stops is a critical element of running an urban railway, but involves a range of actions. Passenger flow, train service, station design, information management and rolling stock design all need to be considered holistically, with the aims of ensuring as smooth and even a flow of passengers as possible between street and train. The impact of bottlenecks in this process (such as the critical train door) needs to be reduced by whatever method is most cost-effective: this issue emphasises clearly the concept of the railway as a system.

Factor	Change	Typical Impact (rate/pass)
Constant term: 1.15 pass/second		
Number of alighters at the critical door	From 10 to 20	+75%
Ratio of alighters:boarders	From 2:1 to 3:1	+1.3%
Ratio of through passengers in vestibule: vestibule capacity	10% increase in vestibule occupancy from 50% to 60%	-6%
Platform on other side of train to separate boarders from alighters	addition	+43%
Vertical distance of gap between train and platform	Each extra 10cms	-13%
Train seating density (seats/m2 of total car floor area)	Each extra seat/m2	-16%
Inter-door distance (m)	Each extra metre	-2%

Table 7.1: *Factors affecting passenger alighting rates. Derived from Harris et al (2014)*

Factor	Change	Typical Impact (rate/pass)
Constant term: 0.093 pass/second		
Number of boarders at the critical door	From 10 to 20	+18%
Ratio of alighters:boarders	From 2:1 to 3:1	+0.4%
Ratio of through passengers in vestibule: vestibule capacity	10% increase in vestibule occupancy from 50 to 60%	-4%
Platform Width	Each extra metre	+0.6%
Steps into the train	Elimination, enabling direct flat access	+49%
Standbacks behind the doors	Each extra 10cms	+2.6%
Car Area/Door width	Moving from 2 to 3 doors per carriage	+4%

Table 7.2: *Factors affecting passenger boarding rates. Derived from Harris et al (2014).*

References

Buchmüller, S, Weidmann, U & Nash, A (2008), 'Development of a Dwell Time Calculation Model for Timetable Planning', Proc. COMPRAIL X pp. 525-534, WITpress, Southampton.

Fruin, J J (1971) 'Pedestrian Planning and Design'.

Harris, N. G. (2006), 'Train Boarding and Alighting Rates at High Passenger Loads.' Jnl. Adv. Transpn., 40 (3), 2006, pp. 249-263.

Harris, N. G., and R. J. Anderson (2006), 'An International Comparison of Urban Rail Boarding and Alighting Rates'. Jnl. Rail & Rapid Transit, 221 F4, 2007, pp. 521-526.

Harris, N G, Graham, D J, Anderson, R J & Li, H (2014), 'The Impact of Urban Rail Boarding and Alighting Factors', Transportation Research Board, Washington.

Heinz, W (2003), 'Passenger Service Times on Trains', PhD thesis, KTH University of Stockholm

London Underground Ltd. (1988), 'Station Stop Dynamics on London Underground', Operational Research Note 88/34, June 1988. (Author: J P McKenna).

Weidmann, U (1994), 'Der Fahrgastwechsel im öffentlichen Personenverkehr', Schriftenreihe des IVT, Zurich, no. 90.

Chapter 8   Fares and Fare Collection

by Nigel G. Harris

8.1   Introduction

Collecting fares from passengers is clearly critically important in ensuring a key income stream for any railway. But how this is undertaken on an urban or suburban railway can itself make a significant difference to the level of commercial operation, since it affects staffing, the use of space at stations, cashflow and the costs of operation as well as the income itself.

In general, a good fares policy needs to relate to:

1. Passengers' willingness-to-pay for the service;

2. The cost of providing that service;

3. A simple way of charging.

Because urban rail journeys are relatively short and the fares therefore relatively low cost and simplicity are perhaps proportionately more important than on longer-distance railways. Unfortunately, the social benefits of urban railways often lead politicians to intervene in urban rail fares policy in ways that may not be to the railway's advantage. Importantly, overall fares reductions may simply reduce income, putting sustained maintenance and investment (hence future service quality) at risk, because Government funding may not always be available to make up any shortfall.

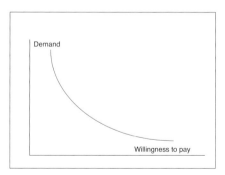

Figure 8.1: *demand curve.*
Source: *N.G. Harris*

In theory, to maximise income, each passenger should be charged what they are able to pay, from which we could derive a demand curve (see Figure 8.1). However, whilst such a policy fails the simplicity test, metros and urban railways do need to take into account some variation in willingness-to-pay. The way this is undertaken is by identifying some broader market segments, between which fares can be differentiated. Not to do this wastes a huge potential opportunity for revenue. Market segments need to be identified to be as homogenous as possible within the segment, whilst as different as possible from other groups. The most common example of a market segment-specific fare on urban rail systems relates to the morning peak (e.g. before 09:30). Here, a combination of:

- overcrowding (leading to higher costs, especially those that are capacity-related);

- journeys to work or on business (implying trips made by those with higher income levels); and

- an unequivocal market segment definition (is it before or after 09:30?)

leads to the ideal conditions for charging a higher rate. Urban railways who do not make some price differentiation by time of day are, again, prejudicing their commercial sustainability, as otherwise high unnecessary expenditure may be required.

The case for evening peak time restrictions is less clear-cut, because of the higher proportion of discretionary travellers (e.g. shoppers) and the lower absolute level of demand often found (resulting from the spread of work leaving times compared to a standard start time of 08:30 or 09:00). However, a key problem for railways arises with setting season-ticket fares for commuting traffic. There are several good reasons for offering discounts for season tickets, including that:

- money is received (often significantly) in advance of the time of travel, giving a cash-flow benefit;

- the number of trips per transaction is relatively high, so that the costs of servicing it are relatively low;

- the absolute level of the fare charged may be very significant, and there is some evidence that passengers are more sensitive to larger physical outlays.

But season ticket discounts can be—and often are—taken too far. Season tickets are purchased by those with jobs, who are (almost by definition) likely to be richer than those without, and hence relatively able to pay. The discounts given for multiple purchase can be excessive—for instance, some railways offer weekly season tickets priced equivalent to only 2.5 daily tickets. But more importantly, season-ticket holders generally travel in peak periods, where they cause greatest inconvenience to other passengers (through crowding) and cost to the railway. It is a common myth that railways make money in the peak, whereas in fact the opposite is true: peak operations are usually loss-making, because of the inefficient use of assets. Many urban railways have trainsets that only make one revenue-earning journey in each direction each day, once in each peak; the remainder of the time these trains sit in sidings earning nothing. Many urban railways also have other physical assets (such as property) only used during peak periods; the opportunity cost of London's Cannon Street terminal (which is very quiet outside peak periods) could easily be £1bn in terms of its potential use for other purposes.

Before changing fares, metros need to understand passengers' likely responses as measured through elasticities (see section 3.3). Because passenger demand falls as fares rise (and vice versa), own-price fares elasticities are negative. (Cross-price elasticities, which relate the demand for one product (e.g. rail travel) relative to a change in the fare of another (e.g. bus travel) are usually positive).

In an urban environment, metros and suburban railways are often in quite a strong competitive position, as road congestion is likely to make car and bus services unattractive. Peak passengers are therefore often able to pay higher fares, implying that the loss of demand per % increase in fare (the elasticity) is relatively small. In the off-peak, road conditions are usually

Conditions	Location	Short-Term	Long-term
Urban transit, peak	Australia	-0.25	-0.5
Urban transit, offpeak,	Australia	-0.45	-0.9
Suburban rail leisure	N England	-0.62	-0.91
Suburban rail commuting	SE England	-0.42	-0.62
London Underground,	Commuting	-0.30	-0.44
London Underground	Business England	-0.08	-0.12 -0.9
Urban transit, peak	USA	-0.2	
Urban transit, offpeak	USA	-0.4	
Urban transit, senior citizens,	USA	-0.21	

Table 8.1: *Own-Price Fares Elasticity Estimates. Sources: Litman (2011); Wardman & Shires (2003); White (2002); TRB (2004)*

easier so that non-rail modes are more competitive and therefore elasticities are larger. Moreover, there is a distinction between the short-term and the long-term; in the longer-term, passengers may undertake much more significant actions, such as buying another car or moving house, so long-term elasticities are substantially higher than short-term ones. Table 8.1 gives some examples from the literature.

Governments usually regulate urban rail fares because, if they did not, railways with low elasticities would increase fares significantly, taking advantage of passengers' higher willingness-to-pay. In addition, if demand fell, it would be possible for rail operators to reduce costs slightly (e.g. by reducing train length), giving a double incentive for them to increase fares. For Governments, though, rail transport may be the only effective way of enabling cities to exist, generating the wealth that national economies need, and providing the related social benefits (time savings, road congestion relief, urban form etc.). The actual level of fares that are sustainable will depend upon market conditions, including the distances travelled, the fares on competing modes, the availability of car-parking and the extent of road congestion, or city centre charges to reduce it, as in London.

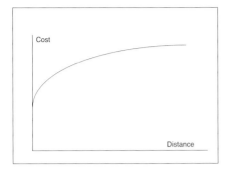

Figure 8.2: *Typical taper on distance-based fares. Source: N.G. Harris*

8.2   Fare Scales

Having decided a general policy of how cheap or expensive to be, railways then have to set an actual fare for each trip. The three common methods are distance-based, zonal or flat-fare. Distance-based fares tend not merely to follow a simple money/kilometre ratio, but to include a base minimum fare element; this avoids the shortest trips having unduly low fares. In addition, distance-based fares normally taper somewhat with distance (see Figure 8.2), so that the per-km rate is lower over longer distances than short ones; this may be seen to be more inclusive for the wider urban area, although it can lead to the effective subsidisation of richer people living further out than poorer people living in inner suburbs.

Distance-based fares can be very complicated, as each station:station pair is likely to be a different distance and therefore requires a different fare. However, the minimum fare and taper elements do bear some relationship to the cost of providing the service; station service costs are not heavily-dependent upon journey distance, whilst increasing journey length may only incur a marginal cost to the railway. This is particularly the case for urban railways carrying a predominance of radial trips, and that may have significant costs associated with city-centre operation (perhaps because railways are underground). The other extreme type of fare is the flat fare, where all trips are charged at the same rate. This is obviously very simple, but issues of equity arise as systems get larger. For instance,

105

following a recent extension of the Orange line, residents of Laval have campaigned to travel on the Montreal metro at the same (flat) fare as residents of Montreal, even though they are travelling from further out. So, whilst flat-fare systems can be appropriate for simple (e.g. one-line) metro systems, the larger the system, the less commercially-astute this is.

Zonal systems attempt to achieve a balance between the other two extremes. Directly-adjacent stations, or those in some small geographic area, are given the same fares to/from all other zones, with the same standard fare for local trips within the zone. Where there is a dominant urban centre (as in Paris), zones may be concentric; where they are not (for instance in Germany's Ruhrgebiet, or North East England (Newcastle/Sunderland)) a system of interlocking hexagonal zones may be used (see Figure 8.2).

8.3   Systems

The next decision for any urban rail operator is to decide what physical systems are to be used to sell, validate and check tickets, as well as managing the associated processes and monetary transactions. Originally, railway ticket office staff were used just to sell single and return tickets, but the volume of business at many urban railways makes this cost-ineffective, if not actually physically impossible. Ticket machines are universally used on urban railways, where many transactions are low-value, and where the number of important traffic destinations may be limited (e.g. to the main urban centre), enabling machines to be kept simple. However, the costs of handling large volumes of cash (as well as the potential for damage or fraud) mean that machines taking credit/debit cards are widely-used instead. Modern machines often use a sequence of displays on a touch-sensitive screen to provide all the relevant options to customers; this can reduce the number of individual buttons required, and hence make machines easier to use by the visually-impaired.

Tickets themselves are increasingly not just pieces of paper, as operators transfer to electronic products with other uses too. Tickets with magnetic stripes are being replaced by Smartcards of various descriptions, of which Hong Kong's Octopus and London's Oyster are perhaps the most famous. These can either be loaded up with season ticket validity, or a smaller

Figure 8.3: *Rhein-Ruhr Verkehrsverbund Zonal Map.*
Source: *http://www.vrr.de/imperia/md/images/verbundg*

amount of value enabling individual trips to be made, with the value of the trip being removed from the stored value when placed on card readers at ticket gates or elsewhere. The ability to add larger quantities of stored value gives the train operator the same type of retailing cost reduction benefit as season tickets, but Smartcards have other benefits to the passenger, including the potential ability to make other purchases. Recent developments in this field in London use a standard bank card, from which a direct debit are made for travel, and which would could lead to the metro not needing to issue its own card at all.

8.4 Ways of Selling Tickets

Whilst the income from selling tickets is obvious, the costs of achieving this must not be forgotten; Lewis (2011) noted that the even cost of sales through Oyster was 14% of the ticket price. Understandably, this is a key factor driving Transport for London's thinking about ticket retailing. The use of staff in ticket offices, in particular, is not cheap, and is relatively expensive for short-distance trips, since the same time may be taken to issue a low-value ticket as a high-value one. Many operators are therefore seeking to stop selling tickets in this manner, although there is some resistance to this both from passengers and Government; the British Department for Transport suggested that it would not normally support closure of suburban rail ticket offices selling more than one ticket every five minutes. Selling tickets at stations also takes up space that, for an urban railway, may be at a premium: the space may be better used either for extra circulation/passenger flow or for more profitable commercial activities.

Selling tickets off the system (e.g. through newsagents) can enhance the reach and visibility of the railway, but commission of several % of the face value will have to be paid, and this may only be feasible for simpler ticket types. Ticket selling also requires equipment, which may be leased; current rates for the annual leasing of machines and gates are each around £15,000. Internet retailing of rail tickets is relatively uncommon (if reasonably cost-effective) for low-value urban area sales but technology is now enabling mobile phone applications as a further alternative. Back-office systems are also required, especially where revenues need to be apportioned between different operators.

Although it may be customer-friendly to offer a range of ticket sales methods, multiple ticket-selling channels can lead to duplicated costs. For instance, ticket office staff may be less-than-fully used once electronic ticketing systems are introduced, but will still need to be paid for the whole shift.

8.5   Revenue Protection Issues

The numbers of passengers on mass transit rail services make manual ticket inspection ineffective, so ticket gates are an important element of revenue protection. Whilst they have the additional benefit of reducing access to the system by vagrants, barrier lines usually need to be staffed, in case problems arise and this adds cost, even if also providing additional customer service opportunities. Paper-type tickets are normally fed through the barrier, for the magnetic stripe to be read, whilst Smart-cards can be read electronically by merely passing them over the reader. Reading times are of the order of 200-300ms, enabling theoretical passenger flows of up to 45 passengers/minute and actual passenger flows of nearer 25 passengers/minute; these figures are of course affected by the familiarity of the system to passengers and the amount of luggage etc.

References

Lewis, P (2011) 'How TfL will operate Oyster card alongside contactless bankcards to increase customer convenience', Rail Revenue Customer Management Conference, Amsterdam.

Litman, T (2011) 'Transit Price Elasticities and Cross Elasticities', Victoria Transport Policy Institute Australia,
available at http://www.vtpi.org/tranelas.pdf

Transportation Research Board (2004) 'Transit Pricing and Fares', TCRB Report 95 Chapter 12, available at
http://www.trb.org/publications/tcrp/tcrp_rpt_95c12.pdf

Wardman, M & Shires (2003) 'Review of Fares Elasticities in Great Britain', ITS Working Paper 573, University of Leeds, available at
http://eprints.whiterose.ac.uk/2059/1/ITS34_WP573_uploadable.pdf

White, P R (2002), 'Public Transport: Its Planning, Management & Operation'

Chapter 9 Interchanges that Improve the Passenger Experience

by John Austin and Felix Schmid

9.1 Enhancing the Attractiveness of Public Transport

Quality of passenger experience is vital to the way travellers perceive urban rail and an important part of that experience is contributed by the interchanges between modes or even between routes in the same mode.

Trams and urban light rail have traditionally been seen in many parts of continental Europe as the backbone of an urban public transport network. However, in order to perform that role effectively they have to complement other elements of the network, such as bus, metro and regional rail services, so that the traveller is able to switch easily between different modes within a single journey. Changing modes is facilitated by good physical interchange arrangements, by appropriate ticketing systems and through the provision of up-to-date and well presented information.

The challenge to provide quality interchange is relevant both where there is a deregulated bus market, as in the UK outside London and where there is 'planned integration', as in London and elsewhere in Europe. Deregulation certainly poses heightens that challenge, forcing the public sector promoter to take account of possibly rapidly-changing and perhaps competing bus services when designing tram and light rail or ticketing and information systems. But it does not change the need for the rail systems to play a key role in delivering a single coherent system that serves the users' needs.

Even where bus services are regulated, it does not necessarily mean that the challenge of getting urban rail to deliver the core of an effectively 'unified' transport system is any easier, particularly if there are different organisations operating the different modes, with different and perhaps 'uncoordinated' financial and performance targets. So how can urban or suburban rail fulfil its central role in a city's public transport network and meet citizens', promoters' and stakeholders' expectations?

Figure 9.1: *An example of a modern, high-capacity, low-floor urban tram vehicle in Porto. Low level platforms are provided at stops to allow level access to the trams. Photo: F. Schmid.*

One way in which rail systems have sought to attract passengers is by raising the quality of the rolling stock. New-generation trams are air-conditioned, low-floor and designed for level access and there have been a number of tram refurbishment or replacement programmes in recent years, including Metrolink in Manchester and the new fleets being introduced in Croydon, Zürich (Switzerland) and in Warsaw (Poland) this follows a natural development as technology and design standards become more advanced. Rail systems are also improving the capacity and visual impact of vehicles. Other ways of making systems more useful is by extending the 'reach' of networks by extending lines into new housing and business districts and by creating short underground corridors in congested areas, such as in the centre of Karlsruhe in Germany.

As mentioned at the beginning of this section though, the rail 'product' can be developed so as to properly perform its role is by improving interchanges and making the transition between themselves and other modes, including park-and-ride, smoother, easier and more pleasant.

9.2 Evolution of Interchange Concepts

The public transport industry in some cities and countries has a tacit understanding that interchange is something that passengers do not like doing and, indeed, that it should be avoided wherever possible. Interchange is seen as removing passengers from the safe environment of the tram (or bus, or train) to an area that is unknown and where they may feel abandoned by the system. For this reason bus operators will often tend to want to run through services rather than connect with rail, if they have the choice. This was a clear feature, for instance, in the relationship of the bus operators with the Tyne & Wear Metro (Newcastle-upon-Tyne, UK) at the time of bus service deregulation.

One way of dealing with the difficulty or unattractiveness of the task of interchange between tram, light rail or metro and other modes is to make the interchange bigger, and somehow 'iconic'. This approach has been adopted by cities such as Madrid with its family of suburban and edge-of-city-centre bus/metro interchanges. Another good example is the Haymarket interchange in Newcastle-upon-Tyne, which has established itself as a landmark for the city.

However, iconic interchanges can be expensive to construct and maintain and may only be suitable for locations with a very high footfall. For smaller interchanges a simplified approach can be more suitable, provided that the use of standardised and cost-effective technologies enables the required functionality and attractiveness to be achieved without making the interchange appear low cost and 'down at heel'.

An important feature for interchanges of all sizes is the incorporation of retail and leisure-focused features, making the interchange an attractive place to wait for the tram, bus or train, and, to a certain extent, turning it into a destination in its own right. Abellio, Merseytravel's contracted operating partner in the Merseyrail urban rail network, has introduced the 'M to Go' concept of combining convenience store retail outlets with ticket offices at Merseyrail stations, based on its experience in the Netherlands.

In Gothenburg, the tram/bus interchange at the centre of the busy Korsvägen road intersection incorporates retail facilities, a café and a waiting room with real-time information. It is important to recognise that interchanges must be functional, enabling easy and convenient transfer and protected as much as possible from the weather, again irrespective of size.

But this is not simply about generating income, it is as much about making the traveller feel looked after. Quality information, an essential feature of a good interchange, is part of that process of caring for the passenger and making him or her feel valued.

Figure 9.2: *Well designed displays for platform information are essential to assist passengers at interchanges and to provide them with a feeling of comfort with the system they are using. Photo: F. Schmid.*

In his challenging book, 'Transport for Suburbia', Paul Mees highlights Toronto as the benchmark for rail-bus and rail-tram interchanges, with what he terms 'free-body' transfers at most underground stations outside the Central Business District. By this he means direct transfer between the modes using a single ticket: in fact the whole rail-bus interchange is inside the station fare gates.

Even though the exact configuration of such close bus/tram interchanges vary from place to place according to the ticketing systems used, the general principal is clear: the distance covered between connecting services must be as short as possible. In the HiTrans Best Practice Guide 2: Public Transport: Planning the Networks (Neilsen, 2005), it is suggested there should be "a five-step distance (with) protection from the weather in a clean and nice environment". This objective is clearly only achievable in the smallest of interchanges but the ambition is laudable.

Another enhancement advocated by Mees is cross-platform interchange between different modes or connecting services. Examples from the UK are Mile End Underground Station where there is cross-platform interchange between the District and Central lines and Stratford, where cross-platform interchange exists between the Central Line and National Rail suburban services to and from Romford. The multi-level station also facilitates interchange with the Docklands Light Railway (DLR) and its Stratford International extension that opened on 31 August 2011.

Stratford International is an intermediate station on the High Speed 1 (HS1) link to mainland Europe, where the Javelin domestic services from towns in the county of Kent stop before they continue to St. Pancras International Station in London. Stratford International creates connectivity with the DLR to the major business district at Canary Wharf and to the City of London via London Liverpool Street. London's Crossrail provides a link to the West End and Heathrow from 2018. Similar features are seen in the centre of Brussels, between the metro, 'pre-metro' and trams at the Brussels Midi station. More recently, three developments have led to a renewed interest in improving intermodal interchange: The first is the continued growth of major cities and the associated growth in rail travel. The second is the growth of more powerful partnerships in cities, with organisations like Règie Autonome des Transport de Paris (RATP) and Transport for London (TfL) being given a much more pivotal role in local rail developments in the last few years. Similarly, Britain's Integrated Transport Authorities (ITAs) have been handed the responsibility for developing the local networks, with the objective of providing better information coherence and coverage. A third key development has been the rapid advance of ITS (Intelligent Transport Systems) and other technologies.

9.3 Interchange Best Practice

Policy-makers and implementers have long grappled with the problem of interchange and a flurry of activity began in the late 1990s with a number of best practice guides. The then UK's Department of the Environment, Transport and the Regions (DETR) and the Chartered Institute of Logistics and Transport (CILT) both produced handbooks in 1998, as did the European GUIDE project in 1999.

The CILT report described passenger interchanges as "a practical way of achieving passenger transport integration" and all reports recognised the need for the interchange to be appropriately sited, with good facilities, attractive imagery, accurate information, good signage and a high level of personal security. This last issue is particularly important where the immediate surroundings could be seen as threatening or where potential assailants could hide out of sight of the traveller. The park-and-ride sites on Nottingham Express Transit (NET), for instance, are monitored by CCTV cameras and patrolled by NET staff. NET emphasises that the sites have been designed "to the latest security standards and include emergency help points with a direct link to the NET control room".

One reflection of the renewed interest in interchange quality was the Better Rail Stations report for the UK's Department for Transport produced in 2009 by Chris Green and Peter Hall and the TfL Interchange Best Practice Guidelines of the same year. The Better Rail Stations report highlighted the need for clear customer standards for stations; indeed it had a robust six-tier hierarchy for categorising stations similar to those used in several other countries, with customer standards matched to the different categories.

9.4   Intelligent Transport System Opportunities

Intelligent transport systems (ITS) developments can add value at both large and small interchanges. They make it easier to automate processes and can transfer activities from being carried out physically at the interchange itself to being carried out on travellers' smartphones (or similar devices, supplied with data remotely via a telecoms link). They can provide communication between the traveller at small interchanges and remote centres via electronic kiosks or help points, substituting for the physical presence of staff. The same system can deliver real-time information on the status of all modes of transport present at the interchange to customers' mobile devices, to handheld terminals carried by local and roving staff, and to information displays. Ticket sales at unstaffed interchanges are rapidly transferring to mobile technology.

At large interchanges ITS now provide a richer customer experience. Software standards have been developed to harness increased computing power to provide location-specific information services and one key standard is the IFOPT Specification (Identification of Fixed Objects in Public Transport) recently developed by CEN, the European Committee for Standardisation. This describes the detailed structure of the information required for a 'Stop Place', such as a light rail station or multi-modal interchange, including entrances, pathways and accessibility limitations.

With IFOPT, it becomes possible to provide electronic information about all the interchange facilities that Better Rail Stations recommends; such as cycle hubs, disabled access, car parking facilities, and bus stops in relation to the rail entrance. Journey planning can be provided in a more detailed way, while on-the-go re-planning becomes possible when detailed digital spatial data is combined with real-time information on incidents and delays.

Work that the author carried out a few years ago for the European Commission's CODE project analysed passenger information-seeking as five different activities: 'Journey Creation', 'End Linkages', and, within the interchange, 'Verification', 'Anticipation' and 'On-the-Spot Orientation'. For regular travellers much of that will not be necessary if the public transport system performance operates reliably. But new or infrequent travellers, on urban systems particularly, wish to check that things are going as planned, look out for possible service disruptions and check that they know where to go, relative to where they are now.

Larger interchanges need to have that information readily visible though physical signs and colour-coding and the presence of clear information boards and, dependant on size, the physical presence of staff. Digitisation of the information also makes it possible to provide it through smartphones and similar devices. With an interchange that has been described according to IFOPT, a smartphone or similar companion device can guide a traveller has pre-recorded his or her travel itinerary. Travellers can be guided 'intelligently' around the interchange, while being provided and provided with personalised alerts that make his or her journey easier.

It can be seen that the interchange needs to be fully described in IFOPT if it is to perform at a robust level. With limited finance available for gathering the necessary data it is essential that the data collection is right first time and done in a standardised way across a conurbation. This is a further reason to have a single body in charge of all interchanges in a conurbation, as the Britain's ITAs are proposing.

Figure 9.3: *Smartphone app showing the train services and interchanges provided with other services at Peterborough, England. The date is provided through a company (Realtime Trains) using open access railway network data. Photo: F. Schmid.*

The fully 'Intelligent Interchange' will be characterised by a number of features, based on hardware, software and thought-ware. Hardware is likely to include barcode and QR readers, electronic kiosks and different types of Near Field Communication (NFC) devices. It is also possible that at larger interchanges, which feature connections with inter-urban or regional services, there might be publicly-accessible but security-controlled areas accessed by means of personal devices, such as car parks and cycle storage.

Software and services will include detailed route planning within the interchange, faster information access, integrated payment systems and information retrieval and could include features such as targeted advertising, passenger counting services and taxi-sharing based on common destinations.

One smartphone facility that is becoming increasingly important is the use of apps and there are now a huge number for giving information and planning journeys on urban light rail, metro and tram networks across the world, from Manchester Metrolink and the Tyne & Wear Metro in the UK, Luas in Ireland, and the Lyon and Paris Métros in France, to the

VBB Rail and Tram network in Germany, the MRT in Hong Kong and various subways in Korea.

There is also plenty of anecdotal evidence that smartphone apps both increase traveller satisfaction and that users are prepared to pay for them, potentially providing another revenue stream. However, many of these applications have been developed by the private sector from integrated information provided by the operators or regulators. It is therefore critical that the necessary information is provided as Open Data to enable developers to produce them.

9.5 Complementary vs. Integrated Modes

Linking efficiently and effectively complementary and integrated modes is always going to be a challenge where different organisations run individual modes under separate contracts, but with only a minimal requirement to integrate fares and where there is a supervisory body that has relatively limited powers.

The tram and (say) bus networks may have been designed to be integrated but without suitably designed operating contracts the integration in practice may be very limited. In fact the practical effect of elements of the contracts may be to dis-incentivise co-ordination between modes. In this respect it is not enough merely to locate light rail or tram stops physically near bus or rail stops and stations. There has to be good directional signage between modes (including good lighting) and clear onward and local area travel information at the stops / stations, including orientation maps.

Multi-modal tickets must be easily obtainable: in Dublin, for instance, multimodal Luas/Dublin Bus tickets cannot be bought from Dublin Bus drivers. By contrast, in Nottingham bus drivers sell combined tram/bus tickets, and this is not just the case for buses of Nottingham City Transport (which has a share in the NET tram operating company) but also for Trent Barton and Premiere Travel for those of their services that are co-ordinated with the tram.

119

9.6　The Importance of Modal Integration

There are four main reasons why modal integration is a key to achieving high passenger numbers and in getting regular travellers to leave their car at home and use the different rail modes of transport. Firstly, the system's potential users will expect a modally-integrated easy-to-use network, as they will know that they have paid towards the rail 'core' through public funds. If the resultant public transport network is not modally-integrated they will inevitably resent it and there may well be a public backlash against using it.

Secondly, if the network is not modally integrated the 'generalised cost' in using it can increase considerably, not just directly through perhaps having to buy separate tickets, but quite possibly due to increased waiting time through uncoordinated connections, and certainly in increased 'hassle'. This all creates a journey that is very far from 'seamless'.

Thirdly, without integrated multi-modal real-time information, the end-to-end journey becomes very difficult to understand and the traveller can feel abandoned and at the mercy of the public transport operators. This is a contrast to the car, which may be slow and frustrating but still feels as if the driver is 'in control'. This issue is exacerbated with the rapid development of technology, where mobile device apps that integrate multi-sourced information are increasingly becoming available to give information to ease the car driver's journey. In order to keep pace with this, public transport needs to provide the same quality of integrated information.

Fourthly, a modally-integrated public transport network becomes a valuable feature of a city's life, which can benefit the city's economy by making local travel easier.

The rapid advances in technology now make it possible to provide much better digital information to urban rail and tram users at interchanges than hitherto, as long as operators and transport authorities grasp the opportunities. As the authors of this chapter have shown, this has to be backed with coherent and consistent physical information and with staff who are 'digitally-equipped' in order that urban networks with trams and light rail at their heart can fulfil their potential.

References

Mees, P., (2010), 'Transport for Suburbia: Beyond the Automobile Age', London, 2010: ISBN: 978-1-84407-740-03

Nielsen, G., (2005), 'HiTrans Best Practice Guide 2: Public Transport: Planning the Networks', EU North Sea Region / Rogaland County Council, Oslo, 2005

Bibliography

CILT (2000), 'Passenger Interchanges: A Practical Way of Achieving Passenger Transport Integration', London 2000.

Chapter 10 Passenger Communications

A case study on London Underground

by Sonja Hedgecock and Carolyn Casey

10.1 Introduction

Since Railways began, communications have often been highlighted as essential in managing incidents effectively and reducing risk overall. Following the fire in the Kings Cross London Underground station on 18th November 1987 in which 31 people died, the Fennell Report into the incident stated: "Good communications are at the heart of a modern system of mass transportation".

Communications and safety often go hand in hand and much work has been done since the Kings Cross Fire to improve communications—not just within London Underground (LU) itself but also between the railway and its customers. However, the rapid progress in communications system technologies have made information almost instantly available to a wide section of the public at large. This has resulted in an increase in customer expectations on how LU communicates service status and updates to passengers. Whilst LU has strived to accommodate this increase with various improvements and initiatives, it has not always been possible to keep up with the customer demand for up to the minute information. That said, there are many different media used to communicate information to customers that have developed over time and we will be exploring some of these media in greater detail in this chapter.

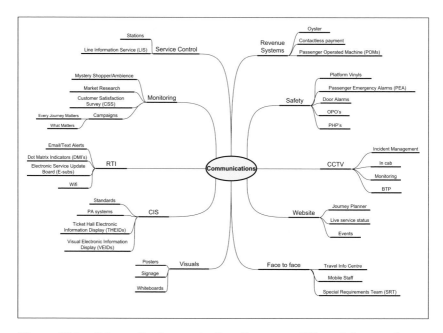

Figure 10.1: *Schematic demonstrating the many different forms of communication that exists within London Underground. Source: London Underground*

LU corporate strategy is greatly influenced by many external factors, such as the changing environment, culture shifts, political influences and technology advancements, to name but a few. In recent years, LU's overall management has moved towards control by the Mayor of London and all London's transport systems have been 're-homed' under the pan Transport for London (TfL) umbrella in an effort to get them managed more holistically. Simultaneously, LU changed its strategy in order to become more customer-focused. The need is to shift the focus to become less about the mode of transport and more about improving the quality of the journey experience for the travelling public. As LU started to understand the importance of Real Time Information (RTI) to customers, it became necessary to measure how well they were performing against customer expectations. Listening to the customer and embracing new technologies in response to customer demand has become central to LU's future. This has resulted in an examination of current practices to see if they fulfil the requirement of today's paying customer. The diagram in Figure 10.1 demonstrates the many different forms of communication that exist within LU. These were evaluated to determine that they achieved their purpose in a practical and meaningful way.

This chapter begins by examining communication on the railway to get an overall picture of the current status and the issues it faces in the future. Then, it looks at the many forms of communication that exist in LU as illustrated in Figure 10.1. We explore the main areas of communication that affect LU customers the most, especially areas that are currently undergoing changes as LU carries out its strategic vision. For example, the recent introduction of WiFi has been a positive step in bringing LU into line with the level of RTI the customer has access to on a day-to-day basis.

We consider how a big issue for LU is that its infrastructure is a major limitation in its attempt to deliver changes in communications. The pace of advancement versus the age of the assets means some of the changes are not that easily achieved. Funding is also an issue—LU has to generate revenue to justify and implement the necessary changes. Also, we note that shifts in human behaviour inform change but also that LU needs to influence customer behaviour in order to maximise the limits of the environment.

To conclude this chapter, we look to the future, considering the changes currently being made and what impact these will have on customer expectations and LU effectiveness in delivering these expectations and we consider the potential paths LU could follow as technology and expectations grow.

10.2 Types of Communication on LU

The LU communication system aims to support and facilitate the functioning of the railway system. The system is expected to provide safe, efficient and reliable operation and, normally, the communication system is expected to support:

- Signalling and train traffic control
- Maintenance and emergency control

- Passenger information systems

- Station management systems

- Trainborne communication systems

- Data communication for signalling, SCADA and automatic fare ticketing

- Functions at stations and control centres

Railway communication, in its simplest form, is provided by a series of telecommunication bearers with links to trains either by wayside signals and/or radio. Historically, railway communications have been based on analogue radio and landline telephony. These communication networks tended to be owned by the railway in order to meet the its particular requirements and, in many cases, it led to bespoke system designs to comply with these requirements.

Signalling and train control is a critical element of railway operation as it is responsible for safe train movements. Traditionally, these were track-based, localised communication systems in the form of track circuits, points and mechanical interlocking. However, signalling and train control have been developing and moving away from track-based to train-based operation using data communication systems. This change came about as a result of continuous improvement to the railway whole-life cycle and parallel moves towards reduced maintenance and operational downtime costs. This has led to the widespread use of new positioning systems and new communications and information technologies to provide better location awareness and more information to help increase capacity and enhance safety and reliability, thereby ultimately satisfying more customers.

Railway communications have evolved and will continue to develop, from the basic mechanical signage to more sophisticated communication systems that allow greater areas to be connected such as communication-based train control, long line PA and CCTV (onboard and wayside). The expectation is that as technology advances rapidly in the communication world, the railway's communication systems will develop either by choice or as a result of obsolescence and interoperability (GSM-R/ETCS) requirements. This has forced the railway to start developing a strategic plan towards a more harmonised railway communication system. The new challenge facing railway telecommunications today is the increasing convergence of internet based technology within the telecom industries. In order for the railway to take advantage of these new technologies and move away from reliance on costly bespoke technology, a clear strategic approach is necessary to ensure effective design and management. The Future Railway Project has published a 2020 vision and strategy (RDG, 2012).

Information systems are now becoming an essential part of the railway delivery process in order to meet the customer demands and expectations created by fast moving mobile technology and smartphone development. The following customer services that can currently be found on the railway network are:

- An integrated transport system, or intelligent transport system as it is now commonly referred to by some. This is to allow dynamic schedule calling and provide real time information to passengers;

- Passenger information systems that provide next train displays, on-time running and delay and disruption details;

- Train operation including incident and performance management.

As stated above, fast development within the telecoms industry is forcing the railway to think strategically in order to address issues such as obsolescence and the movement to digital technology. Within the telecommunications industry, a general approach to digital data exchange was developed around the following internet protocols:

- Data language and formats such as extensible mark up language (XML) for data description;

- Transmission control protocol and internet protocol TCP/IP for networking of applications;

- Public key certificate or digital certificate for security.

There is currently no standardised railway communications approach to digital and internet based technology. The main standardised telecommunications found within the railway are GSM-R (the Network Rail communications system) and TETRA (London Underground's CONNECT communications system). TETRA is also used by the safety services (e.g. fire, police). TETRA is a digital radio system that, amongst other things, enables:

- Group calling;

- Simultaneous voice and data communication;

- Multiple communication channels on a single radio bearer;

- Rapid call establishment;

- Efficient use of bandwidth.

The Future Railway Project (RDG, 2012) and the DfT (2012) talk about railway and the likely changes over the next 20 to 30 years, where the public demographic changes in the form of an increase in older passengers and rises in fuel prices. This will lead to more people relying on public transport. Therefore, the passenger expectation of the services provided will be higher, with less overcrowding, better station facilities, improved functionalities and fewer bus replacement services during engineering works.

Accessibility of trains and stations will be increasingly important as such passengers will expect to be able to plan and navigate their journey from end-to-end, which means that better integrated modes of transport and a unified ticketing service will be required. There is also a need to be able to re-plan journeys en-route in the event of disruption. All this will need to be planned and managed to ensure customer satisfaction. However, since communications systems connect devices, operating systems and people there are many challenges facing the railway operator both today and in the future. These challenges vary from technical to human factors related issues, as highlighted below:

- The railway network is controlled at number of different levels, these are:

    - Drivers, signallers, controllers, stations and maintenance workers;

    - Communication processes between various functions;

- Difficulties in achieving continuous coverage for the railway corridor due to:

    - Propagation and losses especially in the tunnel environment;

    - Interference and intermodulation related issues;

    - The train as a Faraday cage.

- Spectrum and licences issues for the railway;

- Licenced vs unlicenced

- Communication network security issues— Comms infrastructure and technological convergence

Voice communication is vital to the safe and effective operation of the railway. This is even more so when a signalling failure occurs. It is essential that there is a mechanism that enables communication with customers during failures, either between the train driver and customers or directly with the operator in the control centre and/or station.

The increased need to meet customer demands, expectation, growth and the rapid technological development in this area, such as VoIP, communication based signalling, integrated customer information and real time information, is leading to an increased reliance on data-based communication systems. This, in itself, leads to higher data transmission rates than currently achieved and this is driving compression technology development and designs for more efficient use of bandwidth.

To meet these demands, the railway needs to find ways to improve communication systems, moving away from many of the traditional railway signalling and telecommunication systems found today. Network Rail is moving to radio based communication systems, to improve customer experience and cope with increases in capacity. Similarly, LU has been developing and improving its systems with the Victoria Line upgrade and the introduction of Distance-To-Go Radio, enabling 34 trains per hour (tph) operation. This will soon be increased to 36 tph. The Jubilee and Northern Lines have been equipped with Transmission Based Train Control to allow eventually up to 36 tph. Other upgrades now underway will introduce automatic train operation on the subsurface lines and this is also expected to improve customer experience by providing a more integrated customer information system.

The communications infrastructure is included in the upgrade strategy. Communication within underground tunnels has been successfully achieved using radiating cables or leaky feeders. However, to meet the increasing demand for higher data rates, there is a general move within the railway industry towards higher operating frequencies. One particular challenge that is unique to London Underground is the inherent small bore tunnels. Within these tunnels, the trains have the potential to form an effective radio frequency (RF) plug due to the tight gauging and this means that radiating cables are currently used to provide continuous narrowband coverage. The increase in frequencies leads to higher losses associated with the use of radiating cables. Whilst radiating cables currently remain the solution within tunnels, the higher losses make it a less attractive option.

Another key challenge that faces the railway industry is the lack of available spectrums or, more precisely, the cost of obtaining suitable spectrums is prohibiting for the railway industry and this makes the option of an unlicensed band more attractive. However, unlicensed bands come with their own drawbacks, especially with respect to electromagnetic interference, congestion and security related issues. As such, whichever design option is chosen, careful consideration is necessary.

10.3 Strategies for Change

The focus of the Mayor's Transport Strategy (TfL, 2012) is on smarter travel. The shift to bring all the individual modes of travel under one umbrella as Transport for London, realigns the focus towards the customers travel experience, no matter what mode of travel is used. The idea is to travel smarter, therefore making the most effective use of the transport system as a whole, changing the behaviour of the travelling public to utilise what is available.

For London Underground, which has seen a massive increase in demand over the last ten years, it means a large investment in its infrastructure in order to be able to cope with the estimated increase in passenger levels in the coming years. The bigger picture is to provide a reliable service combined with high levels of customer care.

10.4 Forms of Communication

In Figure 10.1 above we mapped out the many different forms of communication in LU. Obvious starting points were the visual and oral systems: Display boards, Public Address systems and radio but other, more diverse forms became apparent as being methods of communication dependant upon the type of information that is being presented to the customer. Also, as communication is a two-way activity, we factored in the need

Figure 10.2: *The public train describer display at Charing Cross terminus, London. The system provides an overall display for the concourse
area. Note also the open and unobstructed concourse. This is essential
for peak periods and especially when the service is disrupted. Individual
train displays are also provided for each platform beyond the fare gate line.
P. Connor.*

to hear the customer's voice, since it informs strategic decision making.

Face to Face

Nothing is quite as effective as communicating face to face. It enables
individuals to pick up communication clues not just from what is being
said but also from body language, facial expression and tone of voice. It
allows the customer to clarify and the member of staff to check understanding and it offers the opportunity for better service to be delivered.
The staff have been seen as a distinct reason for London Underground's
effectiveness as a transport network around the world. However, they are
also a reason why our ticket prices are as high as they are (plus the rela-

tively low subsidy in comparison to other countries) and this is why other means of communication are used as well—you cannot have one member of staff for every customer.

Bearing in mind the value that staff adds to a customer's experience, LU has invested a huge amount of market research into understanding where it's important for the customer to see a member of staff and what customers want to know. LU then measures whether it is meeting these expectations by undertaking at least six Staff Information Surveys (SIS) at every station, every four weeks. These station specific surveys test not only whether a member of staff was available to a customer but also the quality of the information that they gave the surveyor.

In addition to staff at every station, there are a number of Travel Information Centres (TICs) in Central London where specially trained staff can offer tailored advice and information to meet specific customer needs—but this does require the customer to visit the TIC in person.

Signage

Aside from face to face communication, the oldest form of communication on the LU network is the permanent signage around a station and this still has a place in the communications arena. A good signage scheme can ensure that customers move smoothly through a station without stopping and creating potential pinch points. With the network being as complex as it is and with so many stations interchanging with other services, it's important to get signage right to avoid these pinch points as much as possible.

In addition, it's possible to change the signage with 'Way Out' signs that can be illuminated to change customer flows during special events. This can manage customer flows more effectively and prevent overcrowding on a platform between trains.

Customer Information Boards (CIBs) provide at a glance and up to date line specific information at gatelines to enable customers to make better informed travel choices at the start of their journey, and Dot Matrix Indicators (DMIs) at platform level provide next train information. However, new technology installed into the space restricted platform area can obscure existing signage. A delicate balance is required between the revenue-generating technologies that are increasingly being installed at platform level (such as the cross-platform projectors that project adverts to poster sites across the track at stations) and the already existing safety

Figure 10.3: *Platform train describer at Warren St. Underground station, London. Note also the location of the 'Way Out' sign just beyond. Careful siting of signs is necessary, particularly in complex interchange stations. P. Connor.*

and directional signage that has long been in place at platform level. It is a balance that we do not always get right.

Posters and Whiteboards

Station staff have access to a poster printing service that allows them to produce posters via a poster plotter for display on whiteboards at various locations around a station. These posters are normally temporary to highlight a particular issue—such as an escalator out of service being used as a fixed staircase or the forthcoming Engineering Works on the network.

Hand-written whiteboards provide staff with the opportunity to provide short term information while a poster is being produced or simply because the message is personal (such as a "Thought for the Day" message). These whiteboards are a temporary means of information display and cannot be used everywhere as they can pose a safety risk at certain locations as well as being a physical obstacle interrupting customer flows.

Public Address Systems

The Public Address (PA) system allows station staff to make real time announcements as well as recording information that can then be broadcast at set intervals, i.e. every 10 minutes. This can save time and effort and enables staff to spend more time in the customer facing areas of a station, provided the message does not need to be updated, which requires the staff to return to the PA system and record an updated message.

Because of the way these systems developed as they were rolled out around the LU Network, some of the PA systems remain quite restrictive, there being only a short recording time for certain systems in use. When services are severely disrupted, staff are unable to record a full update regarding the problems as the system will not allow the recording length required to do this. This has lead to staff having to become quite inventive in shortening the service information broadcasts to fit within the time limits set by the PA system. Both environmental and behavioural factors can impact on the effectiveness of these.

As LU started to understand the importance to customers of real time information (RTI), so it became necessary to measure how well we were performing against customer expectations, so the Staff Information Survey (SIS) was

Figure 10.4: *'Thought for the day' provided at Earls Court Underground station in London. Such ideas provide motivation for both staff and passengers and help to humanise an otherwise stressful environment. J. Gajeswki.*

born. This survey measures how LU's communications to customers are against a defined set of criteria, for instance, whether a Train Operator makes a PA to customers when a train has been stationary between stations for more than 30 seconds.

Passenger Help Points and Emergency Alarms

Although staff are visible around stations - on gatelines, in circulating areas and on platforms, for customers to speak to face to face; customers can also communicate to station staff via Passenger Help Points (PHPs). These allow customers who require assistance to ask for information or notify the station of an emergency. When a PHP is activated by a customer, a CCTV view of the PHP appears in the Station Control Room, allowing station staff to see the customer as well as communicate with them. At stations where the Station Control Room is not staffed or there is no one available to answer a customer's emergency call, the call will divert to the British Transport Police.

The equivalent of the PHP on the train is the Passenger Emergency Alarm. This allows a customer to talk to the driver directly. This has the obvious benefit of perception of help being at hand for the passengers and allows the driver to make decisions accordingly, whether to stop immediately or proceed to the next station where help might be more readily available.

Door alarms were introduced to give an audible warning to passengers that the doors are about to close. This was an attempt to manage the dwell times of trains in platforms and reduce the number of incidents at the Platform Train Interface (PTI) where customers were struck by doors closing. However, this remains our area of highest risk for customers, in part, because customers do not stand clear of the doors when the chimes start, as they do not want to wait for the next train and for customers wearing headphones who may not hear the chimes.

In an attempt to address the number of PTI incidents, LU is trialling vinyl warning signs fixed to the platform in the areas of highest risk in addition to automatic PA announcements on the train and platform PA announcements to mind the gap. It is too early to judge the success of these additional signs but LU continues to seek new and innovative ways to highlight the risk of the PTI to customers.

CCTV

Closed Circuit TV cameras are installed all over the station, with views of station platforms, routeways and circulating areas available in the Station Control Room (SCR). Station staff can use them to monitor customer flows and identify any issues or situations quickly and take the necessary action to assist. The recordings from the system can then by used by the British Transport Police to review incidents. They also provide a level of security and safety for LU customers.

Website/WiFi

Whilst not strictly part of the management of the railway, the provision of mobile connectivity and positioning services opens up opportunities to enhance applications used by customers, whether before arriving at a station or on-board the train. Allowing passengers to plan their journeys in a more integrated way with live running information together with information from other transport services (e.g. bus, overground and main line routes) becomes feasible at any stage in a journey. Further, the provision of broadband capacity for passengers is becoming a commercial necessity for many railway operators.

The introduction of WiFi now means access to travel updates via websites as well as other mediums such as social media and email. The TfL website offers a Journey Planner and service updates. Customers also have the option to register to receive service information texts and email alerts. Information about any events that may affect travel plans are also available, enabling a customer to plan their journey before they've left the comfort of their home or hotel room.

A new style website was designed to amalgamate the various TfL services—Oyster, Congestion Charging, Travel Information, Emirates Airline, etc. everything with a view to making it easier for the customer to use the multiple modes of travel that TfL offers. The aim was to make it more streamlined and user friendly and more relevant to the user by offering Real Time Information. Improvements have been made to the Journey Planner, search function and maps by incorporating Google Maps, as well as the addition a

Figure 10.5: *An electronic service information display provided at an Underground station in London. This provides early warning of disruptions on other lines as well as the status of the local line. J. Gajeswki.*

'Nearby' function that locates the user's location and gives relevant live information. This is in response to the increase in mobile users, so will give LU customers access to travel information whilst on the move, as well as at home.

10.5 Real Time Information (RTI) for LU Staff

With the development in technology such as sensors and data loggers, remote condition monitoring has been developing. For example, the mainline railway uses 'RailBam', an acoustic monitoring system that provides reliable and repeatable data to identify bearing related issues and manage them in a timely manner. Being able to monitor turnouts or other assets remotely will enable maintenance staff to identify potential failures and respond before they become critical, hence ensuring safety and maintaining reliable services to customers. Whilst this is not directly related to communication with customers, addressing faults and maintaining assets in a timely manner will enable better services to customers and allow for better whole life cycle management of assets.

Now WiFi is available across the network, LU customers are able to receive live information in the stations. Customer Information Systems need to be able to offer the same level of precise and accurate information about our services. Putting WiFi in our stations has made RTI available to our staff so they are on par with the information that our customers receive 'up top' via the internet.

Recently, the operational directorate within LU provided its asset inspection staff with iPhones or iPads for sending real-time inspection data back to a central asset management database and scheduling tool. These have allowed staff to be more productive and are also much lighter and faster than the previous devices used. This initiative was driven by the lessons learnt from the London Olympics. All staff who were involved with assisting on the network during the Olympics were issued iPads in order to be able to facilitate assistance for the vast numbers of customers that were expected to use the underground. This lead to an examination of other LU areas that could benefit from using new mobile technology. The same benefits could apply to station staff having access to real time information to communicate to customers.

10.6 Service Control

Service Control's role was traditionally seen as managing the train service to a timetable but with very little interaction with the customer. Although this remains their primary function, their access to Train Operators via the Connect Radio sees the Line Information Specialist (LIS) based in the Control Room take on an increasingly critical role. Station staff communicate with the LIS when they have assisted large groups of schoolchildren or visibility impaired customers onto a train so that this information can be relayed to the Train Operator of that train. This ensures that the Train Operator knows where the customers are alighting and allows additional time in the platform at that station to ensure the customers are clear of the train before closing the doors.

The LIS will also pass on service status information regarding other lines to Train Operators to allow them to pass this on to customers already on board their train. This, again, allows the customer to make an informed decision when they reach a station that interchanges with an affected line.

10.7 Monitoring/Measuring

Market research is an important activity to assess the perception of the paying customer to how we are doing. This feedback is used to inform corporate decisions on the future and helps us understand what is important to the customer.

Various measures are used:

- The Customer Satisfaction Survey (CSS)—carried out once every quarter where actual customers are asked to score our performance;

- The Mystery Shopper Survey (MSS)—carried out once every four weeks by independent surveyors to measure our levels of cleanliness, lighting, ambience in comparison to contractual criteria;

- The Staff Information Survey (SIS)—a number of surveys carried out every four weeks at every station on the network and on trains by independent surveyors to measure the quality of the information available from various sources on stations and trains;

- Lost Customer Hours (LCHs)—Performance on LU is measured by the number of customer hours lost. Each service affecting incident is allocated a LCH figure depending on the time of day an incident happened and the likely number of customer hours impacted as a result. An incident happening at the start of traffic will incur less LCH than one happening in the middle of the peak, for instance.

10.8   The Future

The full impact of the Mayor of London's transport strategy has yet to come to fruition. It remains to be seen how it will influence the way customers view our staff in trying to meet expectations set by the ever evolving technologies available in the wider world outside the railway industry. Also, it highlights the need to consider how it will change how staff manage customers and how it will affect their day to day activities. As we become more and more reliant on technology, will LU require staff to become more like data managers, potentially needing more back of house staff to manage the constant flow of information available and tailor it for the customer. The shift of focus to the customer experience rather than the mode of transport is changing how we communicate with customers, the emphasis being placed on real time information being precise and frequent.

Interoperability is a factor for railway system as a whole, making our systems compatible across the network and with external services and administrations is essential. The Kings Cross fire of 1987 and the terrorist events of 7th July 2005 proved this. Connect radio has helped improve the situation but there is a need to consider external parties, such as Network Rail where stations interface.

As expected, security is a big issue for technology and data protection is vital. There are the wider implications of these technological developments, such as data storage, legal implications, the impact on staff and their roles. Demand for information will increase, with consumers demanding instant gratification. The expectation will be that LU should be able provide same level of technology as available everywhere else.

The Office for National Statistics reported that in 2014, 38 million adults accessed the internet every day, approximately 58% of those via a mobile device. In line with the issuing of iPads to operating staff, there is a programme roll out expanding on the initial concept. The next steps are to extend the mobile service to surface and corporate staff, to develop a basic TfL App Store with bespoke apps required for all staff, to introduce a process for ordering new Apple and Android devices and also to extend WiFi access to operational buildings.

The addition of Wifi in LU stations has brought a new set of issues. People are checking their phones more frequently than before and earlier than before. Walking along with heads down, looking at their mobiles, has impacted on safety and service disruptions with an increase in accidents, as customers pay less attention to their surroundings. There has been an increase in incidences of mobile devices falling onto the track. LU has had to offset these impacts by introducing floor vinyls warning customers of the gap between the platform and the train and with specific PAs asking customers to keep mobile devices clear of the PTI.

Another impact that came with the introduction of WiFi on stations is that it has raised customer expectations, so LU will once more need to adapt. One can envisage the next step will be a demand for WiFi on trains, but this has huge implications for LU. There are infrastructure issues, such as allowing for the kinetic envelope and there is very limited room for additional cabling for leaky feeders in many of the tunnels.

10.9   Cashless Payment

In 2003, LU introduced the Oyster card and this has proved to be popular, extending its use to the Network Rail system within the London orbital area. This has lead to other initiatives to be explored in order to improve the travelling public's experience of using public transport. There is pressure replace the paper ticket system and extend the Oyster card nationwide. This would make using the railway more holistic and offer customers a more complete service. This then leads to another area that is fundamental in communications—language. The ticket machines (POMs) are limited in their capacity as communication tools. Ideally language options, like those available on ATM's, are required to cater for the many tourists London welcomes every year. LU is currently reliant on the language proficiency of its staff to be able to assist in these situations. Another development being discussed is the introduction of interactive maps in order to give more information options to the customer.

The advent of the Oyster card has shown the benefits of new ticketing technologies to customers and operator alike. The company underwent an Operational Review in 2011, which saw Ticket Office opening hours change in response to the massive shift in the way customers bought and topped-up their tickets. Over the next 20/30 years the expectation is that paper tickets will be all but phased out and replaced with contactless technologies to carry ticket information on mobile phones or other personal devices. It has already been introduced on buses. This integration of ticket with mobile devices will help customers to purchase tickets through their handset or from ticket machines without the need to carry a separate ticket device (e.g. smartcard). This technology would also support some of the demand management technologies described earlier.

This shift has continued, something that the imminent introduction of contactless payment will further impact on. In addition, the company faces a massive shortfall in funding, which has also driven a need to change the way we operate. The Customer Service Transformation Plan aims to involve staff at every level to explore what the options for change and the impacts of these might be, both on staff and customers. One thing is clear—change is coming but what this will look like is currently unclear. Unsurprisingly, this has had a destabilising effect on station staff morale, at a time when future funding will be decided by the company's performance today. So far, this impact has not affected our Customer Service performance in the eyes of the customer but this might not remain the case and consultation regarding the future continues with the Trade Unions.

10.10 Expansion

The Mayor of London has made it known that TfL has an interest in future proposals for taking over certain additional rail routes around London. This has been the result of the success of the London Overground upgrade and subsequent extensions. Potentially this could encompass lines currently operated by Southeastern and other privatised rail operators. The outcome of such as development proved positive with 70% of the stakeholders consulted in support. The first routes to be taken over are the Liverpool Street to Enfield and Chingford services.

Recently TfL has looked to sponsorship to bring in funding for its new endeavours such as Emirates Air line and London Overground and the widely advertised Wifi on stations being via Virgin Media. In order to be able to offer the latest and best technologies it may require future partnerships in order for LU to be able to meet the expectations of the customer.

We have some very long term projects. Making changes to LU assets is not an overnight job, therefore the technology available when you start your upgrade, for example, may be superseded by the time you deliver. The speed of advance today is significant but LU is only able to work with what is currently available.

A hindrance to introducing new technologies will be the ageing infrastructure across railways—LU was 150 years old in 2013. When introducing new data systems a large amount of cabling and hardware is required. Many stations on LU's network were not built to accommodate this technology and working around it is not always straightforward, especially if the structures are Listed Buildings. Obsolescence, the age of the network and its assets and the rapid growth of new technologies are all aspects that cause problems for LU.

The challenges are many; an obvious one is money, but just as likely is the lack of fluidity. The shift in behaviours will only impact on those who use the technology available. The techno-phobic traveller will still expect the same level of communication as those who have immersed themselves in the technological world. Some will need to be educated in order to affect their behaviours to adapt to the impacts of the high level strategy.

The challenge remains in maintaining the pace of communication for our customers, with their expectations of our performance, while balancing the commercial benefits that technology can bring against the technology that helps the company to maintain a safe environment where risks continue to be reduced to as low as reasonably practicable levels. These do not necessarily sit harmoniously together and often conflict directly with each other.

Technological improvements on the network are recognised by customers for only a brief period of time before they become the norm. For instance, the introduction of the dot matrix Indicators displaying next train information on platforms in the 1990's saw massive increases in the CSS scores for information on platforms, only for the scores to quickly settle back to close to their original level when customers came to see these not as a luxury but as a minimum. With the speed that customers can upgrade their own technology, it remains a challenge on how we might keep up with the perception that technological advancement will be so easy on an Underground system that offers so many challenges to delivering enhancements and improvements.

Ultimately, safety is the bottom line for LU in everything that it does. As technical advances affect human behaviour, LU will need to keep abreast, if not ahead, of these changes in order to maintain safety of the travelling public.

References

Department for Transport (2012), Consultation Responses on Rail Decentralisation, November 2012:
https://www.gov.uk/government/uploads/system/uploads/
attachment_data/file/15328/consultation-responses.pdf

Fennell, D. (1988), Investigation into the King's Cross Underground Fire, HMSO, London, 21 October 1988.

Rail Delivery Group (2012), The Future Railway, The Industry's Rail Technical Strategy 2012, Supporting Railway Business:
http://www.futurerailway.org/RTS/About/Documents/RTS 2012
The Future Railway.pdf

Network Rail (2013), Strategic business plans 2014-19:
http://www.networkrail.co.uk/publications/strategic-business-plan-for-cp5.

Transport for London (2012) Mayor's Strategy:
http://www.london.gov.uk/priorities/transport/publications/mayors-transport-strategy.

Chapter 11 Emergency Preparedness

by Richard Morris

11.1 Introduction

This chapter will cover the subject of crisis management. It will describe how to avoid emergencies occurring wherever possible and how to manage them should they occur. It will show that a proactive approach must be the key element of crisis management since it could be said that it is better to be at the front of the bus swerving to avoid an obstacle rather than being at the back of the bus seeing what you have just run over. The concept was summed up neatly in a quotation, "One of the true tests of leadership is the ability to recognise a problem before it becomes an emergency."

This chapter also shows how the aftermath of a crisis brings with it four main elements. Why did the problem occur? How well was it managed? What can be done to stop it recurring? What is the consequence of the crisis? All of these elements can have serious consequences. In particular the fourth element can lead to a major change or reorganisation of the operation and in some cases it can lead to the responsible party being forced out of business altogether.

The importance of considering what risks could lead to a crisis, mitigating them where possible and, should they occur, being ready to deal with a crisis in a well practised and cogent manner cannot be overstressed. But emergencies do occur and, when they do, they must be adroitly managed. Such an approach should produce sound and meaningful plans to deal with

145

emergencies if they arise so that normality can be restored as quickly as possible and with as little inconvenience to customers as possible.

Crises need controlling and pro-activity is important here too. It should be remembered that, "You control an incident, don't let it control you." If you run after a crisis you will never catch it up. If you are always one step ahead, you will be managing the emergency in the optimum way. The technique is referred to as 'business continuity.' Recently an new ISO standard was published, ISO 22301, which sets out in some detail how to introduce such an approach.

This chapter advocates a proactive and risk based culture and explains management techniques that will assist in achieving such an approach. It also describes processes to cater for different levels of crisis so that decisions can be taken at the right time, at the right level and by trained and competent staff.

11.2 Business Continuity

The subject of emergency or crisis management falls neatly into the concept of business continuity. This process is a cogent example of the proactive approach. A good business continuity plan that includes the scope of what is to be done and a description of the areas to be covered is vital to achieve good management in times of crisis. The plans should be agreed and their importance stressed by the top management to give the process its status.

ISO 22301 is the present standard that should be consulted and it will give a good guide to management at all levels of the areas to be covered.

11.3 Risk Analysis

The techniques for compiling a risk matrix are well known and need not be described here in detail[1]. Suffice to say that a good question that any manager should ask is: What three potential crises keep me awake at night? The answers will be the risks that must be your main consideration

---

[1]For example, *Designing an Effective Risk Matrix*, ioMosaic Corporation, 2009

and, if you have been realistic, you will have identified the three risks that are the most likely and have the highest consequences.

In each case, the gross risk is amended by mitigations to a net risk and further management actions could lead, in the future, to a less critical risk. The mitigations are very important. Too often, companies fool themselves into thinking that because they have low scores for net risks, they are in good shape. If they have not paid requisite attention to the mitigations and indeed, if the mitigations have not been carried out, the company could be staring into an abyss. The importance of the mitigations must be stressed and, in particular, each meeting to discuss the matrix should include an audit that will prove the mitigations are still 'in place'.

Regularity of review is important. New risks can appear and present risks can disappear or attain different scoring levels and these considerations must be well monitored. It is important too to carry out the reviews with the risk owners themselves and to present the finished register to the senior management group in order that the top directors have an overall view of the types and states of risk in the company.

Some of the risks will not be as related as others to 'crises' but it will be possible to separate those that fall into the latter category and for the purposes of this chapter, to concentrate on managing them. When the crisis occurs, if a company has fallen into the trap of self delusion, it will not be ready to deal with any of the four questions asked in the introduction and the consequences could be dire.

11.4 Business Interruption Analysis

All businesses rely on a number of computer systems and processes by which they operate. The business interruption analysis must examine each of these and grade them in order of risk, i.e. how serious the impact would be if they would be if they were to fail for any reason.

Once this is known, it is necessary to examine the safeguards that exist around the most important systems. Are there proper back up facilities? If these are found to be insufficient, should more facilities be provided since the cost of that may well outweigh the costs incurred if the systems 'go down'?

The second action in the analysis is to determine what workaround there could be if a particular system were to fail. Whatever method is devised, it must be tested and trained in to all staff that would need to use it. In many cases it would be impossible to retain a workaround for a long period of time. This period should be estimated as part of the analysis so that all are aware that if the system is down at that point, there would be no workaround.

This analysis should be reviewed at least twice per annum, since the world of technology moves very quickly and it is important to keep the analysis up to date.

11.5 Procedures

There are certain generic procedures and processes for managing crises and there are others that will set out the actions to be taken in specific circumstances. Procedures and processes must be written with input from those who understand the situation and any ramifications that could occur 'on the ground'. Thankfully the concept of writing a process or procedure in an office with little or no input from the practitioners has virtually disappeared but it still a factor to guard against.

Most important is the input of stakeholders and partners who are not members of the company but nevertheless fulfil a vital role in crisis management, e.g. the local authority, police, ambulance service and fire brigade. Without their input the procedure can be meaningless and, even if it did contain some meaning, it could be misunderstood, not a useful trait in an emergency.

It is important that any procedure has an objective, a scope, an indicator of how it could be measured and a review date that, in the area of crisis management, should not be more than one year. The procedures for business continuity should be kept in one document so that it is readily available to see what has been written and what scope has been covered. It makes for easy reference and is a useful training aid.

There will be a procedures 'tree'. Overall company procedures will be collated at the top. Underneath these procedures will sit procedures that are more detailed and location specific.

The railway is well known for "falling flat on its interfaces" (according to former British Rail Chairman, Sir Peter Parker) and it will be very easy to review and amend a procedure without consulting or informing other parties that are vital to its success. This must be avoided by showing the interfaces on procedures and by using quality control systems to ensure that those managing the interfaces stipulated are kept in the loop and do sign off any change.

11.6 Generic Procedures

In order to manage both the proactive approach outlined above and the crisis, should it arise, there is a need for a generic set of business continuity procedures. These will set down, amongst other things:

- the communication lines within and outside the company;
- the categorisation of crises that will show the level of management required to resolve the issue;
- the arrangements to summon a crisis command;
- the layout and operation of the crisis room itself;
- the method for conducting crisis command meetings and the subsequent issue of minutes;
- press arrangements;
- particular procedures for calling in alternative transport arrangements including chartering private planes where necessary;
- major derailments; arrangements for handling sensitive issues;
- care of customers, particularly if injured etc.

These will then be developed to provide specific procedures.

11.7 Specific Procedures

There will also be a set of procedures that are bespoke and that set out actions in the event of particular occurrences, e.g. loss of infrastructure and the workaround; loss of communications; loss of an office base vital to the operation, e.g. the control office; loss of systems based on a business interruption analysis etc.

Some of these will take the form of contingency plans, e.g. one line or route, planned to be open, is shut because of an emergency. Contingency plans will set out alternative routes and can sometimes be detailed enough to contain frequencies of trains and calling points. In some cases a more detailed timetable and crew workings are included.

It is the specific procedures that can sometimes play a large part in avoiding a crisis. For instance, if a procedure exists for queuing when services are disrupted and if that procedure is well known to all, the feeling of confusion that is often experienced by customers can turn into confidence that the situation is being managed properly. In addition, crowds can be managed to fill whatever capacity exists instead of the more common 'free for all' that often occurs at such times.

One vital ingredient in the compilation of procedures is the adage that it is most important to keep in front of the incident. This can be achieved by writing procedures that go straight to the highest reasonable level of alert and then allow a reduction of that level when it is seen that the incident is not so serious as first thought.

An example of this followed the first Channel Tunnel fire. As is to be expected, there are many fire detectors of different types located both on trains and the infrastructure. In the original instructions, when the first fire alarm was activated, the original instruction was to monitor the situation and to wait to see if there was a second activation. This would indicate that there was a problem and, at that point, certain actions would be taken. The two tunnels would be closed from each other, trains would be stopped entering the tunnels and trains behind the fire alarm activation would be stopped.

Whilst these procedures were designed carefully, they did mean that the organisation was always slightly behind the incident. It was decided therefore to change this and to configure the tunnel, stop all trains entering and stop trains behind the alarm on the first activation. On most occasions, the second alarm does not activate and in those circumstances it is easy to 'undo' those arrangements with no effect on the service.

What this change has meant is that if the second alarm does activate, the controllers are ready to move to the next phase and remain in command of the incident. This means they are in control of the incident and not being controlled by it.

Another example, returning to the queuing procedures, if information is received that there is a potential blockage of the line and that trains are going to be affected, terminals should start making the arrangements for queuing. If it is found that there is no incident those arrangements can be stopped easily and there is no effect on the customer. If however the situation is allowed to develop and there is a backlog of customers, instituting queues becomes more difficult.

The same approach should be part of every procedure and should be used as a litmus test when devising responses to all information received about a potential incident .

11.8   Procedural Awareness

All too often, once a set of procedures has been devised, they are left on the proverbial shelf to gather dust. When the emergency occurs, it is a common trait that the procedures are found wanting or that the staff who are using them are not trained or refreshed on their use. Confusion will occur and in an emergency, confusion is the enemy of success. It is important therefore, that all those who will have to use the procedures are trained in them and refreshed on a regular basis.

Vital too is a programme of exercises. This not only tests the participants in a simulated scenario, it also tests the procedure itself. Exercises can take the form of a table top exercise where discussions are held on what each of the participants would do next. This affords the luxury of discussion since the scenario is not played out in real time. Exercises can played out using offices as specific locations. Participants rely on telephone communication between different locations 'on site' to play out the scenario and discuss the good and bad points at a hot debrief.

It is occasionally useful to practice in situ i.e. on the line side. Such exercises are expensive in time and resource but can offer great benefits through being in a 'real' situation. They are also very helpful when played with outside agencies as they lead to a better understanding of each others' problems.

Figure 11.1: *Decontamination Exercise in Montreal. Photo: N. G. Harris*

It is important too to devise a number of drills that can be played out at the beginning of or during each shift. These take the form of a simple scenario that can be discussed for no more than two minutes and allow participants to learn by regular practice. The theory is that by practising scenarios over and over again, they become ingrained in everyone's minds. When the incident occurs, the response is automatic and therefore more efficient.

11.9 Crisis Advice

The main location for all information concerning an emergency or crisis is the control office. This office can be related only to a train operating company or a Network Rail region. It is becoming more popular to return to the integration of controls and for all interested parties to sit together. This not only makes for a more coordinated approach but also brings a synchronisation of information flows that are more consistent.

A system of advice, where the control office would be the source, is required to categorise an incident according to its severity; describe the incident; describe the effects of the incident; detail who in the company is responsible for managing the ongoing situation and who else needs to be informed.

This procedure should take the form of an emergency process to which all involved should have immediate and direct access so that, whenever a communication is made, all are immediately aware of the issue and where they fit into the process. The procedure should also have reminders for reference—useful telephone numbers, particularly for outside stakeholders, a map of the route etc. It should also contain references to all business continuity procedures that sit under this overarching document. It is in effect the bible of crisis management.

11.10   Emergencies

If the categorisation of an incident described above has been compiled properly, most incidents will be handled by the control office and on call managers without the need to resort to a full crisis command meeting. It is important that this is so, for it leaves the handling of an incident within the aegis of those who know the systems well and are able to take informed and efficient decisions. Some guidance may be required from further up the management chain but in essence these are the times when controllers and those on the ground earn their money.

There should be reliance on procedures and on contingency plans that, if compiled properly, will mean that all involved know what the basic plan is and will work to it. There should be no surprises.

11.11   Crisis Culture

If preparations have been made as described, the organisation should feel confident in dealing with any level of incident or crisis. It is important that those in authority display that confidence and a calm approach and this will be borne out in training and competence techniques.

Communications, both internally and externally, are very important in ensuring that everyone is aware of where the incident sits.

11.12   Crisis Command

If an incident has grown into a crisis under the terms of the crisis manual described above, it may be necessary to convene a crisis command meeting. It is important that there is a protocol for establishing a crisis command and for disbanding it when the incident is over. This meeting is populated by senior members of the company and is chaired by a senior person who demonstrates the necessary qualities to undertake that role.

It is a common fault of companies to insist that the directors of the company are the representatives on crisis command. This misses a vital point. The managers that are required in crisis command must be well versed in the area they represent and it is the detail that is important in these circumstances. The directors are not necessarily the best people to undertake this role. Their knowledge is not deep enough and they do not necessarily serve the company to the best effect in this role.

All staff who undertake this role must be trained and passed as competent through an annual examination. By this method the company can be sure that decisions that are taken by the crisis command will be based on practical and knowledgeable criteria. In particular the manager of crisis command must also show that he/she is competent.

One method is to issue a log book for each senior on call manager that details the company locations and the areas that they should know. This log book would be completed biennially through the senior representative manager at each location signing it to record a visit from those designated to be in charge of a crisis command meeting and to confirm that a briefing has been given on the particular issues at the location concerned. Professionalism in this area is paramount.

The crisis command must have a clear remit. It is not there to decide detail. It is there to set strategy. It must not interfere with the running of the railway; that is the task of the control office and the terminal staff. It should be the conduit for action if necessary but its purpose is to manage the incident not run it. It will decide on the line to be taken outside the company, assisted by the public affairs representative, and it will be the vehicle through which the method and time of resolution of the incident is conveyed to the company. Minutes of each meeting should be sent around the company using a template that will be recognised by all.

The usefulness of crisis command can easily be destroyed by one or two common faults. A protocol for meeting conduct is therefore vital.

- Speed of communication of strategy is important, as is keeping the message simple.

- Once a policy is set it is important, except under extreme circumstances, that the policy is maintained. There have been many instances where confusion has been caused, leading to meltdown in some circumstances, where a different strategy has been adopted halfway through a crisis for which there is no good reason.

- The crisis command must resist the temptation to become involved with tactics; they are strategic.

- Whoever is on call as the senior manager and therefore the chairman of crisis command, is in charge. If a higher ranking manager wishes to intervene he /she will take charge of the whole crisis. It is impossible for any crisis command to serve two masters.

- No-one who is not a member of crisis command is allowed in the room while the meeting is taking place and no-one in the room is allowed to take a telephone call except the secretary of the meeting who will decide whether the content of the call is relevant and needs to be conveyed to the meeting.

- The representation around the table can be adapted to meet particular circumstances. This will be decided by the chairman.

There is no absolute rule that members of crisis command should all be members of the company. There may be occasions where some outside stakeholders will play a large part in assisting a company by providing their own expertise and resources. In such cases it may well be apposite for a representative of that stakeholder to sit in the crisis command discussions so that their input is available immediately on any strategic matters. They may also provide information on how the resolution is progressing from their point of view.

11.13   Standard Response

The concept of having a standard response to each crisis has many bene-fits. The most important outcome of using this process is to ensure that nothing is missed. Each crisis will vary, even if only slightly, and therefore not all the questions detailed in a standard response will be used every time. That is not important. Not only does it bring order into the res-olution of an incident, it ensures everyone in the company knows what questions will be answered by crisis command.

The response will contain all the usual questions: What is the incident, what is the time for resolution, what is the extent of injury or fatalities, what is the cause if known. There is one question that should be asked towards the start of the list. Who has experienced a similar incident? What did you do well and what mistakes did you make so that the present team can avoid them? Each department should have a standard response to assist in understanding the crisis and to help resolve it.

11.14   Crisis Room

In order to manage a crisis that warrants senior attention, it is necessary to provide a crisis room. It is not always possible for a separate and dedicated room to be available but this would be an optimum solution. Such a facility should be provided with equipment and facilities that will meet the needs of a crisis team. Checking that the equipment is operational and ready to use is a vital part of crisis management.

There is nothing worse than computers or video links that do not work when they are required immediately or that key information cannot be found easily. Weekly checks are a minimum requirement and these should be recorded on a check sheet available in the room.

Video links can be very important in times of crisis. It is useful therefore to consider where any links could be installed. Experience has shown that a link with the rolling stock maintenance depot can be of value. Not only can discussions be facilitated if there is a particular fault with rolling stock that has caused the crisis but it also most useful to receive the input of the rolling stock engineer on availability and whether the strategy that is being decided by crisis command will work with the maintainers.

Links between the train operating company and the infrastructure provider will ease communication and avoid misunderstandings. Each company will have its own particular requirements and it is important that these are carefully considered and equipment provided where it is thought to be beneficial.

Maps of the routes managed should be displayed permanently. They should take the form of a white board so that information can be written on them that will permit a description of the area of the crisis and the type of problem being faced. In addition ordnance survey maps of the route should be available as this will enable the crisis command to understand the terrain around the site of an incident, showing perhaps access points for emergency vehicles. Such facilities enable the crisis command team to understand the physical characteristics of the location and to see what particular part of the area is affected.

A running log should also be displayed that shows what the current situation is and what the prognosis for resolution is. Copies of the relevant business continuity procedures should be available for consultation if necessary.

It will be useful to have a television feed into the room. In many cases a crisis of sufficient proportions can reach the press and it is important that the crisis command team are aware of the tone of public comments in order that they can respond accordingly. Any systems that show real time running can also be useful as a display as it concentrates the meeting on what is really happening.

11.15   The Press

In the case of major crises there will no doubt be a requirement to speak to the press. Training of those designated to speak to reporters is essential. News reporters are keen to sensationalise and want to trap the unwary into saying things they do not want to. Training will assist in preparing for this but even then it is a daunting experience to be faced with a hostile questioner at times when you are not in the ascendancy.

It is useful too, in order to turn an interview into a more reasonable dialogue, to have a series of facts ready so that they can be used to reduce excesses. As an example, in the case of a serious accident, it is useful to balance the sensationalism of "Isn't it terrible that here we are again at the site of major railway accident, do you feel you have failed again?" with a statistic that demonstrates how many million miles trains have run without accidents.

There is also a macabre wish of all reporters to gain an exact figure of the number of customers killed or injured. This needs careful handling and it must be the rule that, if figures are to be given out, they must be capable of being verified and be the figure that all agencies will give so that consistency is achieved. Ensure also that television crews are carefully controlled if they wish to visit your premises. If not, they will be everywhere and their remit will not coincide with yours.

The culture of truth is a matter for each company but it is very clear to a discerning public when the truth is being told and even more so when an issue is obfuscated. Compare the British Midland Chairman who accepted that the crash onto the M1 at East Midlands airport was his company's fault with the statement by Jarvis that vandalism could have been the cause of the Potters Bar derailment. Both were seen for what they were and Jarvis suffered as a result.

11.16   Debrief

Never waste a good incident. There are always lessons that can be learnt from the way each incident is handled. One very important feedback is that of customers. If it is possible to institute a quick current feedback structure, it can be very helpful in judging how well the incident was handled.

In any case, a formal investigation should be held on each incident at the level described in the procedure. The objective of the investigation is to examine the actions taken, to identify any parts of the procedures that did not work, either because they were not implemented properly or because they would not work anyway. Action can then be taken to correct this anomaly.

It is a common fault of investigations that a plethora of recommendations are produced with no prioritisation attached. This merely serves to confuse and in many cases the benefit of the investigation and its recommendations are lost. There should be a minimum number of recommendations and these should be prioritised.

In the case of a major crisis, the senior management group should be made aware of the results of the investigation and the recommendations should be audited until closed.

11.17   Audit of Business Continuity

Audit is an important part of any overall process. At least annually, an audit should be carried out to ensure that all parties are keeping their processes, procedures, training and competence up to date.

In the initial stages of introducing business continuity processes the system will not be complete. The audit therefore, should be quantified and should show clearly where work still has to be carried out. Quantification implies that the more important elements score the most marks. Through a regular series of audits, progress against completion can be monitored and a clear picture given to those audited of the actions that are still required, ranked by their importance.

Too many audits merely show non conformances and give no indication of progress. Merely to count non conformances in not good enough as each non conformance can carry a different weight and merely to say a company has improved because they have less non conformances is not a true indication of their state. The same can be said of moving annual averages, which can hide the real picture and engender a false sense of security. Areas for improvement should be identified and these should be monitored closely at each follow up audit to ensure they are completed.

11.18   Conclusion

Emergencies, crises, incidents will always form apart of everyone's lives at some time. It is important that action is taken to prevent them wherever possible and to be ready if they do occur, with well thought through processes and procedures, managed by well trained and competent staff.

Pro-activity must be the watchword. Try and avoid crises, be ready to deal with them if they occur and keep in front of them the whole time they are running.

Bibliography

Channel Tunnel Safety Authority (1997), 'Inquiry into the fire on Heavy Goods Vehicle shuttle 7539 on 18 November 1996'.

ISO (2012), 'Business continuity—ISO 22301 when things go seriously wrong', International Organization for Standardization, Geneva, Switzerland.

Chapter 12 Railway Infrastructure

by Felix Schmid & Piers Connor

12.1 Introduction

The requirement that the infrastructure of an urban or suburban railway
has to pass through densely populated and highly developed cityscapes
and has to handle high volumes of traffic, represents a heavy investment
commitment that will require governmental support. As an example, the
Crossrail project, where twin full-sized rail tunnels are being bored on
an east-west axis across London, is costing £500million a kilometre to
build, fit with electrical and mechanical systems and equip with rolling
stock. At such levels of investment, the design and construction of any
urban railway route will require a system-wide approach to secure the
optimum life-cycle value for the project and effective transportation for
the community. This chapter looks at the main construction features of
the urban railway.

12.2 Movement and its Guidance

The track of any type of railway, from monorail to maglev, must be designed to form a suitably even running surface for the vehicles. For the
present discussion though, we concentrate on conventional twin-rail, steel
track. The track guides the rolling stock and supports its weight and
thus serves as the interface between the topography of the terrain and the
wheels of the vehicles. Together with the ballast, it forms a structure with

English ft ins	Metric mm	Major Countries & Regions	% of world
2′ 6″	762	China*, India*	1.7
3′ 0″	914	Colombia, Guatemala, Ireland*	0.6
3′ 3¹/₃″	1000	East Africa, Southeast Asia*, Argentina*, Brazil*, Chile*, India*, Pakistan*, Spain*, Switzerland*	8.8
3′ 6″	1067	Southern Africa, Southeast Asia*, North Africa & Middle East*, Australia*, Japan*, New Zealand, Newfoundland	9.0
4′ 8¹/₂″	1435	Europe*, North America, North Africa & Middle East*, Argentina*, Australia*, Chile*, China*, Japan*	58.2
5′ 0″	1524	Former USSR, Finland, Mongolia	12.8
5′ 3″	1600	Australia*, Brazil*, Ireland*	1.2
5′ 6″	1676	Argentina*, Chile*, India*, Pakistan*, Portugal, Spain*	7.0

Notes: *Countries or regions with more than one gauge. Percentages add to less than 100 due to additional, rare gauges

Table 12.1: *Principal Railway Track Gauges in Year 2000. Puffert, D (2001)*

a defined stiffness and thus a dynamic characteristic that is influenced by the specific mass of the rails.

The standard 1435mm (4 ft. 8½ in.) gauge of railway track was determined in the early 19th century and eventually spread world-wide. However, a number of countries adopted different gauges for either political or economic reasons so, today, there are approximately 1,170,000 kms of railway lines world-wide, constructed to a variety of track gauges, as shown in Table 12.1. In general, more recent urban railways have been built to the standard gauge.

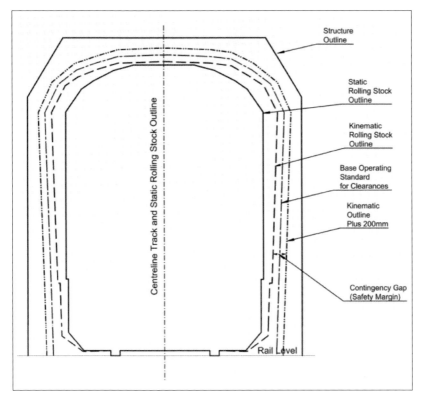

Figure 12.1: *Schematic of components of structure gauge and vehicle motion limits. ARTC (2012).*

12.3 Degrees of Freedom

The number of degrees of freedom available to a mechanical entity is defined as the number of possible motions with respect to a fixed reference frame. An element with six degrees of freedom can move in all three axes of space (translational movements in x, y, z) and rotate around the three axes. An aeroplane normally has five degrees of freedom since it can pitch, roll, yaw, rise and move forward. A typical tramway articulation will allow only two degrees of freedom between body sections, in the pitch and yaw modes. A bogie's motions are restricted by yaw dampers, lateral dampers and the secondary suspension with its bump stops. Unlike cars and planes,

Figure 12.2: *A demonstration of the problem of the platform/train gap with a new train and old infrastructure at Clapham Junction, London. Such problems present both a safety hazard and an increase in dwell times. Photo: P Connor (2014).*

rail vehicles must follow the track, so displacements with respect to all degrees of freedom are therefore strictly limited. The yaw motion of a rail vehicle is defined by the curvature of track and the roll motions are limited to ensure that the vehicle stays within its kinematic gauge, while pitch must be limited to prevent wheel and bogie unloading. The motions are constrained by the flanges of the wheels, the suspension system and vertical and horizontal bump-stops.

At platforms, the gap between train and platform and the dimensions of the stepping distances on and off the train present both safety and time management issues. They are also influenced by legal requirements for persons with restricted mobility. On older railways, where stations were often built on curved tracks, these problems become magnified. Careful management of the platform/train interface (PTI) is necessary to reduce risk to reasonable levels.

Curved track will also affect other aspects of vehicle and infrastructure design (Figure 12.3). The design of the vehicle must take into account the maximum angle of bogie movement, the relationship of the coupling of adjacent vehicles and the range of wire movement over the pantograph. In defining the structure gauge required for the vehicle, the swept area on short radius curves must be allowed for.

164

Figure 12.3:   *This photo demonstrates clearly the effect of curved track on a rail vehicle body. It also shows the angle of the pantograph head on the overhead wire. Photo: C. Watson.*

12.4   Basic Construction

Track is the most obvious part of a railway route but there is a sub-structure supporting the track (Figure 12.4) that is equally as important in ensuring a safe and comfortable ride for the train and its passengers or freight. The infrastructure diagram here shows the principal parts of an electrified, double-track line.

The total width across the two-track alignment will be about 15 m (50 ft) for a modern formation. The 'cess' shown each side of the alignment is the area available for a walkway or refuge for staff working on the track.

12.5   The Sub-Structure

On standard main line railways, the road is built upon a sub-structure that consists of three main elements; the formation, the sub-ballast and the ballast. The formation is the ground upon which the track will be laid. It can be at natural ground level or 'at grade' or it can be on an embankment or cutting. It is important that the formation is made of the right materials and is properly compacted to carry the loads of passing trains.

The formation under the track has a camber, rather like that seen on a roadway. This is to ensure ease of water run-off to the drains provided

165

on each side of the line. The track itself is supported on ballast, made up of stones—usually granite or, in the US, basalt—below which is a layer of sand, which separates it from the formation. For new or renewed formations, the sand is normally laid over some sort of geotechnical screen or mesh to separate it from the foundation material below. In the past, asphalt or plastic sheeting has been used to prevent water seepage.

Drainage will be provided on both sides of a railway. An efficient system of water run-off is essential in securing the stability of the road and thus preserving a reasonable ride quality. It is widely accepted that 90% of ride quality on a railway is based on good track quality. Drainage systems should be regularly inspected and designed for easy maintenance and clearance, with catch pits located at regular intervals.

Catenary masts (if the line is electrified on the overhead system) are located outside the drains and, beyond them, there is a walkway area. This may just be a cleared path for staff to walk safely, avoiding passing trains or, on modernised routes, a properly constructed path. Next to this path will be a cable trough. These were originally concrete but are nowadays often made of plastic. Cables crossing the track are protected by

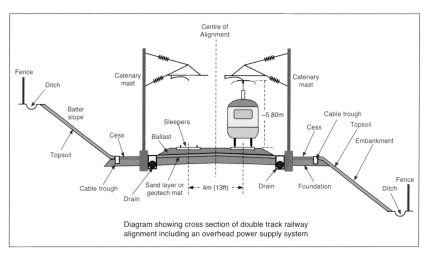

Diagram showing cross section of double track railway
alignment including an overhead power supply system

Figure 12.4: *This diagram of a cross section of a conventional, electrified main line, shows the main parts of railway infrastructure with their commonly used names. Drawing: P. Connor.*

a plastic tube, usually bright orange in the UK. Proper cable protection is essential to prevent damage by animals, track maintenance tools, weather and fire.

Usually, the edge of the railway property is outside the pathway or cable runs. If the line is built through an area requiring an embankment or cutting, the slopes will be carefully designed to ensure that the angle of slope will not take an excessive width of land and allow proper drainage but without risking an earth slip. The slope angle depends on the type of soil available, the exposure, the climate and the vegetation in the area. Drainage routes and pipes are usually added along the edges of cuttings and embankments.

In the UK, fences are always provided along the boundary line of the railway to protect the public from wandering onto the track. Even so, there are a few accidents every year when trespassers are killed or injured by trains or electric conductor rails. Many countries around the world don't fence their railways, assuming people will treat them like roads and look both ways before crossing.

12.6   Ballast

Ballast is provided to give support, load transfer and drainage to the track and thereby keep water away from the rails and sleepers. Ballast must support the weight of the track and the considerable cyclic loading of passing trains. Individual loads on rails can be as high as 50 tonnes (55 US or short tons) and around 80 short tons on a heavy haul freight line. Ballast is made up of stones of granite or a similar material and should be rough in shape to improve the locking of stones. In this way they will better resist movement. Ballast stones with smooth edges do not work so well. Ballast will be laid to a depth of 9 to 12 inches (up to 300 mm on a high speed track). Ballast weighs about 1,600 to 1,800 kg/cu/m. See also Ballasted vs Non-Ballasted Track below.

12.7   Track Form

The usual track form consists of the two steel rails, secured on sleepers (or crossties, shortened to ties, in the US) so as to keep the rails at the

Figure 12.5: *Railway track showing the use of concrete sleepers. Concrete, if correctly specified and manufactured, is a resilient and hard-wearing material but it requires mechanical handling, pre-drilling for fixings and bespoke construction if used as crossing bearers. Photo: P Connor.*

correct distance apart (the gauge) and capable of supporting the weight of trains. There are various types of sleepers and methods of securing the rails to them. Sleepers are normally spaced at 650 mm (25 ins) to 760 mm (30 ins) intervals, depending on the particular railway's standard requirements. The track is supported on ballast to give support, load transfer and drainage to the track and thereby keep water away from the rails and sleepers. Modern, heavy duty track is often laid on slab track instead, as discussed below.

12.8 Sleepers (Ties)

Traditionally, sleepers (known as ties in the US) were wooden. They can be softwood or hardwood. Most in the UK are softwood, although London Underground uses a hardwood called Jarrah wood. Nowadays, they are becoming more expensive and concrete is the most popular of the new types. Concrete sleepers are much heavier than wooden ones, so they resist movement better. They work well under most conditions but they have the disadvantage that they cannot be cut to size for turnouts and special trackwork. A concrete sleeper can weighs up to 320 kg (700 lbs) compared with a wooden sleeper that weighs about 100 kg or 225 lbs. The spacing of concrete sleepers is about 25% greater than wooden sleepers. Typical concrete sleepers are shown in Figure 12.5.

Figure 12.6: *Twin-block sleepers laid on top of ballast prior to topping up the ballast to pack the sleepers and secure the track. Photo: F. Schmid.*

An alternative design is the twin-block sleeper (Figure 12.6). The design consists of two concrete blocks joined by a steel bar. It is 30% lighter than a regular concrete sleeper, allowing it to be moved manually. It is popular in France (where it is called Stedef) and for some lighter track forms like those used for tramway systems. It has some advantage in that its construction provides for better stability in ballast but it is more prone to flex under certain conditions.

12.9   Rail

Different types of rail are used in different applications. For example, tramway rails for road installation are of a different design compared with conventional main line rail. The standard form of rail used around the world is the 'flat bottom' rail. It has a wide base or foot and narrower top or head. The UK introduced a type of rail that was not used elsewhere, apart from a few UK designed railways. This is known as 'Bullhead' rail and is shown in Figure 12.7.

Bullhead rail was originally designed with reuse in mind. It was intended that it would be turned over when the top had worn but this proved impossible because the underside also wore where it had been secured to the sleeper. Bullhead rail has to be mounted in a special 'chair' made of cast iron and secured by a 'key' wedged between the rail web and the chair. The chairs are secured to the sleepers by 'coach screws'.

Figure 12.7: *Bullhead rail laid on wooden sleepers in the traditional British configuration. The design requires special cast iron chairs bolted to the sleepers and rails to be secured with wooden or steel keys. Photo: collection P. Connor.*

Figure 12.8: *Flat bottom rail on ballasted track with concrete sleepers and Pandrol fixings. Photo: P. Connor.*

Flat bottom rails are fixed to a baseplate bolted on to the sleepers. The rail is attached to the plate by a system of clips or clamps, depending on the design. The older UK standard design was an elastic spike with a sprung, curved top that secures the rail. There are a number of variations seen around the world. One of the most popular is the Pandrol clip (Figure 12.8). A resilient pad will be provided between the rail and the base plate and around the securing clip, where required to provide insulation for the track circuits.

The infrastructure owning company in the UK (currently known as Network Rail), has adopted UIC60 rail (which weighs 60 kg/m or 125 lb/yd) as its standard for high speed lines. The present standard is equivalent to the UIC 54 rail, which weighs about 113 lbs/yd or 54 kg/m.

Older track is jointed. In the UK, about 30% of track is still jointed, although this is continuously falling as new rail is installed. Rails were normally laid in standard lengths bolted together by what are called fish-plates in the UK or splices in the US. The joints allowed sufficient space for expansion as they were provided at 60 foot intervals in the UK and 39 foot in the US, allowing them to be carried in a standard 40 ft flat wagon. Nowadays, rail is welded into long lengths, which can be up to several hundred metres long. Expansion is minimised by installing and securing the rails in tension. Provided the tension is adjusted to the correct level, equivalent to a suitable rail temperature level, expansion joints are not normally needed. Special joints to allow rail adjustment are provided at suitable locations.

12.10   Modern Track Forms

There are now a range of modern track forms using a concrete base. They are generally used in special locations such as tunnels or bridges where a rigid base is required to ensure track stability in relation to the surrounding structures. This type of track is usually called 'slab track' or 'non-ballasted' track.

The earth mat is a steel mesh screen provided on electrified railways to try to keep stray return currents from connecting to utilities pipes and nearby steel structures. Earthing must be strictly controlled otherwise serious and expensive problems will occur, made more serious and expensive because they involve other people's property.

Some slab track systems have the sleepers resting on rubber or similar pads so that they become 'floating slab track'. Floating track is used as a way of reducing vibration. Hong Kong Mass Transit Railway is fond of it, since its lines run through very densely populated areas.

12.11   Ballasted vs Non-Ballasted Track

The basic argument for different track designs will be based on the bottom line - cost; cost of installation and cost of maintenance. There are however, other issues such as environment—noise, dust and vibration—or engineering issues such as space, location, climate and the type of service intended for the track. There are a wide variety of track forms and systems incorporating some form of concrete base or support that doesn't need ballast. Almost all of these require less depth of construction than ballasted track. However, the accuracy of installation must be higher than that needed for ballasted track. Slab track will not be adjusted after installation but ballast can be packed to align track as required.

Figure 12.9: *Section of Flat bottomed rail. Photo: F. Schmid.*

The ability of ballast to allow track realignment is one of its most serious weaknesses. The lateral movement caused by passing trains on curved track is one of the major causes of maintenance costs added to which is the crushing caused by axle weight and damage due to weather and water. Ballast damage leads to tracks 'pumping' as a train passes and, eventually, rail or sleeper damage will occur, to say nothing of the reduced comfort inside the train and the additional wear on rolling stock. Apart from regular repacking or 'tamping', ballast will have to be cleaned or replaced every few years.

Another aspect to the ballasted track design, is the dust that is caused during installation and as it wears or gets crushed. It does however, offer a useful sound deadening quality.

Fixed track formations using slab track or a concrete base of some sort do not suffer from such problems. However, the installation of slab track is reported to cost about 20% more than ballasted track. To balance this cost, the maintenance costs have been quoted as reduced by 3 to 5 times that of ballasted track on a high speed line in Japan.

If low levels of use are foreseen, or if low capital cost is a more important requirement, ballasted track would be the choice. For a heavily used railway, particularly one in a structurally restricted area like a tunnel or viaduct, non-ballasted track must be the best option on grounds of low maintenance cost and reduced space requirements. However, care must be taken during design and installation to ensure the best out of the system.

12.12   Structures

To ensure that the path required for the passage of trains is kept clear along the route of a railway, a 'structure gauge' is imposed. This has the effect of forming a limit of building inside which no structures may intrude. The limit includes not only things like walls, bridges and columns but also pipes, cables, brackets and signal posts. The 'structure gauge' will vary with the curvature of the line and the maximum speeds allowed along the section in question.

Although the civil engineer is prevented from allowing his structure to intrude into the train path, the rolling stock engineer also has limits imposed on the space his train may occupy. This space is referred to as the 'kinematic envelope'. This area designates the limits the train can move laterally and vertically along the route. As for the structure gauge, the kinematic envelope will be affected by speed and features of train design such as the bogie suspension and special systems it may have like tilting.

12.13   Gauging

The line of route has to be checked from time to time to ensure that the structures are not interfering with the gauge. A line is always gauged when a new type of rolling stock is to be introduced. It is important to see that the small variations in track position, platform edge, cable duct location and signal equipment hasn't been allowed to creep inwards during maintenance and renewal programmes.

Modern gauging trains are fitted with optical or laser equipment. The optical system uses lights to spread beams of light out from the train as it runs along the line. Suitably mounted cameras record the breaks in the light beams to provide the gauging information. The train can run at up to 50 mi/h (80 km/h) but, of course, the runs have to be done at night. Laser beams are also used but, as they rotate round the train and form a spiral of light, the method suffers from gaps that can allow intrusions to be missed.

Along the line of route various locations are marked by a fixed post in the track or a plate on a nearby structure to indicate the correct level or position of the track. These are called monuments or datum plates. Measurements are taken from these to confirm the correct position of the track.

12.14 Curves

Curves in the track are almost a science on their own. Careful calculations are required to ensure that curves are designed and maintained properly and that train speeds are allowed to reach a reasonable level without causing too much lateral stress on the track or inducing a derailment. There are both vertical curves and horizontal curves. There is also a section of track on either side of a curve known as the transition, where the track is changing from straight to a curve or from a curve of one radius to one of another radius.

Cant is the term used to describe the cross level angle of track on a curve, which is used to compensate for lateral forces generated by the train as it passes through the curve. In effect, the sleepers are laid at an angle so that the outer rail on the curve is at a higher level than the inner rail. In the US, it is known as superelevation.

Of course, there will usually be trains of different types, permitted speeds at different levels, which travel the same curve. Also, there will be occasions when trains stop on the curve. This means that the degree of cant has to be fixed at a compromise figure to allow the safety of stopped trains and the best speeds for all the trains using the curve.

In practice, faster trains are allowed to travel round the curve at a speed greater than the equilibrium level offered by the cant setting. Passengers will therefore feel a lateral acceleration similar to what they would feel if there was no cant and the train was travelling at a lower speed round the curve. The difference between the equilibrium cant required by the higher speed and the actual cant is known as the cant deficiency.

Cant is measured either in degrees or in linear dimensions. On standard gauge track (1435 mm or 4ft. 8½ins.) 150 mm or 6 ins. of cant is equal to 6 degrees. This is the normal maximum in the UK. The maximum amount of cant deficiency allowed is 110 mm (4.3 ins.).

Figure 12.10: *Turnout at one end of a crossover showing, on the right, the electric point motor. Stretcher and drive bars can be seen between the switch rails. Photo: F. Schmid.*

12.15 Turnouts

The word 'turnout' is used to describe the junctions in trackwork where lines diverge or converge so as to avoid 'points' (UK) or 'switches' (US), both of which terms can be confusing. In the railway 'trade', turnouts are referred to as 'switch and crossing work' or S & C.

The crossing is at the location where rails are divided to allow the fixed rails to cross. It can be cast or fabricated. Rails are usually made of steel with a large iron content but a little manganese is added to crossings and some heavily used rails to increase resistance to wear. The trend is to make layouts as simple as possible in order to reduce installation and maintenance costs. The more complex layouts are usually only used where space is limited.

A switched crossing (sometimes referred to as a swing nose crossing or moveable frog) will normally be provided for turnouts with a very acute angle. The crossing will have a powered element that will be set for the required route at the same time as the switch blade is set. The blades of a turnout are normally moved remotely using an electrically operated point machine. The machine contains the contacts that confirm the points are moved and locked in the correct position for the route set. Point machines are normally located to one side of the track but a new generation of machines is now appearing where the mechanism is contained in a sleeper fitting between the rails.

12.16   Wheelsets and Track

The key discovery that led to the early success of railways as a means of mass transport was the realisation that appropriately shaped pairs of wheels, rigidly linked by an axle to form a 'wheelset', had a self-steering property and therefore offered a better ride quality than that provided by road transport. A pair of wheels combined into a wheelset is able to establish an appropriate position on the two rails, see Figure 12.11. The wheel treads are coned to provide the appropriate position and guidance on curves.

The wheelset rolls along the track but it can also exhibit yaw and lateral motions. It tries to follow the vertical and horizontal displacements of the track and absorbs some of these thanks to the radial elasticity of the wheel and, where fitted, rubber elements between the tyre and body of the wheel. The combination of the wheelset motions creates the bogie and vehicle body movements, which include yaw, roll and pitch. The diameter of the tread of most classical railway wheels is between 800 and 1000mm while the height of the flange on main line railways is normally around 27-29mm when new.

The track gauge of the railway is measured between the inner faces of the rail heads and may vary slightly in tight curves or according to the particular standard adopted by a railway company. In the UK, some routes are built to a gauge of 1432mm rather than the standard of 1435mm. As shown in the Figure 12.12, the rails are normally inclined with respect to the vertical axis to provide a better match of the running surface of the rails and the rolling surface or tread of the wheel. The angle to the

Figure 12.11: *A graphic of a railway wheelset showing the principle parts. The wheels are pressed onto the axle (shown in blue) to provide a rigid wheelset. The tyres (in grey) may be manufactured separately but, more commonly, are cast with the wheel in a single bloom. Graphic: P. Connor collection.*

vertical is generally set at 1:20 or 30. The gauge between the flanges of the wheelset is smaller than the track gauge so as to allow the self aligning movements of the wheelset.

12.17   Wheelset Motion

When the rolling radii of both wheels are the same, the wheelset will run in a straight line. Any track distortion or lateral movement of the wheelset results in a change in the rolling radius of one wheel. If the effective diameter of one wheel increases, for example, it will cover a larger distance for the same number of revolutions than the wheel to which it is linked rigidly by the axle. It will therefore create a small yaw angle with the rails and the wheel will effectively run 'down-hill' until both rolling diameters have been equalised. Unfortunately, the wheelset has a linear inertia with respect to this lateral motion as well as a moment of inertia with respect to the angle and will therefore 'over travel' slightly. This leads to a sinusoidal yaw oscillation, even on straight track, since the alignment can never be totally perfect.

At velocities above the critical speed, this motion is constrained only by the flanges of the wheels touching the inner faces of the rails and by the inertia of the body of the vehicle. The motion is effectively sinusoidal. Where the wheelset is part of a bogie it is this that starts to oscillate in a yaw-mode. This motion is called 'hunting', whether it relates to the body of the vehicle or a bogie, or the wheelset on its own.

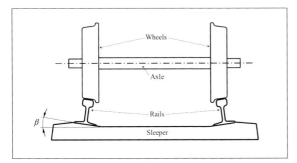

Figure 12.12:   A schematic   of   a railway   wheelset showing   the   coning of the wheels and angled rails.   Graphic: P.   Connor   after Pombo et al.

12.18   Forces Due to Rolling Contact

On main line railways, axle loads range from 90kN (e.g., fully occupied light weight passenger coach of mass 36t) to 300kN (heavy haul freight vehicles). The static load per wheel thus ranges from 45kN to 150kN. As a general rule, axle loads of rolling stock must be reduced as the operating speed increases so as to minimise track damage. The dynamic forces grow as a function of v^2 since they are related to the energy stored in the linearly moving ($E_k = mv^2/2$) and rotating masses ($E_k = I\omega^2/2$) of the wheels, axles, bogies and vehicle bodies. Vertical accelerations on standard track can thus reach values of 300ms^{-2}, that is, 30g or more. Track damage can be minimised by reducing the unsprung mass associated with a wheelset, e.g, transmitting the driving torque through rubber elements can help to distribute the forces acting on the track as a result of a discontinuity. The acceleration and braking performance of rail vehicles, as well as the ride during constant speed running, depend on the quality of the wheel-rail interface.

12.19   Independent Wheels

Several manufacturers have developed arrangements with independent wheels, pioneered by Patentes Talgo in Spain. This manufacturer developed their first articulated train in 1942, using aircraft technology and independent wheels. The prototype, built from steel, had a tare mass of only 100kg per passenger. The alloy production version, launched in 1950 as the TALGO II, was a very comfortable train with a mass of 365kg/p. TALGO III of 1964 represented a major step forward with its ingenious device for radially adjusting pairs of wheels on stub-axles, using the relative motion of adjacent body sections. A later version of the TALGO concept includes tilting performance. Although free running wheels do not achieve self-steering in the same way as wheelsets, they are self-centering due to gravity.

12.20   Design of Wheels and Axles

As we have seen, both the static and dynamic forces in wheels and axles are high, particularly because of the need to transmit traction and braking forces. Wheelsets are thus highly critical components that must be manufactured and maintained to the highest standards. Initially, railway wheels were cast with a hub, spokes and a rim. The hub with its undersize bore was pressed onto the axle with a force of around 5kN/mm of shaft diameter, around 10MN for a 200mm shoulder. A flanged steel tyre was then shrunk onto the rim and secured with a large 'spring ring'. This provided the smooth and tough running surface. Such wheels were light and had low moments of inertia. The tyre could be replaced when it had worn due to traction and braking friction.

As axle loads became larger and trains travelled faster, spoked wheels had to be abandoned in favour of solid wheels with tyres and, later, cast steel or forged monobloc wheels where the tread is machined onto the wheel disk. Today, most high performance trains are equipped with monobloc wheels that are replaced when it is no longer possible to re-profile the running surface and flanges. Generally, monobloc wheels are heated and pressed onto the axle to avoid the formation of pressing ridges and embrittlement of the mounting face. If it becomes necessary to change wheels or inside axle bearings, the wheel can be removed by injecting high pressure oil into an annular groove in the bore of the wheel. This allows removal of the wheel without damaging the seat or bore.

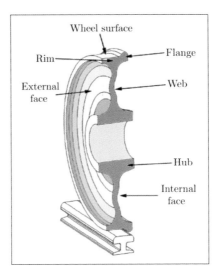

Figure 12.13: *Section of railway wheel. Graphic: After Roux et al*

It is possible to reduce the vibrations transmitted from the wheel-rail interface to the vehicle by designing wheels with integral rubber springs, e.g., the resilient type, illustrated in Figure reffig:Resilientwheel-Bonatrans. This type of design with its low unsprung mass is very suitable for rails set into the road surface without resilient support. A similar design (BA 064) was was fitted to the Intercity Express Mark 1(ICE1) trains to prevent the transmission of rolling noise to the body. This modification had

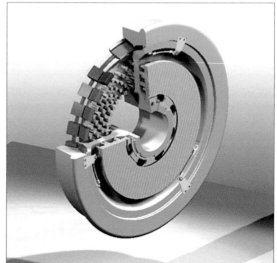

Figure 12.14: *Railway wheel with elastic inserts. The tyre (in grey) is connected to the wheel web with conductor straps. Note also the brake discs (yellow). Photo: Bonatrans*

to be introduced since the coil spring based secondary suspension had insufficient damping. In the BA 064 design, the elastic material is subjected to compression and the tyre of the wheel experiences severe deflections as it rotates. There is, for this reason, a substantial risk of fatigue fracture.

Brake disks can be fitted to the sides of monobloc wheels or they can be mounted on the axle. In the former case it is essential that mounting arrangements do not weaken the wheel by creating stress raisers and in the latter it is important to be aware of the potential for torsional oscillations of the axle. A wheel mounted disc brake arrangement is shown in Figure 12.14. On high speed trains it is often necessary to fit several sets of discs onto an axle to achieve the necessary braking performance.

12.21   Derailments and their Prevention

Derailments can occur because of track failures or because of rolling stock defects. Delays in detecting a derailment present a high risk since a bogie or wheelset that is dragged along the track can destroy long stretches of sleepers and ballast. The kinematic envelope of a derailed vehicle is generally no longer confined to the structure loading gauge and it may therefore collide with a fixed obstacle or another train. Broken rails, damaged wheels and axles and faulty suspensions can all lead to accidents such as the Eschede catastrophe in Germany (3rd June 1998) where the steel tyre of a wheel broke as a result of fatigue.

References

ARTC (2012), Engineering (Track & Civil) Code of Practice, Section 7, p. 5. Australian Rail Track Corporation Ltd. 2012.

Iwnicki, S. (Ed.). (2006). Handbook of railway vehicle dynamics. CRC Press.

Pombo, J., Ambrosio, J., Pereira, M., Lewis, R., Dwyer-Joyce, R., Ariaudo, C., Kuka, N. (2010) A study on wear evaluation of railway wheels based on multibody dynamics and wear computation, Multibody System Dynamics, 24 (3), pp. 347-366

Puffert, Douglas J. 'Path dependence in spatial networks: the standardization of railway track gauge.' Explorations in Economic History 39, no. 3 (2002): 282-314.

Roux, C.; Lorang, X.; Maitournam, H.; Nguyen-Tajan, M. L. (2014), 'Fatigue design of railway wheels: a probabilistic approach', Fatigue & Fracture of Engineering Materials & Structures, 2014, Vol.37(10), pp.1136-1145.

Chapter 13 Infrastructure Maintenance

by Piers Connor & David Oldroyd

13.1 The Need for Reliability

Railways are made up of complex mechanical and electrical systems and there are hundreds of thousands of moving parts. If a railway service is to be reliable, the equipment must be kept in good working order and regular maintenance is essential if this is to be achieved.

The largest investment in any railway is the cost of constructing and maintaining its infrastructure and one of the most significant impediments to the growth of a railway as a business is the investment required for additional infrastructure, combined with the loss of revenue resulting from the engineering works to implement the change. The performance of maintenance itself causes a loss of revenue resulting from the engineering possessions, but a railway will not survive for long as a viable operation if it is allowed to deteriorate because of lack of maintenance.

The functional requirements for Maintenance are to:-

- Avoid spontaneous failures and derailments

- Increase the interval between maintenance intervention by understanding failure modes, wear rate and loss of geometry.

- Monitor by more intensive (or smarter) inspection

Although maintenance is expensive, it will become more expensive to replace the failing equipment early in its life because maintenance has been neglected.

Figure 13.1: *Example of a wet spot on track where ballast and formation are not providing the proper drainage. Such areas require substantial repair to correct them. Photo: N. G. Harris.*

13.2   Earthworks and Formation

The original construction of the foundations of the track is important in securing a stable and reliable base for trains to operate over safely. The rate at which the traditional ballasted track form deteriorates is closely related to the quality of the original construction, in particular track geometry; the heterogeneity/homogeneity of the formation and the strength of the underlying ground, sub-grades and sub-ballast. The track should ideally not be constructed through areas where the underlying ground is soft and/or hydrological conditions are unfavourable. The quality of the subgrade and formation of the track is critically important, regardless of the category of track, and must be capable of withstanding the bearing loads induced by traffic, and other loads induced by external factors such as temperature change and ground settlement.

Many older formations require careful monitoring to ensure they remain safe and capable of providing a suitable ride for trains. This monitoring should be incorporated in the regular inspections of the route, whether visual or mechanical. The same approach should be applied to structures along the route, such as bridges, culverts and tunnels.

Good drainage is essential, both for the formation and the ballast. Track alignment will deteriorate quickly if wet spots (Figure 13.1) are allowed to appear and the condition may require substantial work to repair if it is allowed to remain over a long time.

13.3   Structures

The integrity of bridges, tunnels, station structures (especially platforms), and other buildings associated with the operation and maintenance of the railway must be included in the maintenance regime. Regular inspections of all structures will be required and, in most cases, periods for inspections will be mandated in local laws or building regulations but these periods may need to be reduced in time for particular cases where ground conditions are bad or where damage has occurred from outside influences.

For the safe running of trains, regular gauging of routes is essential to ensure that the structure gauge remains within limits for the line speed at each location. Deviations must be corrected immediately. The risk of deviations is always greater where track renewals or alterations have taken place. Specialist train mounted gauging equipment is available.

In some countries, there is a culture of heritage preservation that includes the railways. Care must be taken to ensure that the maintenance of structures and buildings does not contravene local laws regarding the preservation of buildings or structures. Attempts to modernise buildings to make them more energy efficient or to replace facilities can lead to difficulties in this area. Proper advice should be sought before work is started.

13.4   Boundaries and Cable Runs

The maintenance of a clear and well defined guideway and its boundaries is essential for both safety and security. The ideal is for the route to be fenced, both for safety and ownership purposes but, where this is not possible, regular inspections are required to ensure the route is kept clear of illegal structures and rubbish. In the author's view, all urban and suburban railways should be securely fenced, and this should be mandatory for those that are electrified.

Cable runs are an important part of the railway infrastructure. They provide essential power and communications links and must be designed for and maintained in a robust condition. They must be secure against damage and theft, particularly the risk of infestation by insects or rodents. Theft can be a serious problem because of the high value of metals used in cables.

Cable runs may be located in specially constructed troughs or run along posted supports at the trackside. In modern installations, troughing is a better solution, as it provides security but it must be properly drained and regularly inspected for damage or blockages.

13.5   Track

It is generally accepted that the track of a railway (its permanent way), provides almost all of the ride quality of a train and that the train's suspension system is largely designed to remove the worst failings of many track sections that do not reach this level of quality. It is essential that the track is maintained to the designed cant, gradient, level and line, as these parameters enable the rolling stock that uses the line to traverse them safely and within the limits of comfort for passengers. The maintenance of high quality geometry will also minimise the forces imposed on the track components, which generally results in lower maintenance costs. In a fixed guidance system, the maintenance of that system is a crucial element in retaining the safety and integrity of the system.

The action of rail traffic causes ballasted track to degrade over time. As track alignment falls outside the accepted tolerances, the geometry can be improved using a range of techniques (Prescott & Andrews, 2013), including tamping machines, stone blowers or manual packing. Tamping is the main method for high productivity mechanised correct to track geometry. Stoneblowing was developed as an alternative to tamping, the key difference being that instead of squeezing the ballast beneath each sleeper to effect a change in height, a known quantity of fresh stone is injected beneath each sleeper. This has the primary benefit of leaving the consolidated ballast underneath the sleepers relatively undisturbed.

The high dynamic loads cause the track to move and settle, and abrasion between particles of ballast and between ballast and sleepers gradually reduces its ability to interlock and maintain sufficient vertical and lateral resistance. The track has to be lifted and slewed (i.e. moved sideways) at regular intervals to restore the required level of vertical and lateral track quality, typically using tamping machines. However, the intervals between track maintenance cycles tend to get shorter because the actual tamping process causes the ballast to become less angular and unable to form a strong interlocking structure. As the ballast approaches the end of its life, stoneblowing is a proven method of restoring track geometry and extends the time before ballast replacement is needed.

Eventually, the ballast can get to a point where it becomes un-maintainable (sometimes referred to as 'un-tampable') and it has to be cleaned or renewed. In the case of ballast cleaning, a machine equipped with cutting chains excavates the existing ballast layer, sieves it to remove the fines, then reinserts under the track ballast of acceptable size, along with a proportion of fresh ballast.

13.6   Traction Power

Most urban and suburban railways are electrified, either with third rail or overhead line equipment. Both these systems are essential to the reliable operation of the service and both require regular inspection and maintenance. Proper design and quality installation should eliminate many problems but intensive railway operations such as those experienced on urban and suburban routes increase the probability that faults will arise. Therefore systems are required that will locate a fault before a failure occurs and inform the network operator what remedial work is required (Keen, 1997).

As in other form of infrastructure maintenance, the trend is towards automation of these tasks. The latest systems are mounted on passenger trains, where the condition of, say, the overhead line, can be recorded and transmitted to a control room through a wireless data link. The system can monitor line wear, height deviation, wire tension, hard spots and the locations where arcs occur (Yamamoto, 2013).

13.7   Train Positioning

An essential part of any maintenance regime is train planning. If a section of a route is to undergo renewal or repair and the equipment and tools require the use of an engineer's train, tamping machine, stone blower or high rail vehicle, the origin and positioning of the train or vehicle prior to the start of the work must be planned well in advance. Much track maintenance is mechanised and the special trains and equipment need to be on site at the start of the work period if the equipment is to be used efficiently. It will be useful to position the train before the possession is taken and this may require the train to be run between passenger trains before the end of normal traffic hours. Suitable sidings or reversing points may need to be used to store the train temporarily while the possession is taken.

13.8   Leaves on the Line

'Leaves on the line' is recognised as a serious performance issue for railways across the world. According to Network Rail (2014), there are some 30,000 hectares of railway land in Britain that are home to millions of trees, bushes and other plants and a mature tree can have between 10,000 and 50,000 leaves and each autumn thousands of tonnes of leaves fall onto railway lines across the country.

The leaves are compressed by passing trains to create a thin, black 'Teflon'-like trail on the rail that, much like black ice on the roads, can affect train braking and acceleration as a result of the reduced friction between train wheels and rails. This can affect braking and acceleration and some routes have to introduce special timetables to allow for additional running time.

Figure 13.2: *A Network Rail mili-purpose vehicle being used to treat rail head in order to remove leaf mulch. Photo: N. G. Harris.*

In extreme cases, the build-up of leaf mulch can electrically insulate train wheels from the rails, leading to compromised train detection. This can lead to signal failures and train delays.

In Britain, Network Rail use up to 55 rail clearing trains to clean the rail head by spraying it with high pressure water jets to clear away leaf mulch. 'Sandite', a composite material of sand and aluminium, is also added to aid traction. In some areas trees are replaced with plants that don't shed leaves.

Britain is not alone in this problem, with many countries, particularly in northern Europe and North America, where railways run through large deciduous forested areas, experiencing regular disruption caused by leaf fall. The steps taken in other countries are broadly the same as in Britain, being a combination of proactive vegetation management and specialised technology.

13.9 Weather

Extremes of weather can often cause difficulties for railway operations and maintenance. High winds, snow, ice, flooding and excessive heat can all cause problems for the safe running of trains. Systems for snow and ice clearance need to be set up and available at the vulnerable times of the year. Contingency plans for reduced timetables or diversionary routes should also be set up for non-availability of routes through severe weather conditions. Liaison with other transport and rail operators is essential in these cases.

References

Keen, P.M. (1997), 'Monitoring Overhead Line Equipment' Current Collections for High Speed Trains Seminar (Ref. No. 1998/509), IEE Conference.

Lichtberger, B (2005) 'Track Compendium', Eurailpress, Hamburg (636pp.).

Network Rail (2014), 'Leaves', Website page, http://www.networkrail.co.uk/timetables-and-travel/delays-explained/leaves/, Accessed November 2014.

Prescott, D & Andrews, J (2013) 'Modelling Maintenance in Railway Infrastructure Management', Reliability and Maintainability Symposium (RAMS) 2013, Orlando, Fl., Proceedings, 28-31 Jan. 2013, Pp 1-6.

Yamamoto, H (2013), 'Use of Monitoring Technologies for Inspection of Overhead Line System in East Japan Railway Company', Electrification Infrastructure Congress, 22nd-23rd October, 2013 London, UK.

Chapter 14 Railway Signalling

by Piers Connor

14.1 Background

Signalling is one of the most important parts of the many that make up a railway system. Train movement safety depends on signalling and the control and management of trains uses signalling to maximise the efficiency of the system. Over the years many signalling and train control systems have evolved so that, today, a highly technical and complex industry has developed. This chapter shows, in simple terms, how railway signalling has developed for urban and suburban operations, based on UK standards.

14.2 Pioneer Signalling

Back in the 1830s and 40s in the very early days of railways, there was no fixed signalling, no system for informing the driver of the state of the line ahead. Trains were driven 'on sight'. Drivers had to keep their eyes open for any sign of a train in front so they could stop before hitting it. Very soon though, practical experience proved that there had to be some way of preventing trains running into each other. Several unpleasant accidents had shown that there was much difficulty in stopping a train within the driver's sighting distance because of the low adhesion available with the steel-wheel steel-rail interface.

It was thought that the easiest way to improve train safety was to impose time intervals between trains. Most railways chose something like

10 minutes. They only allowed a train to run at full speed 10 minutes after the previous one had left. They ran their trains at a 10-minute 'headway'.

Red, yellow and green flags were used by 'policemen' to show drivers how to proceed. A red flag was shown for the first five minutes after a train had departed. If a train arrived after 5 minutes, a yellow caution signal was shown to the driver. The full-speed green signal was only shown after the full 10 minutes had elapsed.

This 'time interval system', in trying to use a headway to protect trains, still failed to prevent collisions. Trains in those days were considerably less reliable than they are today and often broke down between stations. It also could not be guaranteed that the speed of the first train would be sufficient to prevent the second train catching it up. There were some spectacular rear-end collisions caused, in each case, because the driver believed he had a 10 minute gap ahead of him and had little or no warning if there was an erosion of that 10 minutes. Even if the time was reduced so much that he could see the train in front, he often did not have enough braking capacity to avoid a collision.

14.3   Line Capacity

Another serious problem, from the railways' point of view, was line capacity. Even if they could rely upon all trains not to make unscheduled stops and to travel at the same speed, the 10 minute time interval restricted the number of trains that could run per hour (in this case six) over a given line. As they needed to run more trains, they gradually began to reduce the time between trains. As they reduced the time, or headway, the number of trains per hour increased. At the same time too, the number of accidents increased. Eventually, they had to do something. The answer was fixed signalling.

14.4   Fixed Signalling

Even with the time interval system, the basic rule of signalling was to divide the track into sections and ensure that only one train was allowed in one section at one time. This is still good today. Each section (or block as it is often called) is protected by a fixed signal placed at its entrance for display to the driver of an approaching train. If the section is clear, e.g. there is no train in it, the signal can show a proceed indication. If the section is occupied by a train, the signal will show a stop indication, usually a red aspect (or horizontal semaphore arm). The next train will be made to wait until the train in front has cleared the section. This is the basis upon which all signalling systems are designed and operated.

14.5   Distant Signals

The basic stop/go signal used to protect each section of the line was OK as long as the driver of an approaching train was able to see the signal in time to stop. This was rarely the case, so a system of 'distant' signals was provided in many locations. These were eventually standardised with a yellow indication to show the associated stop signal was showing a stop indication and should be approached with caution. A red-yellow-green pattern was adopted for colour light signals in the 1920s and eventually used to provide a more sophisticated form of train control.

14.6   Interlocking

Another safety feature introduced in the mid-19th Century was mechanical interlocking of points and signals. The purpose was to prevent the route for a train being set up and its protecting signal cleared if there was already another, conflicting route set up and the protecting signal for that route cleared. The interlocking was performed by a series of mechanically interacting rods connected to the signal operating levers in the signal box. The arrangement of the rods physically prevented conflicting moves being set up. As the systems developed, some larger signal cabins at complex junctions had huge frames of interlocking levers, which gave the name 'lever frame' to the row of operating levers in a signal box.

Eventually, by the time signal levers were being replaced by small (miniature) levers or push buttons, mechanical interlocking frames were superseded by relay interlockings. Electro-magnetic relays were used in series to ensure the safety of route setting at junctions. Complex 'control tables' were drawn up to design the way in which these relays would interact and to ensure safety and integrity.

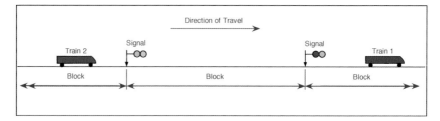

Figure 14.1: *Schematic showing the principles of the signal block section. When a block is unoccupied, the signal protecting it will show green. If a block is occupied, the signal protecting it will show red. Graphic: P. Connor.*

14.7 Blocks

Railways are provided with signalling primarily to ensure that there is always enough space between trains to allow one to stop before it hits the one in front. This is achieved by dividing each track into sections or 'blocks'. Each block is protected by a signal placed at its entrance. If the block is occupied by a train, the signal will display a red 'aspect' as we call it, to tell the train to stop. If the section is clear, the signal can show a green or proceed aspect.

The simplified diagram Figure 14.1 shows the basic principles of the block. The block occupied by Train 1 is protected by the red signal at the entrance to the block. The block behind is clear of trains and a green signal will allow Train 2 to enter this block. This enforces the basic rule or railway signalling that says only one train is allowed onto one block at any one time.

14.8 The Track Circuit

Nowadays for signalling purposes, trains are monitored automatically by means of track circuits. Track circuits were first tried in the US in the 1890s and soon afterwards appeared in Britain. London Underground was the first large-scale user of them in 1904-6.

Low voltage currents applied to the rails cause the signal, via a series of relays (originally) or electronics (more recently) to show a proceed aspect

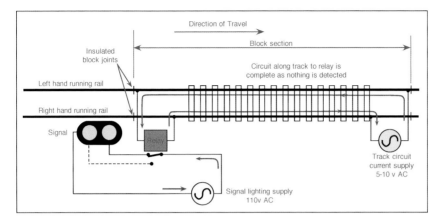

Figure 14.2: *This diagram shows how the track circuit is applied to a section or block of track. A low voltage from a battery is applied to one of the running rails in the block and returned via the other. A relay at the entrance to the section detects the voltage and energises to connect a separate supply to the green lamp of the signal. The system is 'fail-safe', or 'vital' as it is sometimes called, because any break in the circuit will cause a danger signal to be displayed. Graphic: P. Connor.*

(Figure 14.2). The current flow will be interrupted by the presence of the wheels of a train. Such interruption will cause the signal protecting that section to show a stop command. Any other cause of current interruption will also cause a stop signal to show. Such a system means that a failure gives a red aspect: a stop signal. The system is sometimes referred to as 'fail safe' or 'vital'. A proceed signal will only be displayed if the current does flow. Most European main lines with moderate or heavy traffic are equipped with colour light signals operated automatically or semi-automatically by track circuits.

The above is a simplified description of the track circuit. The reality is somewhat more complex. A block section is normally separated electrically from its neighbouring sections by insulated joints in the rails. However, more recent installations use electronics to allow jointless track circuits. Also, some areas have additional circuits that allow the signals to be manually held at red from a signal box or control centre, even if the section is clear. These are known as semi-automatic signals. More complexity is required at junctions.

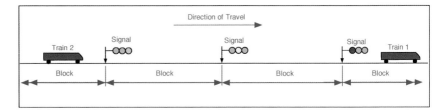

Figure 14.3: *Schematic of 3-aspect signalled route showing the additional yellow aspect provided to allow earlier warnings and thus higher speed operation. Graphic: P. Connor.*

14.9 Multi-Aspect Signals

The basic, two-aspect, red/green signal is fine for lower speed operation but for anything over about 50 km/h the driver of a train needs a warning of a red signal ahead to give him room to stop. In the UK, this led to the idea of caution signals (the distant signals mentioned above) placed far enough back from the signal protecting the entrance to the block to give the driver a warning and a safe braking distance in which to stop. When this was developed for track circuited signalling, the caution signal was provided a block further back from the stop signal. Each signal would now show a red, yellow or green aspect—a multi-aspect signal.

The diagram in Figure 14.3 shows a line with 3-aspect signals. The block occupied by Train 1 is protected by the red signal at the entrance to the block. The block behind is clear of trains but a yellow signal provides advanced warning of the red aspect ahead. This block provides the safe braking distance for Train 2. The next block in rear is also clear of trains and shows a green signal. The driver of Train 2 sees the green signal and knows he has at least two clear blocks ahead of him and can maintain the maximum allowed speed over this line until he sees the yellow.

14.10 Four-Aspect Signalling

The multi-aspect signalling commonly used in the UK today is a 4-aspect system. It works similarly to the 3-aspect system except that two warnings are provided before a red signal, a double yellow and a single yellow. This has two purposes. First, it provides early warnings of a red signal for

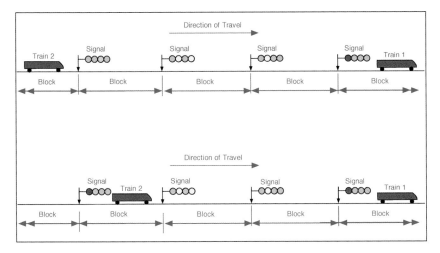

Figure 14.4: *Schematic of 4-aspect signalled route showing the double-yellow aspect. Graphic: P. Connor.*

higher speed trains or it can allow better track occupancy by shortening the length of the blocks. The high speed trains have advanced warning of red signals while the slower speed trains can run closer together at 50 km/h or so under 'double yellows'.

The schematic in Figure 14.4 shows four-aspect signals with (in the upper diagram) a high speed train with three clear blocks ahead of it and (lower diagram) a slower train with two clear blocks ahead of it. The lower speed trains can run closer together so more trains can be operated over a given section of line.

14.11 Warning Systems

In spite of the excellent safety record of railways as a means of transportation, there have been occasions when drivers have allowed their train to pass a point where they should have stopped. Some of these incidents have resulted in collisions, some of these involving loss of life and most involving damage to equipment or property. Most incidents are the result of a driver failing to ensure that his train stops at a stop signal. In Britain, this has become known as SPAD or Signal Passed At Danger.

Such incidents have occurred on railways ever since they began in the early 19th century and various systems have been introduced to try to prevent them. These have taken the form of both warning and train stop systems. In Britain, a warning system is used on most main lines. An alarm sounds in the driver's cab whenever a train approaches a caution or stop signal. If the driver fails to acknowledge the alarm, the train brakes are applied. The system is called AWS (Automatic Warning System).

The AWS ramp is placed between the rails so that a detector on the train will pass over it and receive a signal. The ramp will thus warn the driver of the status of the signal. The French railways use a similar system called 'the Crocodile', the Germans, the 'Indusi'. In operation, the train first passes over the permanent magnet and the on-board receiver sets up a trigger for a brake application. Next it passes over the electro-magnet. If the signal is green the electro-magnet is energised, the brake trigger is disarmed, a chime or bell rings in the driver's cab and a black indicator disc is displayed. The driver need take no action. If the signal is yellow or red, the electro-magnet is de-energised, a siren sounds in the cab and the disc becomes black and yellow. The driver must cancel the warning, otherwise the automatic application of the train brakes is triggered.

14.12   Enforcement

It can be seen from the above that the British AWS allows the driver to cancel a warning as he approaches a signal. This means that, if he cancels the warning and still fails to stop, his train could collide with the train in front. The only way of preventing this is by adopting a system of enforcement.

14.13   TPWS

In spite of the installation of AWS over most of the UK's main line railways, there was a gradual increase in the number of signals passed at danger (SPADs) in the 1990s and some serious collisions as a result. In an attempt to reduce these, a number of suggestions were made to reduce the impact (pun intended) of SPADs. One of these is the Train Protection and Warning System or TPWS, which is now standard across the UK. The idea behind TPWS is that, if a train approaches a stop signal showing a

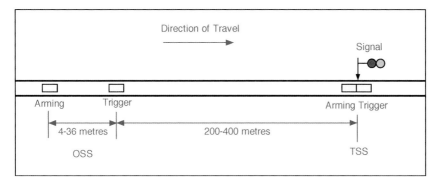

Figure 14.5: *Schematic of TPWS setup on the approach to a stop signal. An Overspeed Sensor System (OSS) is located on the approach to the signal, where the Arming Loop switches on a timer and the Trigger Loop assesses the time elapsed since the arming to determine the speed of the train. If the time is too short, showing the speed is too high, the trigger will activate the train brakes. A Train Stop Sensor (TSS) is located art the signal itself, to trip the train if it passes when a stop indication is shown. Graphic: P. Connor.*

danger aspect at too high a speed to enable it to stop at the signal, it will be forced to stop, regardless of any action (or inaction) by the driver. The equipment is arranged and operated as shown in Figure 14.5.

TPWS has features that allow it to provide an additional level of safety over the existing AWS system but it has certain limitations and does not provide the absolute safety of a full Automatic Train Protection (ATP) system. What TPWS does is reduce the speed at which a train approaches a stop signal if the driver fails to get the speed of the train under sufficient control to allow him to stop at the signal. If the approach speed is too fast, TPWS will apply a full brake but the train may still overrun the signal.

Fortunately, since the train is already braking and there is usually a cushion of 200 yards (183 metres) between the signal and the block it is protecting, there will be a much reduced risk of damage (human and property wise) if the train hits anything. With a possible total distance of 2000 feet (about 600 m) between the brake initiation and the block entrance, trains running over the first loops at up to 120 km/h (75mph) could be stopped safely. TPWS is also provided at many (about 3000) Permanent

Speed Restrictions (PSRs) to ensure that a train does not pass through a restricted section of line (say one with a sharp curve) at too high a speed.

An add-on to TPWS, called TPWS+ is provided at certain signals where train speeds are above 100 mph or 160km/h. The safety effects of TPWS are limited by the fact that it is provided only for stop signals and that it cannot have any effect at caution signals. This means that there is a range of speeds at the higher level that will be excluded from full protection. In spite of this, it is suggested in published data that 60% of accidents due to SPADs are prevented by the installation of TPWS at critical locations. This is achieved, it is said, at 10% of the installation costs of a full ATP system.

TPWS does not replace the existing AWS system. AWS is retained, so the driver will still get the warnings advising him of adverse signals. The TPWS equipment is designed to interface with the existing on-board wiring of trains so that it can be fitted quickly.

14.14   A Safe Braking Distance

The foregoing description of signalling has so far only looked at the concept of warning or enforcement of restrictive signal indications. It has not yet taken into account braking distance or headway. First, there is the problem of braking distances. As we have already seen, a train cannot stop dead. An Inter City train travelling at 100 mph (160 km/hr) will take more than a mile to stop under service braking conditions. Even for a signalling system with enforcement (Automatic Train Protection—ATP) like the London Underground, as described so far there is a risk that a train could pass a stop signal, then be stopped by the ATP enforcement system and still hit the train in front. This situation could occur if the train in front was standing just ahead of the signal protecting it. The problem has long been recognised and can be overcome by the provision of a space for the train to stop in if it overruns the signal, an 'overlap'.

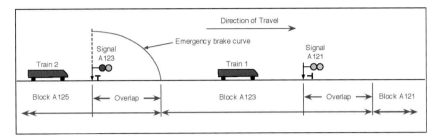

Figure 14.6: *The signal overlap incorporates the emergency braking distance plus a margin beyond the stop signal in case a train overruns the signal. The train is stopped automatically. Some metros and signalling systems adopt a whole block section as a braking buffer between trains so that the block past the signal becomes the overlap. Graphic: P. Connor.*

14.15   The Overlap

In its simplest form, the overlap is a distance allowed for the train to stop in should it pass a signal showing a stop aspect. It is provided by positioning the signal some way before the entrance to the section it is protecting. In Britain it was originally adopted to provide drivers with a margin in case they overran a signal due poor rail conditions or misjudgement. Because it was impossible to calculate all the various braking distances of different types of trains and because it is impossible to predict when a driver might react to a stop signal, a fixed value of 200 yards (185 metres) was adopted in 1978. It has remained the same in principle ever since.

On metros that use ATP systems, the overlap can be calculated by a precise formula based on the known braking capacity of the metro train, the gradient at the location concerned, the maximum possible speed of the trains using that section, an allowance for the sighting of the signal by the driver and a small margin. The result of the calculation is called the 'safe braking distance'. The overlap incorporates this safe braking distance plus a margin. Some metros and signalling systems adopt a whole block section as a braking buffer between trains so that the block past the signal becomes the overlap.

14.16   Metro Signalling

Originally, metro signalling was based on the simple 2-aspect (red/green) system as described earlier. Speeds are not high, so three-aspect signals were not necessary and yellow signals were only put in as repeaters where sighting was restricted.

Many metro routes are in tunnels and it has long been the practice of some operators to provide a form of enforcement of signal observation by installing additional equipment. This became known as automatic train protection (ATP). It can be either mechanical or electronic.

The London Underground and the New York Subway, for example, use a mechanical version known as the trainstop. The trainstop consists of a steel arm mounted alongside the track and which is linked to the signal. If the signal shows a green or proceed aspect, the trainstop is lowered and the train can pass freely. If the signal is red the trainstop is raised and, if the train attempts to pass it, the arm strikes a 'tripcock' on the train, applying the brakes and preventing motoring.

Electrical versions of ATP involve track to train transmission of signal aspects and (sometimes) their associated speed limits. On-board equipment will check the train's actual speed against the allowed speed and will slow or stop the train if any section is entered at more than the allowed speed.

14.17   Automatic Train Protection

On modern metros with electronic ATP, the overlaps are incorporated into the train control system. This may be done by counting the block behind an occupied block as the overlap. Thus, in a full, fixed block ATP system, there will be two red signals and an unoccupied, or overlap block between trains to provide the full safe braking distance, as shown in Figure 14.7 . It should be noted that many ATP equipped systems do not have visible lineside signals because the signal indications are transmitted directly to the driver's cab console (cab signalling).

On a line equipped with ATP as shown in Figure 14.7, each block carries an electronic speed code on top of its track circuit. If the train tries to enter a zero speed block or an occupied block, or if it enters a section at

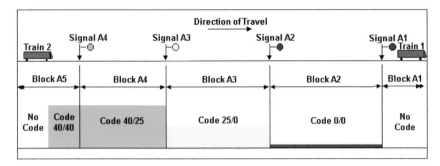

Figure 14.7: *Schematic of ATP Speed Codes Employed on some Metros. Graphic: P. Connor.*

a speed higher than that authorised by the code, the on-board electronics will cause an emergency brake application. This is the system used by London Underground for the Victoria Line from 1968—the first fully automatic, passenger carrying railway. It was a simple system with only three speed codes—normal, caution and stop. Many systems built since are based on it but improvements have been added.

14.18   ATP Speed Codes

A train on a line with a modern version of ATP needs two pieces of information about the state of the line ahead—what speed can it do in this block and what speed must it be doing by the time it enters the next block. This speed data is picked up by antennae on the train. The data is coded by the electronic equipment controlling the track circuitry and transmitted from the rails. The code data consists of two parts, the authorised speed code for this block and the target speed code for the next block.

In the example shown in Figure 14.7, a train in Block A5 approaching Signal A4 will receive a 40 over 40 code (40/40) to indicate a permitted speed of 40 km/h in this block and a target speed of 40 km/h for the next. This is the normal speed data. However, when it enters Block A4, the code will change to 40/25 because the target speed must be 25 km/h when the train enters the next Block A3. When the train enters Block A3, the code changes again to 25/0 because the next block (A2) is the overlap block and is forbidden territory, so the speed must be zero by the time train reaches the end of Block A3. If the train attempts to enter Block A2, the on-board equipment will detect the zero speed code (0/0) and will cause an emergency brake application. As mentioned above, Block A2 is acting as the overlap or safe braking distance behind the train occupying Block A1.

14.19   Operating with ATP

Trains operating over a line equipped with ATP can be manually or automatically driven. To allow manual driving, the ATP codes are displayed to the driver on a panel in his cab. In our example below, he would begin braking somewhere around the brake initiation point because he would see the 40/25 code on his display and would know, from his knowledge of the line, where he will have to stop. If signals are not provided, the signal positions will normally be indicated by trackside block marker boards to show drivers the entrances to blocks.

If the train is installed with automatic driving (ATO), brake initiation for the reduced target speed can be by either a track mounted electronic 'patch' or 'beacon' placed at the brake initiation point or, more simply, by the change in the coded track circuit. Both systems are used by different manufacturers but, in both, the train passes through a series of speed steps to the signalled stop.

14.20   Distance-to-Go

The next stage of ATP development was an attempt to eliminate the space lost by the empty overlap block behind each train. If this could be eliminated, line capacity could be increased by up to 20%, depending on block lengths and line speed.

To remove the overlap section, it is simply a question of moving the braking curve forward by one block. The train will now be able to proceed a block closer (A5 instead of A6) to the occupied block, before it gets a target speed reduction. However, to get this close to the occupied block requires accurate and constant checking of the braking by the train, so an on-board computer calculates the braking curve required, based on the

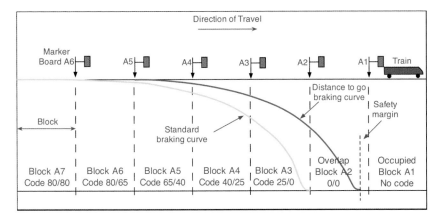

Figure 14.8: *Schematic of Distance-to-Go train control system showing how a block section is saved by continuous speed monitoring. Graphic: P. Connor.*

distance to go to the stopping point and using a line map contained in the computer's memory. The new curve is shown in blue in the diagram. A safety margin of 25 metres or so is allowed for error so that the train will always stop before it reaches the critical boundary between Blocks A2 and A1. Note that the braking curve should reduce (or 'flare out') at the final stopping point in order to give the passengers a comfortable stop.

14.21 Speed Monitoring

Both the older, speed step method of electronic ATP and the 'distance-to-go' method require the train speed to be monitored. In Figure 14.8, we can see the standard braking curve of the speed step system always remains inside the profile of the speed steps. The train's ATP equipment only monitors the train's speed against the permitted speed limit within that block. If the train goes above that speed, an emergency brake application will be invoked. The standard braking curve made by the train is not monitored.

For the distance-to-go system, the development of modern electronics has allowed the brake curve to be monitored continuously so that the speed steps become unnecessary. When it enters the first block with a speed restriction in the code, the train is also told how far ahead the stopping point is. The on-board computer knows where the train is now, using the line 'map' embedded in its memory, and it calculates the required braking curve accordingly. As the train brakes, the computer checks the progress down the curve to check the train never goes outside it. To ensure that the wheel revolutions used to count the train's progression along the line have not drifted due to wear, skidding or sliding, the on-board map of the line is updated regularly during the trip by fixed, track-mounted beacons laid between the rails.

14.22   Operation with Distance-to-Go

Distance-to-go ATP has a number of advantages over the speed step system. As we have seen, it can increase line capacity but also it can reduce the number of track circuits required, since you don't need frequent changes of steps to keep adjusting the braking distance. The blocks are now just the spaces to be occupied by trains and are not used as overlaps as well. Distance-to-go can be used for manual driving or automatic operation.

Systems vary but often, several curves are provided for the train braking profile. One version has three: One is the normal curve within which the train should brake, the second is a warning curve, which provides a warning to the driver (an audio-visual alarm or a service brake application depending on the system) and the third is the emergency curve that will force an emergency brake if the driver does not reduce speed to within the normal curve.

14.23   'Moving Block'

Some train control system suppliers offer what they describe as 'Moving Block' systems. The main component of these systems is data transfer between train and trackside by radio. Often, train location is included. For older versions, like the Seltrac system by Thales (formerly Alcatel), a looped transmission cable is provided along the track and data is exchanged between track and train through the cable. Train control is centralised with areas or 'regions', as they are described by another supplier (Bombardier) monitoring a number of trains at the same time.

A feature common to all these moving block systems is a requirement for fixed target locations such as beacons or loops in the transmission cable that update and confirm the train location at regular intervals. True moving block without any fixed confirmation system is unlikely to be possible within existing technological capability.

Bibliography

Kichenside, G.; Williams, A. (1998)'Two Centuries of Railway Signalling', 1998, Oxford Publishing Company, UK.

Nock, O.S., ed (1980), 'Railway Signalling - A treatise on the recent practice of British Railways', A & C Black / IRSE, London 1980.

Theeg, G.; Vlasenko, S. (eds.) (2009), 'Railway Signalling & Interlocking - International Compendium', Eurailpress 2009.

Solomon, B., (2010), 'Railroad Signaling', Voyageur Press Inc.,U.S, 2010.

Chapter 15 Design Criteria for Tramway Systems

by Mohammad Reza Zolfaghari & Felix Schmid

15.1 Introduction and Background

Horse omnibuses came into existence in the first half of the 19th century, when the world's major cities began to grow beyond a size where any destination could be reached easily on foot in about an hour. However, horse omnibuses were uncomfortable and had limited capacity, due to the poor road surfaces. The operators had to charge relatively high fares, affordable only by well-off people, because they had to cover the cost of the two or more horses required to haul the coaches.

Between 1850 and 1880, recognising the importance of faster and more efficient local transport and the advantages of the steel wheel on steel rail, entrepreneurs and the municipalities themselves started to build basic street railways, modelled on the tramroads that had emerged in the 17th and 18th century for the carriage of freight. Early trams, as the vehicles came to be known, were hauled by horses and, in some cases, small enclosed steam locomotives and underground cables.

Berlin, London, Paris, New York and most other major cities rapidly developed large networks of animal, steam and cable hauled tramways that were electrified from 1890 onwards, to improve performance and reduce pollution. Quickly, electric tramways were built around the globe, often by European commercial interests, with time limited concessions. Many of the smaller networks were abandoned in the 1920s when the concessions expired while others were taken over by the respective municipalities. Most of the major international conurbations had abandoned their tramway networks by the 1960s, in an attempt to free urban space for cars. Metros were built where funds permitted, elsewhere, the tramways were replaced by trolley-buses and motor buses.

As mentioned earlier in this book, tramways became popular again in the 1980s, both in Europe and the United States of America. In the USA they reappeared as Light Rapid Transit, an affordable type of medium capacity, fast urban transport that suited the relatively low density of many American conurbations better than metros such as those of New York City and Washington DC. In Europe, the terms Light Rail and Light Rail Transit were adopted in some cases to differentiate the new systems from the long established tramway with its reliance on sharing most of the alignment with road transport. In the present chapter though, the terms tramway, light rapid transit and light rail will be used interchangeably.

Whatever the terminology used, the requirements for building new street running railways are far more demanding than those that were in place in the late 19th and early 20th century. The planning phase of modern systems often exceeds 10 years from concept to opening. In general, a project starts with a feasibility study.

15.2   Feasibility studies

A feasibility study is an essential first step in any tramway construction project. Any stakeholder or consideration neglected in this phase may result in major flaws in the system and bears the risk of investing public funds in a venture that is rejected by the potential users. This first section thus covers the most important considerations and aims of a feasibility study.

15.3   Identifying Areas to be Served

To ensure the economic viability and sustainability of a tramway system, a successful feasibility study must identify correctly the areas with the optimum population in terms of size and ability to pay fares, the possible commuting demand and the potential for the creation of strategic transport links. The main concept for a successful network should be to link three main types of zones, including central business districts, residential areas and the main public transport hubs, such as railway stations, bus stations and airports. The layout and location of each area, the passenger flows between them and economic justification are the main parameters that can will affect the network planning process. The key to reaching the required passenger flows is the correct identification of areas and creating viable links between them. This concept is illustrated in the traffic generation triangle depicted in Figure 15.1.

Another key factor for a successful feasibility study is a determination of the possible contribution that the tramway network might make to urban regeneration. Nottingham and Sheffield are suitable examples for this. Following the success of the first phase of the Nottingham Express Transit (NET) system, the second phase is expected to add to the contribution that the tram system makes to the Greater Nottingham economy and social fabric.

Nottingham is considered as the regional capital; hence its commercial circle of influence is not restricted to the boundary of the city but also practically affects the other areas around it. In 2014, the Greater Nottingham economy was evaluated at about £10.7 billion and supported about 300,000 local jobs. This statistic shows the importance of the public transport system in providing reliable links between the various districts. At the beginning of the project, during the construction and after the opening of the second phase of the NET line, the benefits listed below were expected:

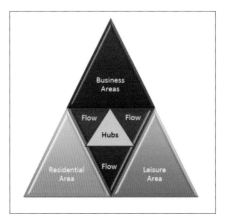

Figure 15.1: *Tramway network planning success triangle (Author)*.

- Significant financial benefits for local companies involved in construction contracts;

- Employment of hundreds of local people;

- Growth in employment, potentially creating 8,000 jobs;

211

- New investment in the city region with a value of £300m annually;

- Contribution to an integrated public transport system for Greater Nottingham;

- Facilitation of modal shift from private cars to public transport;

- Improved access to about 1270 out of 55,000 work places in the city;

- Greater integration with road transport leading to reduced congestion and lower carbon emissions.

The feasibility study for the second phase of NET was intended to ensure that the new lines would improve and sustain the neighbourhood transformation and regeneration strategies in the heart of the city as well as the central areas of Clifton, Beeston and other strategic business and residential areas, including Nottingham University and the Queen's Medical Centre.

15.4   Passenger Flow Prediction

The foundation for predicting reliable levels of passenger flows is the proper identification of areas to be served by a new system, as mentioned in the previous section. In order to avoid confusion and complexity, Bonsall (1997) introduced the matrix method. Generally, in this method, the data generated from linking the traffic zones would be presented in an origin-destination matrix. This matrix can potentially include information on all types of travel by various modes, but Lesley (2011) suggests that tramway network planners tend to focus on transfer from car travel.

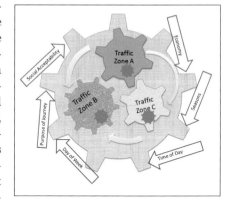

Figure 15.2: *Gearbox-Wheel model for transport planning process - passenger flow prediction (Author).*

The logic underpinning this approach is that the car reflects the most convenient and demanding mode and the highest passenger volume and this helps the planners to be on the safe side. This approach also helps the planners to get the data for potential trips within allocated traffic zones with high passenger demand. Also, planners must assure promoters that there will be enough passenger volume for a tramway network by demonstrating that they have chosen the best routes and alignments.

Apart from these considerations, planners must be aware of passenger flow variations that can be categorised into seasonal, daily and hourly. For instance, occasional markets, seasonal events, seasonal jobs and university teaching periods and vacations can affect the number of trips and passenger flows. At the same time, in the early mornings and early evenings, peak passenger flows are expected because people commute to their work places and schools. The author believes that these considerations can be presented in a gearbox model that shows how different drivers interact to produce traffic demand, see Figure 15.2.

In this model, the whole of the area under study for a new transportation mode is considered as a big wheel. Within the overall network area are some defined traffic zones that are shown as small wheels inside the big wheel. As a gearbox system all of these wheels need to move in the right direction to make the other wheels move and without an exact engineering design and operational plan, the movement of the big wheel will face failure. Obviously, each of the zones A, B and C will have internal traffic and there will be links between the zones that support the

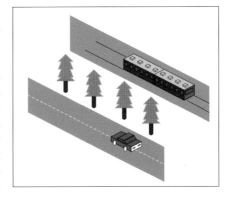

Figure 15.3: *Off-road/Segregated tramway route (Author).*

movement of people throughout the whole network area. Bigger areas can be modelled with bigger wheels. Undoubtedly there are some additional issues that affect the planning, factors such as season, time of the day and the purposes of the journeys. The model can be used in all of the transport planning approaches to deliver a detailed scheme of the area under study.

213

15.5   Route Design

Undoubtedly, route selection and alignment design are an important steps in the process of building a new tramway network. Route design can profoundly affect the time and cost of the project and can impact on the vehicle design, system safety and traffic management. In the feasibility phase, planners should take into consideration the possibility of using existing alignments. This is usually one of the best solutions to address financial and environmental issues and will lead to savings in cost and time in many situations.

15.6   Different Types of Tramway Right of Way

The rights of way for a tramway network can be of different types, depending on the street layouts of the area to be served, on the traffic patterns and safety requirements. Tramway alignment types can be categorised into: Segregated, Separated and Integrated.

A segregated route is a type of alignment that is completely protected from interactions with cars, roads and other traffic corridors. This type of alignment is mostly applicable to situations where tramways or light railways are built on land that is not alongside existing roads and other transport infrastructure. Figure 15.3 shows a schematic arrangement for this type of alignment.

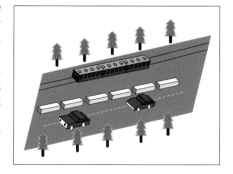

Figure 15.4: *Street running/Separated tramway route (Author).*

A separated route is a type of tram alignment where the tram track is separated from other traffic by a fence or kerb but adjacent to the carriageway. Figure 15.4 shows a schematic of this type of alignment. This arrangement is often referred to as segregated on-street running.

An integrated alignment is a type of route that partially or totally shares the road with other traffic modes such as buses, cycles, motor cycles, cars and trucks. Not unreasonably, planners are keen to design segregated routes wherever possible, since this potentially avoids a number of safety issues, complicated traffic management plans, specific signalling equipment and, to some extent, extra time and cost in the construction process. But there are some inevitable factors that get in the way of designing segregated routes. The most important factors can be listed as:

- Street layout;
- Defined traffic zones and the requirements for connectivity between them;
- Topography of the area;
- Curvatures and width of the streets;
- Vertical curvature of the alignment;
- Political and legal restrictions
- Economic considerations (in specific situations);
- Obstacles such as buildings, roundabouts, historic monuments etc.

The design of tramway systems in city centres is always a big challenge because planners have to cope with these factors and many other unexpected factors that might be encountered during the project.

15.7   Alignment Design Process and Considerations

A tramway alignment or right of way design must meet three main requirements:

- Guaranteed safety;
- Maximum efficiency;
- Optimised cost.

For instance, in the choice of the alignment, planners must try to avoid removing buildings and affecting major road junctions, since the demolition process and traffic diversions might not be cost and time efficient.

As previously mentioned, defining the traffic zones and origin-destination matrix of the network is the foundation of a successful route design.

After this step, planners need to start collecting relevant data, based on the available information and restrictions, suggest routes and try to validate them based on proper scientific approaches. At a high level, Multi Criteria Decision Making (MCDM) can be used as an approach to selecting the best option amongst various choices. By contrast, Swept Path Analysis (SPA) is a detail design tool that facilitates the assessment of design requirements, such as the minimum width required for footways, parking, bus lanes etc. These tools can also assist in the design of level crossings.

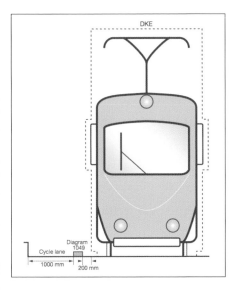

Figure 15.5: *Clearance required between cycling lane and tramway (Source: ORR).*

In Great Britain, these approaches are important in meeting the ORR (Office of Rail & Road) requirements for tramways. Figure 15.5 shows an example of ORR guidance for the clearance between a cycling lane and a tramway. There are many factors such as gradients, curvature, kinematic envelope and vertical clearances that impact on the design criteria.

15.8   The Impact of Construction

The Birmingham Centre for Railway Research and Education (BCRRE) conducted a study to identify the technical and non-technical issues that have arisen during the work to extend the initial line of the Midlands Metro (MM) from Snow Hill to New Street Station. It is expected that the results of this case study can be used for assessing the impact of similar projects in the future.

The studies and planning for the project to extend the MM from Snow Hill to Five Ways started in 2000. Financial constraints resulted in the project being limited to a new section between Snow Hill and Stephenson Street, alongside New Street Station. However, the choice of Curzon Street for the Birmingham HS2 terminus will rekindle the interest in extending the MM to Curzon Street and beyond, as well as to Five Ways. After a development period of more than 10 years, construction of the extension started in February 2014.

More than 400 small, medium and large businesses operate around this area, some of which have opened recently but others have been operating for a long time. Large commercial buildings in Colmore Row, like the House of Fraser building and small premises such as takeaways, are examples of the numerous businesses that are affected by the extension work. The most important problems are described in the sections that follow.

15.9   Interaction between Construction and Local Businesses

At the beginning of the construction of each section of track, installing barriers and blocking some of the access pathways are inevitable. Depending on the location of each individual business, the nature of the business and the income and the number of customers of each business, blocking the access affects the business to a greater or lesser extent. For example, some small takeaway shops that have only a small number of customers tend to be at risk of losing all of them.

There have been numerous and time-consuming efforts to address the complaints of the management and customers of a hotel affected by the works. Balfour Beatty considered these issues and adopted some changes in the construction process; some of the issues are still ongoing. Significant issues were as follows:

- The owner of the hotel also owns some other business units. There were complaints about construction noises;

Figure 15.6: *The interface between the construction site of the Birmingham Metro extension works and the Burlington Hotel. (Author).*

- The residents of the hotel complained of noise due to the crushing of concrete slabs;

- There were frequent complaints about noise of material delivery vehicles;

- The contractor had to change the schedule for breaking up the concrete remaining from Birmingham's first generation trams;

- A separated delivery area was arranged to avoid passing trucks in front of the hotel;

- Improved barriers with resilient bases were used to mitigate the effects of vibration and noise;

- The negotiations started about 3 months before work commenced but the contractor was still struggling with the hotel management team at start-up.

All these considerations and changes in the programme impose extra time and extra cost to the project. Allowances must be incorporated for similar problems in the costing of any new project.

15.10 Impact of Construction Noise, Vibration and Dust

The construction process included excavation and concrete vibration. Also some sections of the route are along the line of the original Birmingham tramway, so in those sections there was a need to crush the old concrete track structure. The severe noise and vibration transferred to the surrounding buildings. In one old commercial building, a number of offices overlooking the works eventually had to be abandoned. The windows were old and were not double-glazed. The office staff were suffering from the high level of noise and vibration. The contractor had provided some noise barriers but, in practical terms, they were not effective. Eventually, the office occupiers had to move to a new building.

Figure 15.7 shows two prestigious business buildings located on Colmore Row. These buildings accommodate some well-known companies and the managers are very concerned about the noise, vibration, access road and any other little issue that affects the buildings. For example, the cleaning of the windows for this particular building cost about £15,000 (in 2014). Thus, the contractor had a difficult task to help the managers to understand the problems and consequences of the construction process and to assist in mitigating those consequences.

15.11 Impact of Construction Works on Road Access

Large businesses, such as House of Fraser, located near the construction sites that receive, on a daily basis, delivery consignments carried in big trucks. Road closures can seriously affect the delivery process.

The best choice was to find an alternative route along parallel streets to provide for truck access and rubbish collections. This process required precise traffic management and in some sections a new traffic management system became inevitable. Implementing the new system required lengthy risk and safety assessments and approval processes and these resulted in higher costs and longer timescales for the project.

The approvals process profoundly affected the management of the project and its cost and time budgets. In some sections, the contractor had to

Figure 15.7: *The interface between the construction site and new commercial buildings overlooking the Midland Metro extension works (Author).*

split the track into separate sub-sections. This had the potential to affect the quality, integrity and resource allocation policies of the project. It also led to severe problems for people and local businesses because of multiple changes to the delivery and access routes and the effects on traffic management.

Hence the authors suggest a comprehensive study prior to starting the construction of tramways in city centres to determine the consequences and the priority of track development in order to achieve the optimum traffic management, utility diversion and mitigation of environmental impacts, such as noise and vibration.

15.12 Impact of Track Characteristics on Vehicle Design

Track geometry and curve radius and length directly impact the choice of the tram vehicles and their design. The most important parameter in design is consistency. For the whole extent of a network, the same standards must be applied. The interface between track and vehicle is influenced by a range of factors. According to the US Transportation Research Board (TRB, 2012)), in order to set up the procurement of a tramcar, the following requirements must be taken into account:

- Weight of vehicle. Both empty and fully loaded weights are important;

- Clearance issues including required track-platform location tolerance, essential clearance between cars and adjacent tracks, considering car dynamics, required clearance for bridges, tunnels etc.;

- Gap between vehicle door sill and platform edge that affect wheelchair access;

- Wheel dimensions including wheel profile, diameter, wheel gauge and wheel back to back gauge;

- Lateral component of vehicle force on track;

- Longitudinal vehicle/track interaction forces.

It should be noted that the form of track potentially affects the clearance envelope. For instance, ballasted track can drift during its life-cycle and this can affect the kinematic envelope.

The TRB (2012) suggests that all track, vehicle and control system designers should be coordinated from the first stage of design. The suggested approach is to produce a comprehensive manual for design criteria and then update the manual by adding information as the project progresses. The defining characteristics of a stationary tramway vehicle are demonstrated in Figure 15.8.

Figure 15.8: *Light Rail car body characteristics (Author).*

The dynamic characteristics of a light rail vehicle have a greater impact on track design criteria than the static ones. The vehicle dynamic envelope (VDE) of a railway vehicle defines the maximum space that the vehicle can occupy when it moves on the track. Identifying the tram car dynamic envelope is the vehicle designer's job. Figure 15.9 shows the most important factors in VDE.

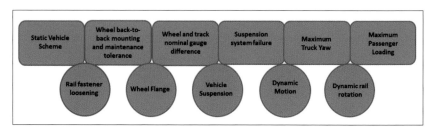

Figure 15.9: *Factors affecting the dynamic excursions of a light rail vehicle (Author).*

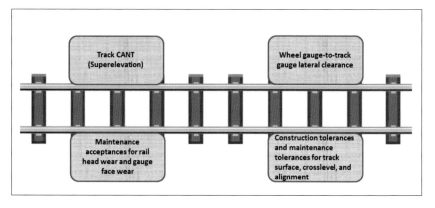

Figure 15.10: *Features of track affecting vehicle dynamic envelope (Author).*

To assure compatibility of light rail vehicle dimensions with specific track geometry restrictions in urban areas, track designers and vehicle designers must collaborate properly. Depending on the situation, track designers need to consider the vehicle specifications based on some key factors and then develop the track geometry. On the other hand, the vehicle manufacturers should be able to modify the vehicle according to the minimum requirements imposed by track geometry. The key factors and considerations can be briefly mentioned as below:

- Horizontal curvature relating to minimum turning radius of vehicle;

- Vertical curvature relating to minimum crest curves;

- Combinations of horizontal and vertical curvature;

- Vertical alignment with respect to maximum gradients;

- Maximum allowable twist of the track;

- Ride quality.

15.13 Electrification Systems

The ORR (Office of Rail & Road) is responsible for regulating for all types of rail systems in Great Britain. As regards tramway systems electrification, the ORR has some provisions and guidelines that must be followed by tramway network developers in Britain.

In Britain tramways are generally supplied with electric traction power via overhead lines. The maximum allowed voltage on public roadways is 750 V DC. Different voltages might be permitted in special cases, subject to technical and safety agreements. AC power supply is normally not permitted for on-street systems.

Overhead lines require support structures along the track length where the electrification equipment cannot be suspended from roadside buildings. These structures and the associated overhead electric traction equipment require careful siting. They should not hinder traffic on the road or street and at the same time they need to be safe from possible damage caused by road vehicles. Different types of poles are being used to support the overhead wires, according to location and local conditions. Apart from the shape and type, all of them need to be installed considering the regulations and considerations. Figure 15.11 shows a typical configuration as used on the Nottingham tramway network (NET).

Figure 15.11: *Overhead line electrification in Nottingham (Author).*

15.14 Design and Installation of Poles

According to ORR guidelines, overhead lines and supporting poles in public area must be designed and installed considering some important standards and regulations, which are briefly listed here:

- Protection against climbing: Electric poles in public areas must be designed and installed to prevent climbing. Poles must be secured against vandalism and not accessible for improper use;

- Insulation: Electric poles in public areas must be insulated properly;

- There must be provision for electrical protection in case of pole failure.

Minimising the vulnerability of any single supporting equipment and pole needs to be a major goal of the design. The collapse of any single support can potentially impose tension in the overhead line system. Incidents can occur when repairing buildings where electric system anchors are mounted, when poles are struck by road cars, affected by a fire etc. The design must be able to prevent live equipment from dropping lower than 5200 mm above the road or highway. In the case of off-highway rights of way the limit can be lower but only if it is safely out of reach of pedestrians. Connections between the pole and the contact wire must be physically weaker than the contact wire to guarantee that in case of a pole being damaged or collapsing, the connection will break before the live equipment is pulled down.

15.15 Using Electric Traction Poles for Other Functions

In some areas, in order to save space and costs, electric poles are used to mount the street lighting system or other similar electrical equipment. The ORR obliges contractors to consider the required safety and technical issues. For example, in the case of failure conditions, a traction system must not badly impact the other systems. In the case of two different electrical systems being present on the same pole, double insulation might be required. It is important that any other pole mounted electric system, such as street lighting, must be installed such that its maintenance has no effect on the tramway power supply system.

15.16 Safety Management of Traction Power Supply Systems

ORR instructions clearly state that the design of any electric traction power supply system must guarantee that the maximum touch voltages do not surpass 60 volts. Since the positioning of electrical sub-stations can be potentially significant, minimising the return resistance by the use of sufficient rail section or additional return current conductors must be taken into account. Higher voltages might be permitted in low-risk areas, subject to specific inspections and considerations.

Isolating switches are important and need to be provided. This ensures that the operators have effective and efficient control of the power supply system, even in emergency conditions. The switches must be protected from intrusion by unauthorised persons and located without creating any kind of hazard. The guidelines suggest that isolators be positioned in secure trackside cupboards. In case of mounting the switches on trackside poles, required safety and protection must be in place. There should be adequate signage to inform people to keep away from live parts. Authorised people must be trained to use this equipment safely.

In some areas, depending upon the owners' consent and safety requirements, electric overhead lines or equipment might be mounted on the roof or walls of trackside buildings. In these cases, the proximity of the buildings to the equipment, the location of windows and the possibility of touching equipment during cleaning activities must all be considered carefully with a view to ensuring safety.

15.17   Stray Current Management

The power circuit of any direct current supplied electric tramway can be considered as including four essential components (Steel, 2014):

- The substations, from which the direct current at the selected nominal voltage for the line is supplied;

- The positive conductor (the overhead line) connecting the supply to the trams;

- The load (trams);

- The negative conductor over which the current is returned to the substations.

According to Ohm's law, in any conductor the passage of an electrical current will result in a voltage drop along its length, proportional to the resistivity of the conductor. As a result of this phenomenon, sections of the rails will be at a voltage, which is different from that of other equipment buried in the earth, such as metal pipes and cables and urban utilities.

Figure 15.12 shows the ORR (2014) suggestions for the design and configuration of tramway power supply systems to avoid stray current flow. The voltage is dependent on the location and power flow within the system and could be positive or negative, depending on the local earth. Since the earth is not a perfect insulator, the potential difference between the rails and adjacent buried conductors causes that part of the traction return current to 'leak' to earth and some of this total leakage to return to the substation, in part, through the buried pipes. The level of leakage depends on the relative total resistance of the many possible return paths,

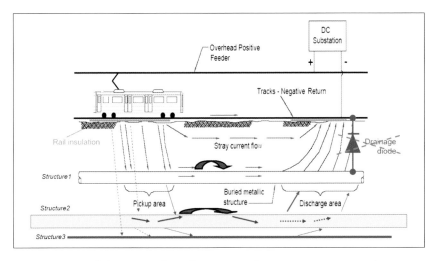

Figure 15.12: *Schematic of configuration of tramway power supply system to avoid stray current flow. (ORR)*

through the rails and through other metallic pipes, earth shields of cables and the ground itself.

The impact of stray currents on buried metal objects is electrolytic corrosion. This mostly results in loss of material. Undoubtedly this is an unwanted phenomenon in locations where metal pipes carry gas or water, since leakage and rupture will impose very significant safety and operational risks to the tramway, people and the environment. With regard to utility cables, especially old lead covered types, such losses arise even more quickly and can lead to failure of the unprotected inner insulation of the cable. It is important that utility companies and other organisations which own equipment buried in the ground beneath the track, accept that, even with a proper design and satisfying all the requirements, there would still be some leakage. Hence the buried equipment and devices must be protected properly.

Constant monitoring and maintenance are key factors to assure control and mitigation of return current losses. Steel (2014) in the ORR tramway technical guidelines, suggests a useful strategy that can be used as reference for tramway developers in modern cities. Tramways are recommended to designate a stray current working party (SCWP) for each project. All stakeholders that are likely to be affected by stray currents, should contribute to this working party. The most important steps in this strategy are listed below:

- Agreement on the establishment of a register of vulnerable assets. It is important to note assets that are metallic and close to the tramway rails, and capable of creating an effective path between different parts of the tramway. The ORR paper (2014) suggests some measures. For example, buried metal apparatus further than one metre away from the rails in any direction are not considered to be vulnerable to stray currents;

- Proper communication is required to allow awareness of programmes where the utility companies replace the cladding of equipment currently metal with plastic or similar, therefore reducing the range and extent of vulnerable devices;

- Agreements on the level of testing of measures to mitigate stray current throughout the construction phase of the system;

- Agreements on the level of monitoring of change in these measures during the operation phase of the system;

- Appraisal of the outcomes of testing during construction;

- Investigating the issues as they arise during the operation phase of the system;

- Regular meetings with stakeholders, legal bodies, constructors and companies during the construction phase. In the operation phase these meetings can be less frequent but must still take place regularly.

In general, the design, siting and installation of supportive structures for tramway power supply systems can play a significant role in the success, reputation and safety of a tramway network. In some urban areas, especially where the trams are running on narrow streets and there is not enough space for electric poles, promoters need to negotiate with the owners and residents of the local buildings to reach agreements to attach the OHLE equipment to the walls of the buildings. Availability and appropriateness of buildings from technical, aesthetic, and architectural/historic sensitivity points of view are some of the key factors. The Croydon Tramlink project experienced great difficulties in siting for electric poles while the Edinburgh tram project was able to use trackside buildings to attach and fix the power supply systems and equipment.

15.18   A Modern Concept of Traffic management

In this section the authors will not discuss the technical components of traffic management but will present a modern tramway project management strategy that is much more accurate and energy efficient. This should give the tramway promoters a good idea of how they should design tramway control systems for modern urban areas.

In 2011, Christian Gassel from Dresden University of Technology presented an idea for enhanced transport quality and tramway energy efficiency by multi-modal traffic management systems. "Intelligent Transport Systems can significantly contribute to a cleaner, safer and more efficient transport system". Figure 15.13 shows his schematic view of the different components of traffic management systems in modern urban areas and the interactions between them.

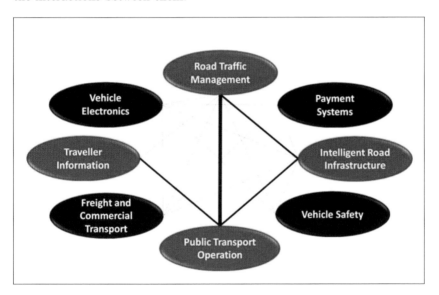

Figure 15.13: *Traffic management components in modern urban areas (Gassel, 2011)*

The traffic management system components in Dresden, Germany, in a case study based on Gassel (2011), provide a good overview of the requirements that need to be defined when developing similar systems in other modern urban areas. In Dresden the main authority bodies for traffic management are:

- Intermodal Transport Control System (ITCS): This section deals with location and dispatch of the vehicle fleet;

- Passenger Information Services: In Dresden this centre monitors 12 tramway routes and 28 bus routes.

- Traffic Control Centre (TCC), which deals with road traffic condition monitoring. This system is in charge of traffic flow detection. The applied equipments are single- and multi-induction loops, infrared and video detection, taxi FCD (about 1200 sensors);

- This system also deals with traffic control and information using changeable traffic signs, parking information etc.

The TCC used to suffer from poor awareness of public transport issues. The main goal was to improve the traffic quality by setting priorities at traffic lights depending on private transport conditions, punctuality of public transport, the dynamics of connecting services and a reduction in tramway energy consumption. Figure 15.14 illustrates traffic flow control and prioritisation in Nottingham at a junction that is a critical section where trams are running on street.

In Dresden (Figure 15.15) the traffic management system was based on the idea that traffic prioritisation would be intelligent and based on the real-time situation at each junction, using a 'priority decision system'. As each vehicle approaches a junction, the priority decision system obtains information on a few key factors. The most important factors include headway, punctuality, connecting services and local traffic conditions. Basically this approach adds reliability to the decision making process since each decision will be made according to exact information arising from real-time considerations.

Figure 15.14: *Traffic prioritisation using traffic light in junction, NET, Nottingham (Author)*

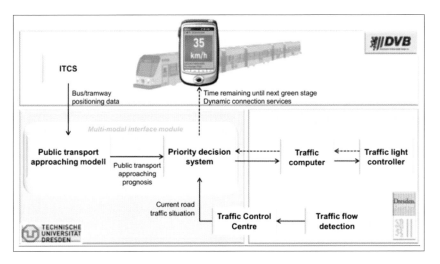

Figure 15.15: *A Multi-modal traffic management system modified by adding priority decision making process. (Author, based on Gassel 2011).*

References

Alkubaisi, M. I. T. (2014) 'Predefined Evaluating Criteria to Select the Best Tramway Route', Traffic and Logistics Engineering, vol. 2, pp. 211-217, 2014.

Gassel, C. (2012), 'Cooperative Traffic Signals for Energy Efficient Driving in Tramway Systems', 19th ITS World Congress, Vienna , Austria, 2012.

Lesley, L. (2011), 'Light Rail Developer's Handbook', J.Ross Publishing Inc., 2011.

Steel, A. (2014), 'Design Standards Stray Current Management' in Tramway Technical Guidance Note 3, ed. http://orr.gov.uk: ORR, 2014, p. 16.

TRB (2012), 'Track Design Handbook for Light Rail Transit'. The Transportation Research Board, Washington DC, USA, 2012.

Chapter 16 Electric Railway Systems

by Felix Schmid, Colin Goodman & Piers Connor

16.1 Background

The rail mode of transport, using steel wheel on steel rail technology and mechanical traction, is over 200 years old. Although steam power was the main source of locomotion, Davidson used batteries as early as 1842 to power a small electric locomotive that could pull 7 tons at 4 mph. Electric traction with an infrastructure-based power supply has a history of 130 years. Werner von Siemens demonstrated third rail current collection at 150 V DC at the Berlin Exhibition of 1879 and Volk's electric railway in Brighton has been operating with the same technology since 1883. Thus, both the mode and one of its major subsystems may be viewed as mature. However, they are still subject to constraints that derive from the natural characteristics of the rail mode of transport.

Characteristics of the Rail Mode of Transport

As shown in Figure 16.1, there are four fundamental physical characteristics that are intrinsic to the railway mode of transport. Three of these features are inherent to the guidance and support system formed by the steel wheel running on the steel rail and the fourth derives from the way in which the assets are distributed to reach rail's dispersed customers. The single degree of freedom of motion, low coefficient of friction and stiff interface between wheel and rail determine the general strengths and weaknesses of the mode (shown as G in the table) and facilitate the electric operation of railways (E). The single degree of freedom of motion permits infrastructure-based power supply systems while the energy efficiency of

Characteristic → ↓ Aspects		Motion restricted to single degree of freedom along track	Low coefficient of friction between wheels and rails	Stiff interface between wheels and rails	Distributed linear infrastructure subsystem
Strengths	G	• No steering required; • Predictable motion; • Narrow swept path; • Linked consists (trains); • High standard of safety.	• Low rolling resistance; • Low rolling surfaces wear; • Efficient propulsion; • High speed operation; • Energy efficiency.	• Low energy dissipation; • High tonnages / period; • Low forces in track bed; • Predictable motion; • Smooth operations; • Potentially long track life.	• Product reaches customer; • Production process controllable throughout system; • External events rarely affect all of system; • Part opening of new routes.
	E	• Track-based power supply.	• Energy recovery potential.		• Multiple feeder options.
Weaknesses	G	• Guidance function cost; • High route blockage risk; • Low network flexibility; • Complex route changes; • No collision avoidance.	• Limited braking rate; • Low acceleration rate; • Seasonal adhesion variation; • Line of sight inadequate; • Low rolling surface wear.	• Stiff rolling interface; • Low inherent damping; • Noise & vibration issues • Cost of track & structures; • Cost of inspection.	• Environmental impact affects linear strips of terrain; • Remote management of local problems difficult.
	E	• Complex electrification; • Limited design options.	• Risk of slip and slide; • Torque control required.	• High impact environment for traction drives.	• Voltage drop along route; • Many supply points needed.
Technical requirements	G	• Variable geometry elements; • Train position detection; • Locking of route elements; • Junctions & stations.	• Signalling system; • Adhesion control; • Artificial wear required; • Regular maintenance.	• Load rack design; • Testing & inspection; • Accurate maintenance; • Regular maintenance.	• Provision of redundancy; • Protective features (tunnels, galleries, fences etc.).
Operational requirements	G	• Timetabling & planning; • Strict rulebook for all staff.	• Path allocation to trains; • Stringent safety rules.	• Strong procedures.	• Scheduling of services; • Several layers of control.
Management tools	G	• Rigorous selection of staff; • Modelling of train services.	• Simulation of individual train behaviour.	• Maintenance management; • Technical understanding.	• Delegated authority; • Strong supervision.
Training	G	• Responsibility; • Staff competence.	• Environmental awareness; • Safety ethos.	• Strong engineering skills; • Safety ethos.	• Rule based behaviour; • Adaptive behaviour.

Figure 16.1: *Table showing the Characteristics of the Rail Mode. F. Schmid.*

the wheel-rail interface provides the basis for the return of braking energy to the supply.

Background to Electric Traction on Railways

Electric traction for railways was originally developed in an urban context. The growth of cities in the late 19th century led to the use of horse-drawn cars on street railways to improve the movement of the population over longer distances than had hitherto been required. The proliferation of horse-drawn tramways increased the nuisance of dung and its removal and the high costs of keeping and replacing horses led to ways of making street railway systems more efficient. After a number of excursions into cable, steam and pneumatic systems, electric traction was eventually seen as a viable way of replacing the horse. The first reliable, commercial electric tramway was opened in Richmond, Virginia in 1888.

Many elements of a modern electric railway would be entirely recognisable to a late 19th century pioneer of electric traction, notably the power supply arrangements and aspects of traction motor design. The methods of control though, would be a complete surprise. Today's advanced electronic components and systems, including high-power silicon switches and complex data and information processing devices, allow smooth control of torque and speed over a wide operating range.

Several generations of technical solutions for controlling the tractive effort and performance of trains have appeared and become outdated since the early 1970s, with a particularly rapid phase of development during the last decade. Modern control systems are orders of magnitude more complex than their predecessors and require much greater input in terms of engineering design and development.

Other subsystems of the railway have also advanced technically, with the most significant progress in the areas of train control and signalling and in rolling stock running gear. This has resulted in a need to analyse the interaction between multiple elements of the railway when there is a change, rather than just considering the impact on one component and the associated subsystems. Today's traction engineers must apply systems thinking to the railway and must consider it as an integrated whole.

Impact of Recent Industry Changes

The need for an integrated approach and more advanced engineering design approaches has caused the railway manufacturing industry to undergo major realignments, leading to the emergence of a very small number of large multi-national equipment suppliers.

European railway operators and infrastructure managers have also been forced to restructure, at the behest of the European Union. By 2005, most national railway organisations in Europe had been divided into infrastructure and operations functions, at least in accounting terms. Most restructuring has involved some element of tendering and, in a few cases, privatisation. The intention was to allow train operators to focus on providing passenger and freight transport services in a cost-effective manner while the infrastructure management was handed over to specialists. Unfortunately, this has led to a tendency to leave the engineering design to the manufacturers and their sub-contractors, not always with the intended result of improved performance.

16.2 Critical Components

The authors of this chapter attempt to identify and describe the critical component elements of an electrified railway that need to be understood at a reasonable technical level in order to gain an appreciation of the overall system. They will also highlight some of the success factors associated with railway electrification schemes. The main elements are:

- Traction motors and associated control equipment;

- Power supply conductors and trackside substations;

- Signalling equipment, especially track circuits and trackside communications links.

The key interactions that will be discussed include:

- Susceptibility of signalling to traction-generated interference;

- Relationship between substation loading, conductor voltage drop and train performance;

- Supply current distortion due to power electronic drive systems.

In Figure 16.2, the authors provide an overview of the full set of subsystems that come together to form an electrified railway. The blocks of relevance to this chapter are the Traction and Braking System, Elec-

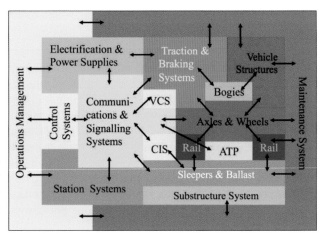

Figure 16.2: *A Railway system diagram. Graphic: F. Schmid.*

trification and Power Supply, Rails to carry the return current and the Communications and Signalling Systems.

The illustration is intended to show, for example, that the traction system interacts with the rails by means of the axles and wheels, both mechanically and electrically. Propulsion and braking torques are transmitted to the axles by means of gear-boxes and brake discs. The wheel to rail interface then turns these torques into acceleration and braking of vehicles and trains. Traction return currents are conducted through axle-end brushes.

16.3 The Railway Traction Duty

A sound appreciation of the fundamental mechanical aspects of accelerating and braking trains is essential to understanding the basic economics of providing a given service, that is to say, the purpose for which the electric traction system exists. Therefore, in the first section of this overview chapter, the authors discuss the constraints arising from the limited adhesion of the steel wheel on the steel rail and how these lead to decisions regarding locomotive haulage or multiple-unit rolling stock.

The resistance of a train to motion is essentially given by the Davies Equation (Rochard, 2000):

$$R(v) = A + B \cdot v + C \cdot v^2 + M_\text{t} \cdot g \cdot grad$$

A, B and C are coefficients determined by means of so-called run-down tests where a vehicle's motion is recorded as a function of time while it is allowed to slow down to rest from a representative speed without interference. Value v is the instantaneous speed of the train, M its mass, g is gravity and $grad$ is the ruling gradient. A negative value of $grad$ reduces the resistance to motion of the train. Some authors use per unit values for A, B and C, thus making the whole equation a function of M_t.

Since the tractive effort TE of the train is also a function of the speed v, the calculation of the theoretical rate of acceleration at for any speed of the train is as follows:

$$a_\text{t} = [TE(v) - R(v)]/M_\text{t}$$

Value a_t reduces to zero at the balancing speed of the train, signifying that the sum of all the resisting forces is now the same as the available traction force. At high speeds, aerodynamic resistance largely determines this balance.

The frictional force available between the steel wheels of the train and the steel surface of the rails is the fundamental physical property that limits the acceleration and braking rates of trains and, hence, their performance. The coefficient of friction μ, sometimes referred to as adhesion, determines the fraction F_t (tangential force between wheel and rail) of the perpendicular force F_v acting on the rails that can be exerted before slip occurs in motoring or slide in braking.

$$TE = F_t = \mu \cdot F_v = \mu \cdot M_t \cdot g$$

The higher the required adhesion level during motoring and braking, the more likelihood there is of damage being caused to wheelsets, rails and traction motors due to the phenomenon of wheel slip and slide. The adhesion levels accepted for normal operations vary between railway authorities, with maximum levels of 18% to 22% assumed for calculations for acceleration performance and 9% to 15% for braking (Wilkinson 1985). British and other railways accept up to 32% for creep controlled low-speed operation, e.g. in yards and during starts. In conventional rolling stock employed in urban mass rapid transit systems, the maximum accepted brake rate is viewed as limited by rail to wheel adhesion and rarely exceeds 1.3m/s^2 (Gill and Goodman 1992).

The assumed adhesion level between the wheel and the rail, together with the proportion of the weight carried on the motored axles, determines the maximum electric traction and braking effort that can be achieved safely. As the friction level is independent of the train design (other than with sanding systems), raising the proportion of motored axles is the only way to increase the maximum usable tractive effort. A similar argument applies to braking. Assuming an equal distribution of the train mass M_t amongst all axles of a train, the achievable acceleration a_t becomes:

$$a_t = g \cdot p \cdot \mu$$

where p is the proportion of motored axles and g and μ are used as above. In mass rapid transit systems and high capacity suburban railways, high rates of acceleration and deceleration are required to obtain the shortest possible inter-station run-times. Due to the limited adhesion available, a

238

high proportion of motored axles is necessary in such situations, leading to the choice of multiple units as rolling stock.

Based on a typical acceleration rate of 1.0m/s^2 and an adhesion μ of 0.2 or 20%, the proportion of motored axles p, is given by the equation (approximating g as 10 m/s^2):

$$p = \frac{a_\text{t}}{g \cdot \mu} = \frac{1.0}{10 \cdot 0.2} = 0.5 \ (Goodman\ 2001)$$

Therefore, at least 50% of such an EMU's axles must be motored. Acceleration rates as low as 0.6m/s^2 are characteristic of 25% motored stock whereas the higher figure of 1.4m/s^2 would usually require 67% or 75% of the axles to be motored (ibid.).

The percentage of motored axles could be increased to achieve a higher acceleration rate and a greater traction performance. However, this would be at the cost of installing more power equipment, resulting in an increase in weight, first cost and maintenance cost. There is also a deceleration limit of about 1.5m/s^2 for passenger comfort reasons. In summary, the best electric motoring and braking performances are obtained by using the maximum economic number of motored axles.

There is a natural trade-off between short journey times and high energy costs. This can be optimised in metro type conditions by using coasting (freewheeling). This technique is closely linked with high acceleration rates and regenerative braking. Conditions applicable to main-line services are very different and other aspects of the same fundamental physics become dominant.

It is perhaps worth noting at this point that the main reasons for using electric traction with an infrastructure supply are to be found in the inexhaustible nature of this type of traction energy supply and the high power rating that can be achieved on locomotives and multiple units, up to 1.6 MW at present, per axle. The ability of electric traction to regenerate energy during braking is another important incentive. Diesel traction is limited both by the need to carry fuel and by the space required for the engine cooling systems.

To From	DC Machine	AC Machine
DC Supply Source	Switched Resistance or Chopper Control	(Chopper Input and) 3-phase Inverter
AC Supply Source	Transformer and Phase Angle Control Rectifier	Transformer and PWM Input and Inverter

Table 16.1: *Conversion Options for Electric Drives*

16.4 Electric Traction Subsystems

Electric machines work thanks to interactions (attraction and repulsion) between the magnetic fields present in the stator and rotor. To create a mechanical output torque, there has to be an instantaneous angle between the fields. In a DC machine, this is achieved by means of the commutator, a rotating mechanical switch whereas, in a 3-phase AC motor, an angle develops naturally.

Modern power electronic devices and the associated micro-processor based controllers have made it feasible to supply AC or DC traction motors from AC or DC sources with almost equal ease. Some of the options available today are shown in Table 16.1.

All the four drive arrangements shown in Table 16.1 exist in substantial numbers on the world's railways, although it is now normal to supply new builds with AC 3-phase induction machines, also known as asynchronous motors, rather than DC motors.

The chief reasons for the preference for asynchronous machines in traction applications are:

- Elimination of the commutator and brushes that are an inherently maintenance intensive feature of the DC machine;

- The increased power density of the machine itself; and

- Scope for a 'sealed-for-life' motor that should require almost zero maintenance.

Against these advantages has to be weighed the requirement for accurately controllable, variable-voltage, variable frequency (VVVF), 3-phase power sources on the train. Until recently, high-performance electronic converters were more complex than the controlled rectifiers and choppers (see section 16.7) used with DC machines and, arguably, both less reliable and more expensive. However, the latest generation of power electronic inverters based on IGBTs (insulated-gate bipolar transistors) are simpler, more compact and more reliable than the previous generations based on thyristors and GTOs (gate-tum-off thyristors). They can now control all but the largest machines without series-parallel grouping of large numbers of switching devices.

16.5   Traction Motors

In terms of the achievable train performance, there is little to choose between the machine types. Both DC and AC machines are basically assemblies of iron and copper and are subject to the same limitations: The flux density is limited by saturation of the iron while the current is limited by the permissible heating of the copper windings or, more accurately, the capability of the insulation material used and the performance of the cooling system. Since the output torque of a machine is essentially the product of flux and current, all machines have an inherent torque limit, related to size.

The other key factor is that the 'back electromotive force' (e.m.f) reduces the ability of the supply to feed current into the machine. This is

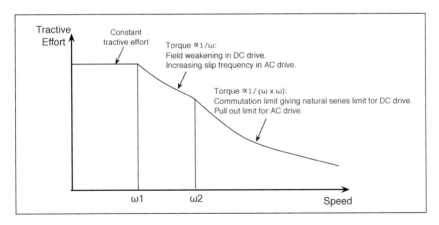

Figure 16.3: *General Shape of Tractive Effort (or Torque) vs. Speed Characteristic of a Traction Drive. Authors.*

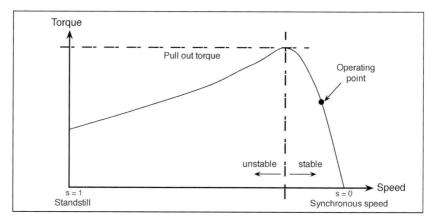

Figure 16.4: *Motor Torque vs. Speed Characteristic for an Induction Machine at a Fixed Supply Frequency. Authors.*

inescapable since the 'back e.m.f. voltage' is developed by the rotating machine acting as a generator and is, basically, the product of flux and speed (Faraday's Law; rate of cutting of flux). Electric circuit theory dictates that it is the difference between the source voltage and the back e.m.f. voltage that determines the motor current and hence the torque available and, ultimately, the tractive effort.

Current and voltage determine the amount of electrical power that can be supplied into the machine. Thus, the voltage fed to the machine must rise with increasing speed whilst the flux is maintained at its maximum. This creates an initial constant torque region in the torque vs. speed characteristic of all traction drives. Figure 16.5 shows a generalised tractive effort versus speed relationship that is typical of all traction drives.

Once the controller output voltage has reached the maximum that can be made available from the particular supply, the flux has to be reduced in inverse proportion to the speed to keep the back e.m.f. below the now fixed supply voltage so that the current continues to flow. In both the DC and AC cases, the result is the beginning at $\omega 1$ of a region of constant power operation where the torque falls as 1/speed, as shown in Figure . To reduce the flux in the DC drive, the current in the field winding must be lowered, whether it is of the series connected or separately excited type. How this is achieved in practice depends on the type of motor. In an AC

242

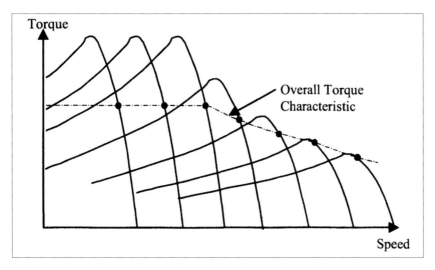

Figure 16.5: *Induction Motor Torque vs. Speed Characteristics at Variable Supply Frequency. Authors.*

drive, the flux is reduced by increasing the frequency of the 3-phase stator voltage supplied to the machine, while keeping its amplitude constant. In the AC machine case an increase in the slip frequency has to be accepted that is caused by a move further up the torque vs. speed curve at a given frequency. This is needed to compensate in part for the fact that the basic AC motor characteristic scales vertically with the square of the supply voltage.

Figure 16.4 shows a typical induction motor operating characteristic where the narrow range of stable operation between peak torque and zero torque at zero slip (s = 0) indicates why the only feasible means of speed control for this machine is to change the supply frequency. This creates a family of similarly shaped curves, as shown in Figure 16.5. Eventually, when the voltage limit is reached, the peak values of the curves start to fall as a function of 1/speed, because the motor current is falling.

This pull-out limit means that for even further increases in speed, the torque will have to fall as $1/\text{speed}^2$, thus a third region of operation is entered, as shown on the diagram in Figure 16.5. There is a corresponding, but quite different, phenomenon in DC machines that also limits the width of the second region (between $\omega 1$ and $\omega 2$) and causes a third region to exist. In this case, there is a limit to how weak the field can be made in the presence of full armature current, due to the resulting flux distortion. Thus, eventually, the current and flux have to be reduced together as functions of 1/speed, resulting in the torque falling as $1/\text{speed}^2$. This effect is sometimes described as the commutation limit since it manifests itself as sparking at the commutator as the voltage between the bars becomes very unevenly distributed.

Some use has also been made of synchronous traction motors, notably on several generations of Trains à Grande Vitesse or TGV in France. The advantage of the synchronous machine is that it commutates naturally and thus requires less complex electronics; however, it is larger than an asynchronous machine of the same rating and requires mechanical or electronic transmission of a magnetising current to the rotor, e.g. by slip-rings.

The authors are not considering linear motor drives here although there are a number of railway systems in operation worldwide where a reaction plate is mounted between the rails, with a linear motor installed on the train. Following a prototype implementation on the Scarborough Light Rail line in Toronto, such systems now exist in Vancouver (Skytrain), Kuala Lumpur and Japan. They feature high acceleration and deceleration rates because they do not rely on wheel rail interface adhesion, however, the methods of control are similar to those for normal AC machines.

16.6   Permanent Magnet Motor

The next development in electric motor design is the permanent magnet motor. This is a 3-phase AC synchronous motor with the usual squirrel cage construction replaced by magnets fixed in the rotor. The motor requires a complex control system system but it can be up to 25% smaller than a conventional 3-phase motor for the same power rating. The design also gives lower operating temperatures so that rotor cooling isn't needed and the stator is a sealed unit with integral liquid cooling.

A number of different types of trains have been equipped with permanent magnet motors, including 25 AGV high speed train sets, trams in France and Prague and EMUs in Europe and Japan. The reduced size is particularly attractive for low floor vehicles where hub motors can be an effective way of providing traction in a compact bogie. Development of motor design and the associated control systems continues and it is certain that the permanent magnet motor will be seen on more railways in the future.

16.7 Power Electronic Controllers

Power electronic controllers convert electrical power from one type (e.g. AC) to another (e.g. DC) or from one level to another (e.g. constant voltage DC to variable voltage DC) using high-power silicon switches and diodes. Because of the high currents involved, such devices are not operated in an amplifier mode but either switched on fully or kept in the off state, thus minimising losses and reducing the need for cooling. Forward voltages are in the region of 0.7V to 1.1V while the devices are conducting and losses are significant at rated currents of several hundred amperes. There are two basic methods of obtaining variable voltages by means of electronic switch action, with a number of application-specific variants.

With an AC supply, a thyristor or similar device is gated (switched on) at some delay angle with respect to the start of the mains supply cycle and thus only part of the sine-wave is applied to the load. Since the mains supply voltage reverses polarity in the middle and at the end of each full cycle, even the current in an inductive load will eventually fall to zero some way into the negative (or positive) half-cycle and the thyristor will be commutated off naturally. This is known as phase-angle control and produces a DC output with substantial ripple.

With a DC supply, commutation does not occur naturally and devices such as GTOs (gate turn-off thyristors) are needed as these can be turned off via the gate by removing charge from the conduction region. IGBTs are turned off simply by removing the gate voltage, thus moving the device from saturation to blocking. With this capability, it is possible to use Pulse-Width Modulation (PWM), where the widths of a series of rectangular pulses, usually at constant frequency and amplitude, are adjusted to deliver the required average voltage to the load. In its most basic form, this is the principle of DC chopper operation.

With a relatively high carrier frequency (say 1kHz) and variation of the pulse widths in sympathy with a modulation frequency representing the

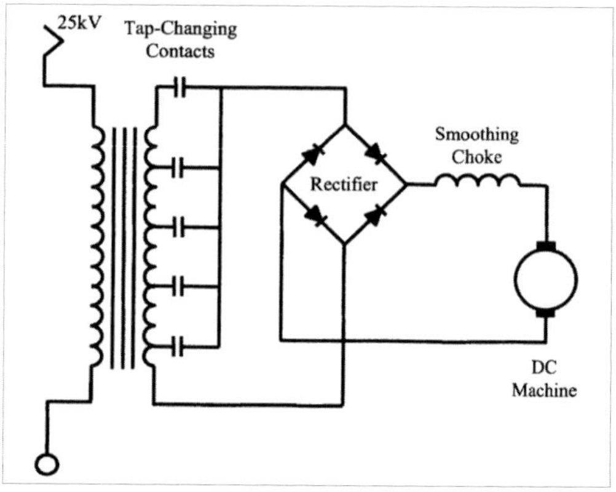

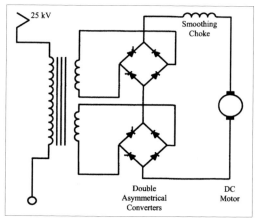

Figure 16.6: *Schematic of Diode Bridge Rectifier and Tap-Changer Converter Scheme for DC Drive with AC Supply. Graphic: F. Schmid*

Figure 16.7: *Schematic of Double Asymmetrical Phase-Angle Controlled Converters Scheme for DC Drive with AC Supply. Graphic: F. Schmid*

output AC frequency required, this same basic chopping technique enables an AC output to be derived from a DC supply. To create the three phases to drive an induction machine and both polarities of the output voltages, a bridge with six 'switches' (GTOs or IGBTs) and six anti-parallel diodes is required.

16.8   AC Supplied DC Drives

There have been two main stages in the development of AC supplied DC drives for traction purposes, namely, systems incorporating a mixture of

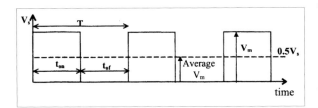

Figure 16.8: *Principle of duty-cycle control to vary average motor voltage with a chopper drive. Graphic: Authors.*

electro-mechanical and electronic 'switches' and purely electronic systems. In the former, an uncontrolled diode-bridge rectifier is supplied with an AC voltage from the main transformer and this is varied in steps by means of a tap-changer. This is a combination of mechanical switches that allows adjustment of the proportion of the secondary voltage that is applied to the rectifier and thus the load, as shown in Figure 16.6. It is possible to switch to the primary winding, using a so-called high-voltage tap-changer but this is no longer common. A variable DC voltage can also be achieved by means of phase-angle controlled rectifier bridges, with thyristors turned on as a function of the current requirement of the DC traction motor. To improve power factor it is usual to have at least two bridges in series, which are ramped up one after the other from 0 phase angle to maximum phase angle. The asymmetrical bridges shown in Figure 16.7 provide an automatic flywheel path for the motor current.

Although the DC machine is perfectly able to regenerate power to provide electrical braking, neither of the above arrangements can pass this power back to the supply. Back to back controlled converters can do this but exhibit poor power factor and harmonic performance.

16.9 DC Supplied DC Drives

Originally, DC machines fed from constant voltage DC supplies were controlled by sequentially shorting out and re-combining resistances connected in series with the armature of the machine, in such a way as to maintain the current reasonably constant as the speed increased. Indeed, so-called cam-shaft controllers did this automatically, based on measuring the load current. In regions 2 and 3, diverting resistances reduced the field current in stages. Most conventional schemes used self-regulating series

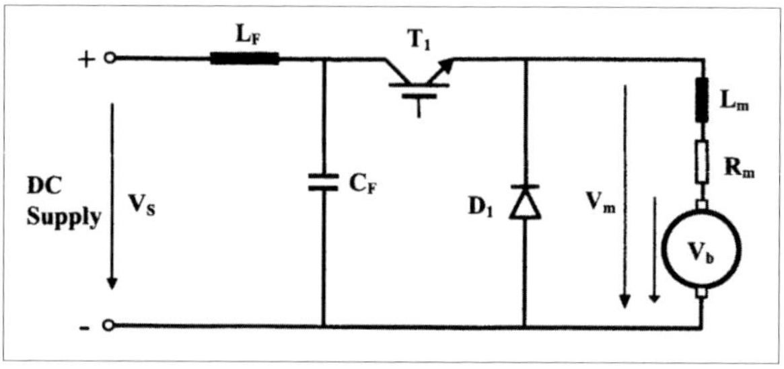

Figure 16.9: *Basic Chopper Circuit for DC to DC Conversion. Authors.*

machines. Many trains using this type of technology are still in operation on the world's metros and tram systems.

16.10   Motor Voltage with a Chopper Drive

Many DC motor control schemes use separate chopper controllers for the field and armature. These operate at a fixed frequency and use so-called pulse-width modulation to change the average voltage, as shown in Figure 16.8. This is often referred to as duty-cycle control in this context. Closed loop control is used to obtain the required armature and field current characteristics, as demanded by torque control and driver traction demand. In order for the chopper to operate correctly and to prevent chopper harmonics from entering the supply, it is necessary to have a substantial LC (inductor-capacitor) input filter that can appreciably affect the economics of what is a fairly simple drive. The corresponding circuit arrangement is shown in Figure 16.9. Relatively simple additions to the circuitry make stable regenerative braking very straightforward, e.g. electro-mechanical switches.

16.11   DC Supplied AC Drives

An arrangement of six diodes and six controllable on-off switches, connected as shown in Figure 16.10, can create a VVVF three-phase supply directly from the DC input, although filtering and pre-conditioning of the supply may be needed in some situations. An additional chopper can be installed, for example, to reduce the input voltage and to tune it to the needs of the inverter.

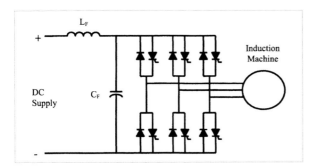

Figure 16.10: *Input Filter and Basic Inverter Power Circuit. Authors.*

The key process here is the application of sinusoidal pulse-width modulation or PWM, the concept of which is illustrated in Figure 16.11. Generated by comparing a sine-wave at the desired motor frequency with a triangular wave at a particular carrier frequency, the resulting output is a sequence of rectangular pulses, with a height equal to the DC supply and a width that is proportional to the local value of the sine-wave.

As the motor is essentially a low-pass filter, it only responds to the fundamental component of this complex wave, i.e. the desired motor supply frequency. The key parameters for the approach are the modulation index M_1 and the frequency ratio M_r, derived as follows:

$$M_1 = (amplitude of modulation)/(carrier amplitude)$$

$$M_r = (carrier frequency)/(modulation frequency)$$

The combination of inverter and induction motor is intrinsically able to regenerate and can to do so directly into a DC supply.

16.12   AC Supplied AC Drives

A system known as a cycloconverter is able to convert a fixed-voltage, fixed-frequency supply directly into a variable-voltage, variable-frequency output but it is totally unsuitable for a traction drive, not least because it is not suited to a single phase supply. Cycloconverters are used on 16.7 Hz railways to obtain a supply from the 50 Hz industrial system. In practice, the only viable on-board arrangement for AC supplied AC machines is to rectify the incoming AC to supply a DC link that feeds a VVVF inverter, as shown in Figure 16.12.

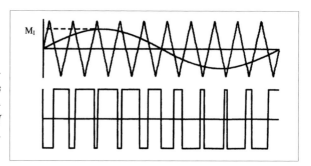

Figure 16.11: *Conceptual Process of Generating Sinusoidal PWM Waveforms. Authors.*

The rectification can be achieved simply by means of a diode rectifier, as in the example in the figure. Alternatively, a thyristor bridge converter can be used, as discussed in Section 16.8. With a converter, a constant voltage link can be established or, if so desired, a variable voltage link, as mentioned in 16.8.

Most modern AC-AC drive systems feature what amounts to a single-phase inverter operating in reverse for most of the time, i.e. a PWM rectifier or 4-quadrant converter, shown schematically in Figure 16.13. This approach is highly beneficial since it offers unity power factor, low harmonics, common constructional features with the inverter and the ability to return power back into the overhead line down to very low speeds.

Except for those situations where a direct DC supply is used, the inverter fed induction motor drawing its power from a DC link, set up by a PWM converter (both the inverter and converter being built with IGBTs), is probably the 'state of the art' for traction drives. In certain circumstances, there are arguments for using synchronous motors, which are reviewed below.

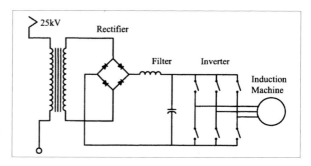

Figure 16.12: *Schematic of AC-AC Drive with Rectifier Front End. Authors.*

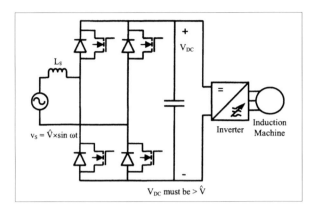

Figure 16.13:
Schematic of AC-AC Drive with PWM Converter Front-End. Authors.

16.13 Traction Power Requirements

Trams, light metros and high capacity metros generally operate with relatively low voltage supplies, ranging from 600V to 1500V DC. Power ratings differ widely, from 150 to 200kW are common for a tramway vehicle and 1.5 MW and more for an underground train with eight vehicles. Currents from 300A to 2000A during acceleration and peak braking are common.

Traction power requirements for main line railways are yet more substantial, whether trains are used for heavy haul freight or for high speed passenger services. The high rated power levels of such trains are only achievable with an infrastructure based supply of traction energy, as stated at the end of Section 16.3. Diesel locomotives, even with six axles, rarely reach ratings greater than 4000BHP (3MW) and often work in multiple.

Power ratings of traction units for main line electric railways are generally given in MW_{el} (106W or 1,330HP) where the subscript 'el' for 'electrical' indicates that the power at the wheel, available for traction, will be somewhat lower. Typical locomotive ratings for the 3kV DC systems in Belgium and Italy are $3.5MW_{el}$ (resulting in a current of 1200A) and more than $6.4MW_{el}$ for the 15kV 16.7Hz supply in Switzerland (around 420A) and the 25kV 50Hz system in Finland and France (around 250A).

In all these cases the locos have only 4 powered axles. Eurostar trains with their 12 powered axles draw 13 MW_{el} when operating at 25kV 50 Hz on the lignes à grande vitesse (LGV) in Belgium, in France and on Britain's High Speed 1 (HS1), resulting in a line current of 450A. They absorb 6 MW$_{el}$ when running under Belgium's 3kV DC overhead line (2000A), France's 1500V DC overhead line (4000A) and, in the past, when travelling on Britain's 750V DC 3rd rail network (8000A). This current and power is collected by a single pantograph in the case of the higher voltage (AC and DC) sections and was picked up by several collector shoes when Eurostars were still using the 750V DC 3rd rail supply between Fawkham Junction and London Waterloo.

Due to the linear nature of the railway infrastructure, the power use is distributed and varies not only in time but also in space. Usually, there will be more than one train or electric multiple unit in a section fed from a particular substation, increasing both the maximum current drawn and the variation between minimum and maximum demand, a difficult duty for the infrastructure systems.

16.14   Traction Power Supply Systems

All traction systems, whether using AC or DC to transport the electrical energy to the trains, feature regularly spaced sub-stations that distribute power to some form of conductor system positioned in alignment with the track. As mentioned, trains collect the current by means of pantographs or pick-up shoes. The electrical equipment on board the train will only function correctly if the power is provided continuously and at a voltage in the specified range. Modern electric trains on the 3rd rail network in southern Britain, that is, Electrostar trains of classes 375/377, will trip out if the voltage on the third rail at the location of the train falls to less than 450V, given that the nominal voltage is 750V DC (Abbott, 2005).

Pioneer electrified railways, whether tramway or main line, frequently obtained the power supply from their own generating stations. They did this because there was no electricity supply industry or because they needed a particular type of voltage. Today, in almost all cases, traction supplies are derived from the industrial utility supply at a level within the hierarchy of the grid system that is appropriate for the power being drawn. For metros and trams (or light railways) this tends to be at 11kV or 33kV and for mainline applications at 132kV, 275kV, or, in a recent development, even at 400kV.

16.15   Criteria for the Choice of System

It is important to appreciate that modern power electronic control equipment makes it feasible to use AC or DC traction drives (motors and associated controllers) on the vehicles, irrespective of whether the train is supplied with AC or DC current from the infrastructure. Ignoring historical constraints for the moment, the fundamental choice between AC and DC transmission to the train must be based on the following compromises:

- Minimising the voltage of the supply to avoid the obvious safety risks created by exposed conductors carrying high voltages;

- Maximising the voltage of the supply to minimise the current and thus the amount of copper needed to carry the current while still maintaining the transmission losses at a low level;

- Optimising the conductor system, the type and number of substations and the on-board controllers in whole life cost terms;

- Ensuring that a supply is available at all times and that it satisfies the requirements of the rolling stock.

These issues will be referred to again shortly. However, it is useful to examine the existing systems before discussing how they have come about. We shall see later that history actually has a tremendous bearing on decision taking processes in railway systems design, not just in the domain of railway electrification.

16.16   The Choice: AC or DC Supplies?

Relatively low voltage DC supplies dominated most early electric railways, with DC traction motors on the train, primarily because of the comparative ease with which the speed of a DC motor could be controlled on-board the trains with switches and resistances (rheostats). However, as suggested in Section 16.15, the fundamental economics of electric power transmission dictate the use of as high a voltage as possible, thus enabling a given power to be delivered with the smallest current I, since,

$$Power\ P = V \cdot I$$

DC supplies have a serious problem in this respect: It is very difficult to break fault currents in a high voltage DC circuit because of inductive effects. This is an insurmountable problem since the supply voltage never goes below zero and, thus, natural commutation does not occur. In practice, therefore, DC supplied systems are limited to a maximum of 3kV, although research was conducted in Italy to demonstrate the viability of 12 kV DC for traction supplies.

The need to minimise the current was one of the main drivers for the adoption of AC for industrial power supplies: AC is easily and efficiently stepped up and down in voltage by means of transformers. Economic and mechanical design[1] arguments led to the near exclusive use of 3-phase supplies in industrial systems. Some of the pioneers of electric traction experimented with the 3-phase system, e.g. for the high speed trials between Zossen and Marienfelde in Germany.

Italian State Railways operated a few lines where twin overhead conductors and the rails carried the three phases. A very few tourist railways still use such a 3-phase system but it is no longer a viable option for railways, despite the very real problems caused by the single-phase system of electrification that will be discussed later. The ease of regeneration did not compensate for the complexity of the twin overhead line electrification for any but the most basic railway layouts.

AC at the industrial frequency of 50Hz or 60Hz is reliably available from national grids, certainly in all developed countries, and is easy to transform to different voltages, both at the trackside and on the vehicles. Now that the onboard control of torque (and thus tractive effort) is no longer limited to inserting and removing resistances between the supply and the motor, there is a strong rationale for all new schemes to use AC, ideally at 25kV and 50/60 Hz[2]. Trams, metros and some suburban railways are the

---

[1] 3-phase systems do not require a separate return conductor (an economic benefit) and the presence of multiple magnetic pole pairs results in a smooth motion where power is used in machines. The distribution of coils around the circumference of the machine also reduces out of balance behaviour.

[2] The Technical Standards for Interoperability demand that all new high-speed lines in Europe must be electrified at 25kV AC 50Hz, unless a so-called derogation applies.

exceptions to this rule. AC transmission does in fact have its own drawbacks and these become significant where it is not possible to utilise high voltages or where the frequency of service is high and distances between stops are short.

For street running, safety requirements limit voltages to around 750V. Indeed, 600V DC was for a long time the de-facto standard for tramways throughout most of continental Europe. Similarly, in deep bored tube tunnels it is not economic to provide the clearances for operation at 25kV AC, resulting in the adoption of 1500V DC where power requirements are high. However, as soon as the voltage is constrained by such external factors, the current becomes correspondingly greater and the series impedance of the conductor system becomes important.

For the same conductor arrangement, the AC series impedance is considerably higher than the DC impedance. This is partly because of the loop inductance (flux between the 'out' and 'return' conductors) of the overhead conductor system of about 1mH/km and partly because of the 'skin effect' in the return rails, a phenomenon that increases their apparent resistance (by about 40% at 50 Hz). Effectively, the AC current tends to be concentrated at the surface.

The proportion of voltage 'lost' along the supply and return conductors is therefore higher in a low voltage AC system than in a DC system. Since this is the factor that determines the spacing between substations and, hence the number required, the economics are in favour of DC for low voltage and high current railways, such as metros, where substantial savings may be obtained from returning braking energy to nearby accelerating trains via the supply. An additional benefit is the reduction in the mass of trains thanks to the absence of transformers.

16.17 Conductor Systems and Supply Voltages

Over time, a wide range of 'standard' voltages and transmission arrangements were developed for different applications although it is difficult to give clear reasons for some of the choices made. A fundamental choice though is that between ground-based conductors and overhead supplies. The original implementation of the former system still exists on Volk's electric railway in Brighton with a top-contact third rail installed between the running rails, powered at 200V DC. Similar systems can be found in amusement fair rides.

Other early systems, such as that of the Southern Railway in Britain, feature a third rail on the outside of one of the running rails, with pick-up shoes making contact from the top. Side-contact systems were also popular for a while.

Top and side contact third rails are dubious when viewed from a modern safety perspective so many modern systems use shrouded third rail installation, as used on London's Docklands Light Railway, with under-running pick-up shoes (known as bottom contact). Voltages for third rail systems are generally below 1200V DC. It may be worth noting though, that China is moving to 1500V DC third rail for its metros, for both aesthetic and economic reasons. The linear motor driven Tianjin metro was the first network to go 'live' with this system. The Tobu Kyuryo urban Maglev Line in Nagoya, Japan, opened in 2005, also features a conductor rail energised at 1500V DC. Modern systems mostly use composite third rail sections with a stainless steel wear surface that protects a high-conductivity aluminium current rail.

Overhead line electrification can be of the trolley type (single conductor wire) or of the catenary type (one or two conductor wires suspended from one or two catenary wires, linked by so-called droppers). In confined areas, such as in tunnels and under low bridges, we also find solid conductor systems formed of an aluminium extrusion carrying a copper conductor. This system requires very accurate installation if excessive wear of the pantograph's contact strip, due to high forces, is to be avoided. Special multi-pole arrangements, similar to overhead crane supply rails, are used on people-movers, such as the Bukit Panjang line in Singapore, internal airport links and the Kuala Lumpur, Malaysia Monorail system. All of these operate at relatively low speeds, with low voltage 3-phase or DC and very simple collectors.

16.18   DC Systems in Common Use

600-1200 V DC
Trams, light metros and heavy metros tend to be supplied at 600V to 1200V DC. Occasionally, shorter distance suburban railways also use

such low voltages, sometimes for historic reasons. As mentioned in Section 16.17, the conductor is arranged either overhead or as a third rail at the side. The former is the obvious solution for street running and where it is necessary to reduce the risk of electrocution in depots and during maintenance. The latter is chosen for aesthetic reasons or, more commonly, to reduce cost since the third rail supplies minimise the cross section of the tunnels required.

Until recently, London Underground was unique in that its system employs an outside third rail (supply at +420V) and a central fourth rail (return at -210V with respect to the running rails). This approach reduces stray earth current and eliminates 'touch voltage' problems caused by the traction current returning via the running rails. As mentioned above, there is now a similar system in Kuala Lumpur.

The Forch railway in Switzerland uses 600V DC on tracks shared with the urban trams while it is supplied at 1200V DC on the long interurban route. The metro system in Hamburg in Germany uses 1200V DC third rail while Barcelona metro changed from 1200V DC third rail to a rigid conductor overhead electrification.

1500V DC
1500V DC is the most popular and economic solution for light and heavy metro operations, as well as for interurban tram systems. Main line railways in the East and South of France and throughout the Netherlands still feature 1500V DC overhead line electrification for both passenger and freight services. In both cases this is for purely historic reasons although it could be argued that the Dutch network has some metro characteristics The Tyne and Wear Metro in Newcastle, Britain, uses 1500V DC on its own network as well as on the route shared with heavy rail diesel services. Recently though, as already mentioned in Section 16.17, several Chinese metro operators have decided, under political pressure, to use third rail for 1500V DC, ostensibly for aesthetic reasons but also to minimise the number of substations.

3000V DC
All systems supplied at 3000 V DC that are known to the authors use overhead electrification. Extensive installations of this type exist on suburban and mainline railways, especially in Belgium, Italy, Poland, Spain and many countries of the former USSR, as well as in South Africa, etc. No new systems are being built, except for extensions to existing networks.

16.19 AC Systems in Common Use

11kV and15k-16.7Hz

16-Hz (today standardised as 16.7Hz) electrification at 15kV was the original AC system[3] in the early part of the 20th century and was developed in Switzerland and Germany because of the limited commutating ability of early single- phase variable speed AC motors. These motors, some of which are still in use today, were essentially the same as the 'universal' fractional horse-power motors in electric drills and similar appliances.

Effectively, the original motors used with the 16.7Hz system are DC machines operated from an AC supply and thus rely on the field flux and the armature current reversing together. Principally because of field current flux lag, resulting from eddy currents in the iron, this does not work well at higher frequencies, hence the need for a special low frequency supply. With the advent of robust static rectifiers for on-board use, this original reason has long since disappeared, however, the enormous investment in the infrastructure means that 16.7Hz will see continued use in Austria, Germany, Norway, Sweden and Switzerland, for a long time. AMTRAK, the American passenger rail operator, still uses electrification at 11kV, 25Hz for parts of the high-speed North East Corridor for similar reasons (Duffy, 2004).

As mentioned in Section 16.15, there was an early 3-phase system in Northern Italy, supplying power by means of two parallel trolley wires and the running rails, energised at 3.6kV 16Hz. This made it possible to return energy to the supply easily, when descending long gradients. This system was abandoned in the late 1960s because of the complexity of current collection with double pantographs, especially in areas with points and crossings. The system also required quite complex phase-changing apparatus on the traction units to create the two or three synchronous speeds. So-called water-resistors were used to smooth the transitions, resulting in electric locomotives that emitted great clouds of steam when accelerating.

25kV 50/60Hz

25kV 50/60Hz overhead electrification is viewed today as the world standard for main line railways and also for high capacity suburban railways,

---

[3]Some railways use 11kV instead of 15kV because the networks are relatively small but include many tunnels.

unless there are insuperable constraints in the shape of tunnels or the presence of a significant existing electrification system. As will be mentioned later, the system requires special transmission features to reduce ground current.

50kV 50/60Hz
The 50kV 50/60Hz systems is occasionally used for dedicated heavy-haul railways, such as the 1067mm iron-ore mining railway from Sishen to Saldhana in South Africa that features some of the longest trains in the world. The infrastructure and locomotives require larger clearances and special vacuum circuit breakers to cope with this voltage. There is a 100kV, 60Hz railway in the USA.

It is important not to confuse the 50kV 50/60Hz arrangement with the '50kV auto-transformer scheme' where only the transmission to the overhead line feed points is effected at 50kV (25kV - 0 - 25kV). The locomotives receive 25kV, as will be explained later.

16.20   Electrification Paradise

The city of Kuala Lumpur, Malaysia, is of great interest to the electrification infrastructure engineer since it features a wide range of power supply systems. The steel wheel and steel rail based PUTRA LRT is powered by linear induction motors and has a DC supply at +375V and -375V with respect to the 0V potential of the rails. This was opened in November 2001. The STAR system is fed at 750V DC from a third rail with a standard running rail return. The standard gauge Airport Express and the metre-gauge national railway both use 25kV AC electrification.

16.21   DC Power Supplies

DC traction substations initially used motor-generator sets and later mercury arc rectifiers. Although some equipment such as this still exists, e.g., on the Isle of Man, substations are nowadays equipped with solid state rectifiers or even converters, able to return braking energy to the mains supply in inverting mode. Substations no longer draw their supply from the railway's own generating station but from locally available AC utility feeders. The main components of a typical substation, shown in Figure 16.14, are as follows:

- Duplicated input transformers to provide the correct input voltage for the rectifier bridges from the incoming 3-phase AC, typically at 11kV;

- AC circuit breakers for fault protection;

- AC switches and isolators for the selection of the in-coming feeder, transformer etc. and to permit emergency feeding conditions and maintenance access;

- Silicon diode rectifier bridges. Usually, each rectifier consists of two 6-pulse bridges, connected in parallel for 750V or in series for 1500V, thus producing overall 12-pulse output ripple;

- DC switches and isolators to select which rectifier is to be operational, for isolating track sections, etc.

- High-speed DC circuit breakers for protecting the track and trains. These are highly specialised and costly components but necessary because of the physical difficulty of breaking a large DC current in an inductive circuit.

- Similar high-speed breakers are also installed on board the trains to avoid tripping of the supply due to a localised fault and also to disconnect braking currents of other trains in the case of a fault.

Depending on the traffic density, supply voltage and conductor arrangements the substation spacing on a DC railway will typically be between 3 and 9km. Overhead conductor systems provide a loop resistance of 35-90mω/km and third rail systems 8-20ω/km. In order to make the best use of the conductors and rails, it is normal to bond the return rails together and to cross-connect the catenary or third rail at points midway between substations. This is done with further sets of DC isolators in a 'track-paralleling hut' or as an overhead pole mounted arrangement and this also provides further means of emergency operation.

A major issue with DC systems is the stray current that leaks from the rails into the ground and eventually returns to the substation negative via its earth mat or the nearer part of the rails, if no deliberate earth is provided. Stray current can cause electrolytic corrosion damage to gas pipes and reinforcing steel in civil engineering structures and its control

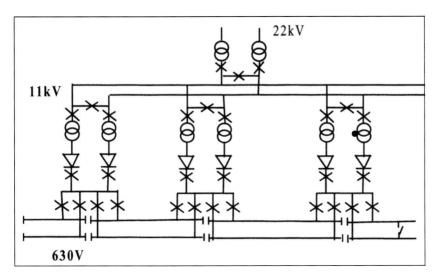

Figure 16.14: *Schematic of typical London Underground DC substation feeding arrangement. Authors.*

is thus very important, albeit something of a black art, in practice. Attempts to insulate the rails are common and modestly successful, although achieving more than about 10ω/km reliably is a fantasy of specification documents. Paradoxically, keeping the current in the rails worsens the problem of 'touch voltage', i.e. the voltage between the rails and local earth.

Modern power-electronic devices and control electronics make it feasible to control the output voltage of a DC substation in such a way that it has no voltage regulation (i.e. fall) as the load increases or even so that its output voltage rises to compensate for conductor volt drops. It is also possible to provide inverters in parallel with the rectifiers so that current from regenerating trains may be absorbed and the energy passed back to the AC supply. Considerable efforts were needed to justify the economics, reliability and maintenance issues and the introduction of regeneration to the 3rd rail DC system in Southern England was only achieved through a combination of modern rolling stock and sophisticated control systems. The difficulties have so far not encouraged other railway operators to adopt them widely.

16.22   AC Power Supplies

Arrangements within an AC substation have the same basic objectives of duplication and emergency feeding as those of DC substations. Figure 16.15 shows typical features, chief amongst which are:

- Duplicated incoming transformers, connected to different pairs of phases to try and balance the load on the three-phase supply. These change the voltage to 25kV or 50kV from the 132/275/400kV duplicated feeders. Typical ratings are around 20MVA for each transformer;

- Circuit breakers and isolators for protection against track faults or faults within the substation and to allow various emergency feed arrangements. Normally, each transformer feeds from the substation to a point midway to the next substation in the 'single-end fed' mode;

- Breakers and isolators at the mid-point parallel the catenaries and allow feeding beyond the mid-point when necessary. So-called intermediate track-sectioning cabins are sometimes provided to reduce the impedance and to give greater flexibility for working trains during catenary outages.

The feeds to the substations are taken from as high a level as possible within the utility supply network because the traction load is intrinsically a 'dirty' load and imposes significant imbalance, flicker and harmonics on the industrial supply. If the point-of-common coupling can be at a level where the railway load is a small proportion of the available power, these effects are mitigated to some extent.

In remote areas, the locomotive power may be as high as 1-2% of the short-circuit capacity at the connection point and this can cause significant problems on the AC supply. There are many examples of static-VAR compensators and harmonic filters being fitted at substations, as well as power factor correction circuits on-board the trains. Modern PWM converters on the trains, discussed in the next section, substantially eliminate the harmonic and power factor problems, but cannot help with the flicker and unbalance.

As with DC systems, ground leakage current is a major issue in AC systems, but for different reasons. Electrolytic corrosion does not usually occur with AC currents although there are a few known examples of problems arising where rectifying contacts have been unwittingly created. However, once the current has escaped from the rails, it distributes itself deep into the ground and the path taken by the 'virtually combined' current can be several hundred metres into the ground. This results in a substantial magnetic field being established between and around the conductors. This has two effects:

- The self inductance of the supply loop is considerably larger (around 2mH/km) than if the out and return currents can be kept closer together (around 1mH/km). This, in turn, increases the volt drop and requires closer substation spacing;

- The external field links into line-side telephone and signal cables, causing induced interference or even hazardous voltages under overhead fault conditions. The effect spreads well outside the railway's own estate and dictates that some mitigating measures are taken to force the current to return through the rails as far as possible.

In a 25kV 50/60 Hz system, the normal way to reduce the ground current is to provide a return conductor mounted high on the structures and connected in series with the secondary windings of a sequence of 'booster transformers' (BT) whose primaries are in series with the contact wire itself. Such transformers are installed at about 3km intervals, as shown in Figure 16.16. The ampere-turn balance imposed by the

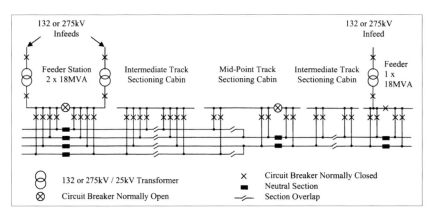

Figure 16.15: *Typical AC Feed and Substation Arrangements. Authors.*

'current-sucking transformers' (a literal translation of the German term 'Saugdrosselspulen'), forces the current to flow through the nearest mid-point connection into the return conductor where, being fairly close to the overhead, it tends to cancel the field that is created due to the catenary current.

An alternative to the BT scheme is the auto-transformer (AT), shown in Figure 16.17. Although the principal reason for its use is to halve the current and to increase the feeding distance, it also has the effect of forcing the current into the auxiliary feeder, which is again mounted high on the structures, thus partially cancelling the field created by the overhead line conductor. However, the auxiliary feeder needs 25kV insulators, of course, unlike the return conductor in the BT scheme, which is at earth potential. This complicates installation under bridges and in tunnel sections.

ATs are fitted at roughly 10 km intervals, which lessens their effective-ness in reducing external fields, compared with the BT arrangement. By their nature, neither the BT scheme nor the AT scheme can prevent some ground current flowing in the section where the train is drawing current, unless it is close to a rail connection point.

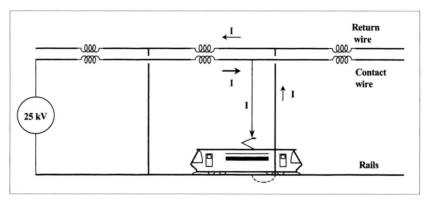

Figure 16.16: *Schematic of AC booster transformer supply scheme. Authors.*

16.23 Interference and Compatibility

Electric railways inevitably create numerous possibilities for interfering with other types of electrical or electronic equipment. The most obvious targets for interference are the railway's own assets, such as the signalling and telecommunications systems, although it is important not to lose sight of the potential impact on other installations adjacent to the railway. There are four basic mechanisms that can couple a source of interference to its victim:

- Conduction;

- Magnetic fields (mutual inductance);

- Electric fields (capacitive coupling);

- Electromagnetic radiation (RF interference).

More than one of these mechanisms may play a part in any given situation. The problems of DC leakage current as a general threat to metal structures within some quite considerable distance of the railway have already been mentioned. The DC external magnetic field can also interfere with delicate magnetic measurements and even cause colour distortion in monitors. With AC supplies, the external magnetic field is intrinsically

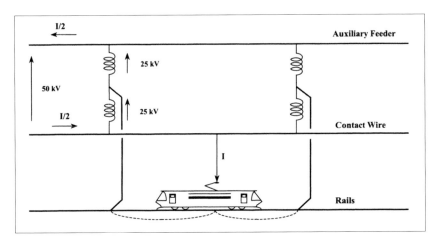

Figure 16.17: *Schematic of AC auto-transformer supply scheme. Authors.*

changing at the supply frequency and therefore induces voltages into any conducting path parallel to the track. Again, the requirement to limit this field by means of booster transformers, or similar, has already been mentioned. Even so, it is necessary to use properly screened, twisted-pair telephone cables alongside a railway and to limit the length of any signal cores.

A prime target for interference is the train detection part of the signalling system, especially track circuits where the rails form the differential circuit to detect the trains. The original DC track circuits had been invented some time before other engineers decided to use the running rails for traction return. Clearly, DC track circuits could not be used with DC traction and, thus, low frequency AC track circuits (e.g., 33^1/$_3$Hz, 50Hz, 125Hz and others) were developed for use with jointed track circuits on DC railways, as shown in Figure 16.18. With the introduction of rectifier supplies for the DC supply though, 50Hz track circuit relays no longer represent good practice in systems engineering. For this, and several other equally cogent reasons, modern track circuits usually involve some form of digital coding of audio frequency carriers.

Whilst such coded track circuits offer a high degree of immunity to traction interference, they also offer targets for interference at audio frequencies. Reed relay type sensors operate at a few hundred Hz and the coded types

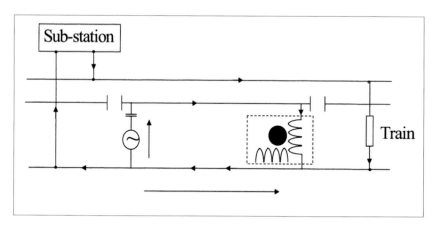

Figure 16.18: *Schematic of Direct Conductive Interference from a 3rd Rail DC traction supply into a Jointed Track Circuit. Authors.*

at 1000 to 3000Hz. Power electronic drives have to comply with some very severe limits with respect to the amplitudes of harmonic currents that they can produce. The limits apply over a whole complex of different frequencies to avoid affecting the low frequency track circuits already mentioned.

For DC choppers, this may not be too onerous, as they can be designed to operate at just one or maybe two carefully chosen frequencies. By their very nature, AC drives produce motor supply frequencies in a typical range of 0.5 to 150Hz. They use carrier signals in the 600 to 3000Hz region and are therefore capable of producing harmonics at almost any frequency, up to high audio bands and even beyond. However, it is possible to reduce the interference currents to levels that do not pose a threat to most track circuits, with suitable input filtering and by the appropriate choice of carrier frequencies and a sound modulation strategy.

The problem of signalling compatibility is an area where the rigorous adoption of systems engineering principles is paramount. Ultimately, a safely working railway can only be achieved if all its subsystems are compatible. However, this must also be achieved at a sensible overall cost and the most economic solution to signalling compatibility will almost certainly involve design compromises in both the traction and signalling equipments. Both must be designed together as a whole system, to the extent that historic constraints will permit.

16.24   Concluding Remarks

An appreciation of the requirements and operating principles of an electric traction system starts from an understanding of the basic physics of motion. Despite the recent major advances in the capabilities of power electronic converters and microprocessor controllers, the overall tractive effort vs. speed characteristics are still much the same as in the early days of electric railways and trains services are subject to the same limitations, such as adhesion and power limits.

The authors of this chapter have attempted to provide an introduction to these basic factors. They have also reviewed the wide range of implementations of electric traction drives that can be observed in operation. The detail design of the equipments involves experts in many branches of electrical, electronic, mechanical and software engineering and good systems engineering management is essential to achieve optimum results.

It should already be apparent that the railway is a complex system and that the different components all have to work together closely. The overwhelming need is for all those involved in the engineering design of railway equipment to develop an overview of the full system so that they can practice the much-vaunted, but rather less often practiced, art of real railway system engineering.

References

Abbott, J, 'South Eastern Trains: the State bows out in Style', Modern Railways, Vol. 62, No. 680, p. 44, May 2005.

Gill, D.C. and Goodman, C.J., 'Computer based Optimisation Techniques for Mass Transit Railways', lEE Proceedings-B, Vol. 139, No.3, May 1992.

Goodman, C.J., 'Overview of Electric Railway Systems and the Calculation of Train Performance', lEE Sixth Residential Course on Electric Traction Systems, 2001, lEE Publications.

Mellitt, B, 'The Impact of Electrification Systems and Traction Control on Signalling and Communications', lEE, Seventh Vacation School on Railway Signalling and Control Systems, 1998.

Rochard, B.P., and Schmid, F., 'A Review of Methods to Measure and Calculate Train Resistances', Proceedings of the Institution of Mechanical Engineers, Vol. 214, No. F4, pp185-199, Journal of Rail and Rapid Transit, London, 2000.

Wilkinson, D.T., 'Electric Braking Performance of Multiple Unit Trains', GEC Review, Vol. 1, No.1, 1985.

Chapter 17   Commuter Train Design

by Felix Schmid and Piers Connor

17.1   Trains for Commuting

Urban and suburban railways have to carry large numbers of commuting passengers on a regular basis and they must be capable of maximum utilisation at peak times. The design of commuter trains has long been based on the multiple unit principle where power and auxiliary equipment is distributed along the train and, where possible, located above or below the possible passenger space.

Passenger train vehicles always consist of at least the following elements:

- vehicle structure and associated hardware;
- running gear (axle, guidance, bogie and primary suspension) and secondary suspension;
- traction & braking equipment;
- couplers and drawgear;
- hotel requirements (lighting, heating, air conditioning, seating, etc.).

Getting the specification right for new vehicles or for a refurbishment project is an important part of the train procurement process. The design of a new rail vehicle or the improvement of an existing design can only be successful if the design process is based on a clear and agreed specification for the transport conditions to be experienced by the load - both passenger and propulsion plant. This overall, user oriented specification must then be translated into a technical specification, taking into account the constraints imposed by the physical and, where necessary, regulatory environment. The user specification must include the following criteria:

1. Maximum levels of permitted acceleration and deceleration under normal and abnormal operating conditions.

2. Permitted body transmitted vibration and noise limits.

3. Acceptable levels of catastrophic failure.

4. Rates of change and peak forces in the case of an impact.

5. Performance, maintenance, availability & reliability required to achieve travel time targets.

6. Air and temperature control requirements (for passenger comfort).

7. Ease of loading/unloading (passenger access).

8. Loading density (passengers per m^2).

9. Visual benefits (internal/external).

To a large extent, ride quality is dependent on track condition and maintenance but allowance must be made for a proportion of standing passengers when considering quality limits. In performance ranges, the maximum acceleration is usually $1.4m/s^2$ for emergency braking except for trams mixing with road traffic where it might be as high as $2.2m/s^2$ to allow for road vehicle conditions.

For passenger density, the criteria are usually measured in passengers per m^2 over a range between tare and 'crush' loading. For design purposes, the crush load may be set at a high level (say $10/m^2$) in order to take structural requirements into consideration.

Loading and unloading requirements are important to ensure dwell times at stations are kept to a minimum. The design of doorways, circulating areas and seating all play a part in the effectiveness of boarding and alighting speeds. This must also take into account the type of service being operated and the length of the majority of journeys.

A technical specification for the design or modification of rolling stock can be devised once the user specification, environmental specification and regulatory frameworks have been established. The specification must cover issues such as configuration, layout, crash worthiness, safe loads and

Figure 17.1: *Photo: of a 6-car urban multiple unit train in Vienna, Austria. The train is made up of 3 x 2-car units coupled together. Any unit could be used as a 2-car train. Photo: P. Connor.*

loads imposed on the infrastructure. Constraints imposed by the physical environment of the vehicle must be summarised in the environmental specification that will include some or all of the following criteria for both routine and non-service operation:

1. Track gauge.

2. Loading gauge (maximum permissible physical envelope of the rolling stock).

3. Maximum allowable mass per unit length of the vehicle.

4. Maximum permitted axle load imposed by the structures and track design.

5. Maximum gradients and rate of gradient change.

6. Maximum curvature radius and transition curve length.

7. Maximum and minimum levels of super-elevation in curves.

8. Wind velocities and temperature ranges.

9. Deviations from design values.

Alongside the user and environmental specification there are requirements that rail vehicles conform to the regulatory and legislative framework. This includes standards imposed by the railway undertaking or infrastructure owner, national safety authorities (e.g., for track side maintenance

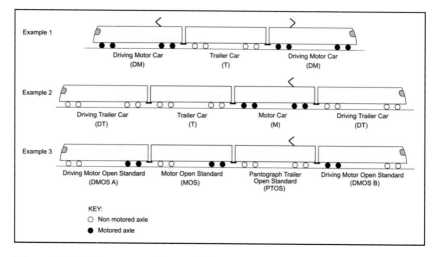

Figure 17.2: *Schematic of typical formations of multiple unit trains. The three examples show (1) a 3-car unit with 66% axles motored, (2) a 4-car unit with 25% axles motored and (3) a 4-car unit with 60% axles motored. In Example 3, the standard British main line vehicle designations are used. Graphic: P. Connor.*

work), UIC standards committee (e.g., end loads, loading gauge), Technical Specifications for Interoperability in Europe (TSIs) and international standards organisations (e.g., software proof of safety).

Most of the standards that currently apply to railway design in Europe have been developed over many years and cover a wide range of issues, from end load requirements to door control systems. Some of the standards are advisory while others are mandatory. This proliferation of regulations and legislation is one of the reasons for the large size of tender documents; any specification or regulation can invoke other specifications and regulations.

17.2   Train Formations

The use of multiple unit trains for urban and suburban railways is common world wide both for electric and diesel traction. The design offers variable formations, variable capacity and efficient operation. The choice of unit can range from a 2-car unit upwards to any length that the operational and maintenance facilities will accommodate, although the 16-car articulated formation of the 394m long Eurostar is the longest fixed formation train in Europe. In general, trains are formed of 2-, 3- or 4-car units. This provides a reasonable off-peak length while permitting longer trains for peak hour services by adding a unit or units.

Each unit will normally be equipped with a driver's cab at each end and all the required traction and auxiliary systems necessary for train operation, safety and passenger comfort. Where possible, designs are arranged so that all high voltage equipment is carried below floor level with only low voltage systems above the floor.

Some designs have adopted a split system, using two single-ended[1] units coupled back to back to provide a long train. This allows the train to be split at the middle point to allow a unit to access a short length workshop. It also reduces the number of driving cabs. There are also designs that use 2-car married pairs with a cab at each end and some where full cabs are not provided but unit ends have shunting control positions for depot use.

Multiple unit trains (Figure 17.2) have a distributed traction system usually arranged under more than one vehicle in the unit, whereas push-pull trains have all the power located on the locomotive at the end of the train. This space is not available for passengers. Both designs allow a rapid turnaround at terminals, important for both rolling stock utilisation and clearance of platform space.

Although the design of commuter trains has long been based on the multiple unit principle, a number of operators have adopted a push-pull system with a locomotive at one end of the train and a coach with a driving cab at the other end, known as a 'cab car' in the US. These systems are generally seen on those mature routes where the traffic levels are low and the expense of ordering a special fleet of multiple units trains cannot be justified.

A further consideration in commuter train design is the power to be provided and the number of motored axles required as a result. As one might expect, a wide variety of solutions have been chosen over the years. At the top end of the scale is the 'all axles motored' solution, where high acceleration is required and the line's signalling and power supply is designed to

---

[1]Single-ended units have a driver's cab at one end only.

accommodate it. At the lower end of the scale is where a multiple unit has only 20% axles motored, the short time acceleration performance being less of an issue for routes with long distances between stops. The British Southern Railway Class 442 5-car units are such an example.

Today's passenger railway undertakings mostly use four axle bogie rolling stock. However, articulated designs using Jacobs bogies have been adopted for some passenger applications (e.g., TGV trains) since they have good curving characteristics and make efficient use of the available train length. More recently, light rail vehicles have emerged with single axle bogies and special arrangements involving independent wheels and drives using stub-axles.

The choice of train formation tends to be route specific. Careful assessment of the existing infrastructure, the signalling capability, the frequency of service, the expected loads,the power supply facilities, the station designs and the maintenance facilities is necessary when considering a new train design. It may be more cost effective to incorporate a line upgrade when new rolling stock is required and to incorporate some or all of the infrastructure and support systems in the procurement cycle.

Double-deck passenger vehicles are popular in North America and some countries in Europe with a suitable structure gauge. They are not seen in the UK because of the restricted structure gauge. Double-deck cars have the disadvantage of slower loading and unloading times due to the volume of passengers and the restricted availability of doorways.

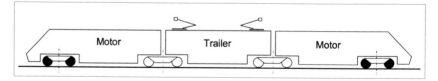

Figure 17.3: *Schematic of articulated 3-car multiple unit train using Jacobs bogies at the articulation points. Graphic: Pombo et al (2010).*

17.3   Choice of Motive Power and Traction System

Petrol and diesel engines dominate road transport while jet engines power
most commercial aircraft. Railway engineers have more choices since rail
based transport lends itself to operations using electric power: accurate
guidance of the vehicles eases current collection, while the low coefficient
of rolling friction reduces the need to minimise tare load. Indeed, there is
no substantial penalty associated with including several stages of energy
conversion on board a rail vehicle. A modern AC motored diesel locomotive, for example, includes the following conversion stages: chemical -
thermal - mechanical (translational) - mechanical (rotational) - electrical
(fixed frequency AC) - electrical (DC) - electrical (variable frequency AC)
- mechanical (rotational) - mechanical (translational). This complex arrangement represents an optimum in terms of traction performance even
though each conversion requires some equipment and reduces overall efficiency.

Electric transmission systems are generally favoured on heavily used routes
because of their controllability and the good conversion efficiency. Batteries and fuel cells are not yet acceptable for major railway applications
since the energy content of the former is still too low while the latter are
expensive and not fully proven. Electric traction systems are described in
Chapter 16

17.4   Vehicle Capacity

The capacity of a railway vehicle is a crucial part of the railway system.
For passenger vehicles, it is always a compromise between what is acceptable to the passenger in terms of accessibility and comfort and what is
acceptable to the operator in terms of efficiency and cost. The results are
not necessarily ideal for either.

The range of vehicle capacity depends largely on the use of the vehicle or
its expected journey distance. In this respect, for a short average journey
as experienced on urban routes and metros, capacity will be at the top
end of the range, most passengers being expected to stand while, for
longer journeys, capacity will be reduced by the need for more comfort,
more seating, more amenities and the consequent reduction in standing
space.

The other aspect of capacity is determined by the design of the loading and unloading system - where passenger doors are located, their size, their design and their operating system. A wide variety of systems are available and they will have an effect on dwell time management and vehicle capacity.

17.5   The Compartment Coach

From the earliest years of the 19th century railway, two basic passenger coach designs appeared — the compartment coach and the saloon. The compartment coach was based on the horse-drawn stagecoach, which contained two facing bench seats either side of a central transverse passage (Moon 1934). The access was through doors provided at either end of the passage.

The design was soon multiplied for railway coaches where the number of compartments expanded with the length of the vehicle, which was stretched as far as the infrastructure constraints would allow so that, by the beginning of the 20th century, 60ft (18m), 10 compartment, 4-axle vehicles were in use on commuter routes (Jenkinson 1996). With 5 persons being seated on each bench, such a vehicle could accommodate 100 passengers plus standees. Later versions managed to squeeze in 6-seater benches. The quality of the seating was variable but quantity was the main criterion for the lower classes of travel. Even in a compartment with a length of 6ft (1.8m), it was possible to get 5 persons standing between the knees of 10 seated passengers. First class seating was provided in some vehicles, allowing fewer, wider seats and and a longer compartment length. One typical example, recorded by Jenkinson (1996), showed that the reduction in capacity in a First Class vehicle amounted to 50% compared with an equivalent 3rd Class Coach.

The big advantages for the compartment coach were in its capacity for large numbers of seated passengers and its ability to unload them quickly. With one doorway for 10-18 passengers (depending on the standing load), it was possible to unload a whole commuter train arriving at a London terminus in 30 seconds. Many experienced commuters would open their door and alight from the train while it was still moving and some were agile enough to be able to arrive at the end of the platform before the front of the train.

Figure 17.4: *Interior of British Class 378 showing all longitudinal seating to allow maximum standing space. Some tip-up seats are provided (right) to give space for wheelchairs. Photo: P. Connor.*

Loading was not much slower but it suffered from the disadvantage that it relied upon passengers opening and closing the doors themselves. Regular commuters did, from education and habit, but there were always some doors left open and it required a number of platform staff to ensure all were closed before dispatching the train. This was expensive in staff and sometimes caused extended dwell times. It was also inherently unsafe, in that door could be opened while the train was moving. Such coaches survived in Britain until 2005.

17.6 The Saloon Coach

The other popular passenger coach design was the saloon. This type originated in the US, where the standard 19th century vehicle had end access through (usually) open platforms leading onto the seating area via a central walkway. Original examples of this type had open end entrance platforms but later examples were enclosed. The end platform also allowed access between vehicles, something not introduced in the UK until 1892.

This type of vehicle had to have a stronger body shell than the compartment type, simply because of the lack of internal structure. Its advantage over the compartment vehicle was the improved interior circulation but

Date	Stock	Seats/m length	Standees/m length	Pax/m length
1922	SE&CR Compartment Coach	5.55	2.78	8.33
1945	Southern Compartment EMU (4-SUB)	6	2.5	8.5
1947	Southern mixed Comp./Saloon EMU (4-SUB)	4.96	2.81	7.77
1972	Southern outer suburban EMU (4-VEP)	2.72	2.81	5.53
1994	Class 365 EMU	3.29	2.5	5.79
2002	Class 444 EMU	3.41	2.5	5.91
2010	Class 378 EMU	1.7	7.05	8.75
2009	LU 2009 Tube Stock	2.16	8.97	11.13
2010	LU Surface S Stock	2.27	9.12	11.39

Table 17.1: *Seating & Standing Capacity of Selected Suburban Rolling Stock. Table: Authors*

the loading/unloading was slower. Later versions of the saloon coach were adopted for long distance routes in Europe and elsewhere and various designs included mixed layouts combining compartments and a side corridor. In the UK, a hybrid compartment style saloon coach was used on many suburban routes, where the side doors were retained between sets of seats arranged either side of a central walkway. Transverse seating allowed 10 spaces per bay.

17.7 Measurement of Vehicle Capacity

Measurement of passenger vehicle capacity has two purposes, passenger planning and vehicle engineering, and comprises two distinct parts, passenger seating and available standing space. Seating is normally fixed, although some metro operators have vehicles equipped with a proportion of tip up seats. Standing space is calculated on the basis of floor area, less allowances for seating and other interior equipment. Various methods and standards are used. Some examples are offered in Table 17.1.

For new train design in Hong Kong, a $10/m^2$ engineering load is specified and $8/m^2$ for passenger planning. In the US, a basic $5/m^2$ is considered the worst case allowable planning standard (Kettleson et al 2003) with $6/m^2$ or above for engineering requirements. Also, to calculate loads for engineering purposes, an individual weight per passenger is required. This may range from 70 to 75kgs per person and includes a luggage weight factor.

A further consideration is the provision of toilets on trains. If these are provided, a certain percentage has to allow for disabled access. This will affect seating capacity by up to 20%. It is also usual to have a load factor applied to capacity calculations. This is to allow for uneven loading on individual trains and for the 'peak within the peak' often experienced on urban and inner suburban routes. These factors range from 70% to 86%.

17.8   Passengers in excess of capacity (PIXC)

In Britain, a target for restricting overcrowding on rail vehicles is set as 'Passengers in excess of capacity' (PIXC). This was defined by the government as greater than 10% of the vehicle's seating capacity or of an allowance of $0.55m^2$ per passenger depending on the type of vehicle. Some variations were subsequently introduced for London suburban routes and the 110% figure increased to 130% in 2008. Government literature (House of Commons 2003) suggests that there is much confusion over definitions.

The London Overground routes operator defined overcrowding as, 'more than 1.6 passengers per square metre' (TfL 2009) or 38% over the total number of seats. This data was issued when Class 313 trains were in use and there was an average of 77 seats/vehicle. The replacement Class 378 vehicles have an average of 35 seats/vehicle, less than half the replaced stock. In engineering terms, the question is simply to find the floor loading requirements of the vehicle structure and the consequent energy and braking requirements under the heaviest loading conditions. London Underground, for example, adopts a variable load, setting a standard of 8 passengers/m^2 between doorways and $6/m^2$ elsewhere. For passenger planning purposes, $7/m^2$ is adopted as the 'crush' load condition.

17.9   Door & Seating Configuration

The layout of doors and seats provides a significant impact on vehicle capacity. Doors need to be designed for optimum dwell time requirements while sufficient seating is essential to provide reasonable comfort for a majority of longer distance passengers. Some operators provide a guide to the maximum length of journey time passengers should be expected to stand. In the US (Kettleson et al 2003) and the UK, this time is typically 20 minutes.

The standard commuter train does not exist. There is a wide range of floor plans, beginning with the typical British mixed distance design Class 377 (Figure 17.5), which shows an attempt to include as many seats as possible but which offers little capacity for overcrowding. Standard class seats are arranged in both 2+2 and 2+3 configuration in an attempt to offer better seating for longer distance passengers.

The trains have an average of 66 standard seats per car. There is not much additional space for luggage. This will be crucial for trains covering longer distances or for airport services. The location of the side access doors is at the typical $1/3$ and $3/3$ positions along the body used on suburban routes, whereas the trains are largely used on long distance cross country routes. The doorways have no standback spaces and their 1200mm width is too narrow to allow more than 1 person through at a time.

An inner suburban example is the Class 455 as used by South West Trains for their routes out of Waterloo. These have a similar door layout and an average of 68 seats per car in their rebuilt state. In their original state, there was an average of 79 seats per car. The reduction in seating has allowed an increase of standing space.

At the other end of the scale, many heavy metro car designers adopt a minimalist approach to seating. In Hong Kong, the MTRC originally specified a 24m car with 5 sets of 1400mm double doors per side and wide connecting gangways (Ball & Vint, 1981). The cars had all longitudinal seating for about 50 persons. Each car was designed for a full load of 375 persons. This principle has been maintained for all subsequent builds. The design capacity was originally based on $7/m^2$ for standing passengers. This was later increased to $8/m^2$. Similar levels of occupancy are used in other Asian cities. A similar, open plan design has been adopted

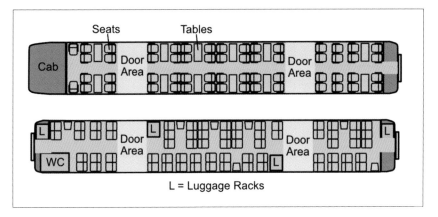

Figure 17.5: *Seating plan for two cars of British Class 377 showing a mix of 2+2 and 2+3 seating in two cars of the same 4-car unit. One car of the unit (not shown) has a disabled toilet and spaces for wheelchairs, resulting in a loss of 16 seats. Graphic: P. Connor.*

for some London routes, including the Overground Class 378 units (Figure 17.4).

In London, interior seating on Underground cars has been reduced to the minimum tolerable in order to cope with the increasing traffic loads experienced on the system. Taking the Victoria Line as an example, the original stock had a capacity of 264 seated and 926 standing (TfL 2007).

The driving cars had two 1400mm double doorways and one single 700mm doorway with 40 seats. The original cars were provided with a 200mm 'standback' space adjacent to each door. This was designed to reduce the impact of the obstruction to access caused by passengers standing against the draught screen. The design was continued up to the 1990s when internal refurbishments eliminated it on many trains.

The new vehicles for the Victoria Line (2009 Stock) have fewer seats and increased overall capacity. Seating is reduced to 252 and the standing capacity to 1196. It should be mentioned that TfL (2007) stated that the observed capacity is 28% less than the planned capacity (Figure 17.6).

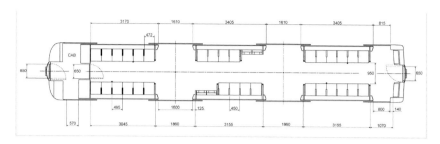

Figure 17.6: *Seating plan for a London Underground 2009 Tube Stock. Note the large door openings (1600mm) and the all longitudinal seating layout. Graphic: P. Connor.*

The increased capacity also meets the new requirements for disabled access by allowing a 900mm wide gangway throughout the car. Doors are increased to 1600mm width but stand-back spaces are lost due to the extra pillar dimensions required for the all-aluminium car body structure. A feature of many new vehicles intended for the heavy urban routes around London is for seating near doorways to be removed and for tip-up or 'perch seats' to be provided.

Railway vehicle capacity requirements vary widely according to the length of route and density of occupation. Generally, standing spaces are measured as passengers per square metre. These range from $4/m^2$, considered tolerable in the US and Western Europe to $8/m^2$ in Asian cities. These variations can be said to be due to both physical and cultural differences. Load factors should be applied to account for variations in train loading. Longer, commuter and outer suburban routes tend to limit standing to 20 minutes for any journey and any more than 10% above seating capacity was regarded as overcrowded. The UK Department for Transport raised that limit to 30% in 2008.

Designs for vehicles should taken account of the loading and unloading requirements and allow space for stand-back at doorways. Some regard for the storage of luggage may be required for longer distance or airport services. Care should be taken in deciding the capacity requirements for rail vehicles. An ideal layout designed for a particular route will largely restrict the use of this vehicle for its whole life, particularly if large width or multiple doorways are chosen. A more versatile vehicle may end up

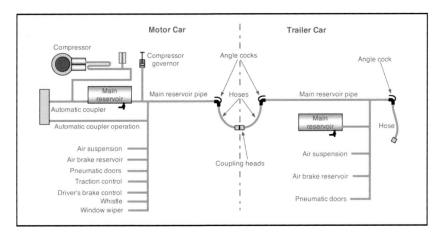

Figure 17.7: *Schematic of compressed air system showing distribution of air supply over a motor car and trailer car of an EMU. Graphic· P. Connor*

as a compromise, not ideally suited to any route. A forward looking and system orientated approach is essential to obtain the best result.

17.10   Auxiliary Systems

The modern passenger train provides a number of on-board services, both for passengers and control systems. They are almost all electrically powered, although some require compressed air and a few designs use hydraulic fluid. Since a train is virtually a self contained unit, all the services are powered and used on board. They may be broadly divided into pneumatic and electrical.

Compressed air
A compressed air supply is almost always required on urban and suburban trains, since it is used for brakes and sometimes for powering doors or unit coupling systems. It was also once popular for powering traction power switches or contactors. It is normally used for raising pantographs on overhead line systems. The compressed air always needs drying after compression to avoid moisture from condensation getting into valves. The compressor is normally driven directly from the main power source (the

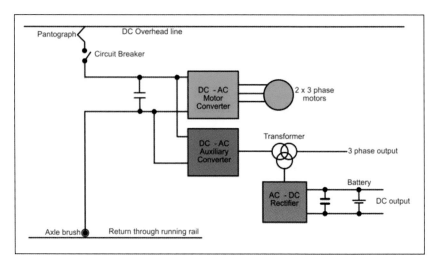

Figure 17.8: *Schematic of auxiliary electrical system showing the division between power and auxiliary electrical systems of a DC EMU. Graphic: P. Connor*

overhead line or third rail on electrified lines or the main generator on diesel powered vehicles). In some recent commuter train applications, the compressor is supplied from the on-board auxiliary converter.

17.11   Auxiliary Electrical

The auxiliary electrical or 'hotel' equipment on a passenger train will have a battery—essential as a basic, low voltage standby current supply source and for start up purposes when livening up a dead vehicle. The battery is normally charged from the on-board auxiliary power supply. This can be a generator or alternator on older vehicles or converter on more modern types.

The traditional source on a train for on-board, low voltage supplies was a generator. The generator is a DC machine driven by the diesel engine or, on electric locomotives, by a motor powered from the traction current supply. On a coach, the generator was often driven directly off an axle (a

Figure 17.9: *Photo: of a wagon with the typical European with a screw shackle coupler (in red), air hose and side buffers. Ideally, the shackle should be coupled and tightened when the buffers are in compression so as to reduce the shock loading. Photo: P. Connor.*

dynamo), a large bank of batteries providing power for lighting when the train was stationary.

The alternator was the replacement for the generator. It provides AC voltages instead of DC for auxiliary supplies. AC proved better than DC because it is easier to transmit throughout a train, needing smaller cables and suffering reduced losses. A rectifier is added to convert the AC for the battery charging and any other DC circuits.

The converter has now replaced the alternator. This is a solid state version of the alternator for auxiliary current supplies and can be a rectifier to convert AC to DC or an inverter to convert DC to AC Figure 17.8. Both are used according to local requirements and some designs employ both on the same train. The name converter has become generic to cover both types of current conversion.

17.12   Coupling Systems

Initially, vehicles were formed into trains using chain-links that were soon supplemented by shock absorbing buffers (Figure 17.9). In Europe the chains were replaced by a standardised hook and shackle system while American railways preferred a simple automatic coupler that combines the draw and push function into one unit that also absorbs shock loads— the Knuckle or Buckeye coupler. However, the American coupler has very limited lateral play and therefore requires that the overhang at vehicle

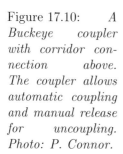

Figure 17.10: *A Buckeye coupler with corridor connection above. The coupler allows automatic coupling and manual release for uncoupling. Photo: P. Connor.*

ends be minimised. Both European hook and the US system require manual coupling of air lines and control cables.

For multiple unit trains, the trend is now for semi-permanent couplings between the vehicles of a unit (Figure 17.11) and automatic couplers at the cab ends. Maintenance of the unit is carried out for all vehicles at one time and, although a single defect on any vehicle will cause the whole unit to be removed from service, it has been shown, by experience, to be more efficient overall than individual vehicle removal and replacement.

Semi-permanent couplers will normally only be accessible from within a maintenance facility. The mechanical link between the vehicles will incorporate some of the buffing gear and will provide for some absorption capability in case of a collision. Jumpers and hoses will normally be separately coupled between the vehicles and these may be required to be located either side of a gangway between the vehicles.

Often it will be necessary to provide duplicate jumpers and hoses on either side of the coupling point between vehicles. This is required so that, if vehicles are turned in service, it will still be possible to effect coupling. Railways where duplicated connections are not provided, for example, on some London Underground types, careful management of train utilisation is required to avoid incompatible ends being offered for coupling. Similar issues arise for automatic couplers.

Figure 17.11: *Photo: of a semi-permanent coupling on an electric multiple unit coach. The coupling provides the mechanical link between the vehicles (the larger element) and the compressed air supply link (the smaller element). In this example, the mechanical link also absorbs the buffing loads. Electrical jumpers are separately connected. When vehicles are uncoupled, the coupler should be covered to reduce corrosion and contamination. Photo: P. Connor.*

Automatic couplers may only be needed at the ends of units where train lengths are required to be altered during the traffic day. Otherwise, a simple coupler system for rescue purposes (a push out) may be sufficient. There is a large variety in the number of automatic coupler designs, most of which are not compatible with one another. A mistake made when privatisation took place in Britain in the mid-1990s, was the lack of a requirement for standard coupling arrangements. This has led to numerous difficulties when trains are required to be rescued and a suitably equipped form of traction is not available.

Automatic couplers are usually highly complex and require regular use and an active maintenance regime in order for them to remain operable. They are also vulnerable to severe weather, particularly snow and ice and may require to be covered at exposed ends of trains under these conditions.

Figure 17.12: *An automatic coupler on the driving end of an electric multiple unit coach. The coupling provides the mechanical, pneumatic and electrical connections and the buffing system between the two units when coupled. The mechanical connection uses a male/female side-by-side system with the small pneumatic connection fitted centrally below them. The connection is locked pneumatically. Electrical connections are made through butt contacts mounted in a covered box immediately below the mechanical head. Photo: P. Connor.*

Appendix 1

Many railway engineering projects express rolling stock loading requirements as follows:

- AW0, empty weight,

- AW1, weight with seated passenger load,

- AW2, weight with average peak-hour passenger load,

- AW3, crush loaded weight.

Some variations include AW4 as an engineering load above AW3.

For US standards, passengers are usually assumed to weigh an average of 155 lb (70 kg). Peak-hour passenger load is normally based on 0.4 p/ft^2 (4 passengers/m^2) of floor space in North America, 0.4-0.5 p/ft^2 (4-5 p/m^2) in Europe and 0.5-0.6 p/ft^2 (5-6 p/m^2) in Asia, after discounting space used for cabs, stairwells and seated passengers at 0.2/ft^2 (2/m^2).

Crush loads are 0.6, 0.6-0.7, and 0.8 p/ft^2 (6, 6-7 and 8 p/m^2) respectively. Caution: some systems and manufacturers use different designations, some systems report loading in excess of 0.8p/ft^2(8 p/m^2) (Kittleson et al 2003).

References

Ball, N D; Vint, J (1981), 'The Electric Multiple Unit Trains of the Hong Kong Mass Transit Railway', Proc. I. Mech E. Railway Division, London.

Bolton, G., Turner, S. (2009), 'S Stock - A new train for London's Sub-Surface Railway', Presentation.

Harris, M. [1966]. 'Great Western Coaches from 1890', David & Charles, Newton Abbot.

Hobbs, G (2009), Attachment to Letter to Transport Committee, London Assembly, 12 January 2009.

House of Commons Select Committee on Transport (2003), Seventh Report, 25-38, London.

Jenkinson, D. (1996) 'History of British Railway Carriages 1900-1953', Pendragon, 1996.

Kittleson & Associates Inc. for Transit Cooperative Research Program (2003), 'Transit Capacity & Quality of Service Manual', TCRP, Washington DC.

Moon, A.N (1934), 'One Hundred Years of Railway Carriages', Journal of the Institute of Locomotive Engineers, London.

Passenger Focus (2007), 'The Pennine Class 185 experience: What do passengers think?' Passenger Focus, Warrington, UK.

Pombo, J., Ambrosio, J., Pereira, M., Lewis, R., Dwyer-Joyce, R., Ariaudo, C., Kuka, N. (2010) A study on wear evaluation of railway wheels based on multibody dynamics and wear computation, Multibody System Dynamics, 24 (3), pp. 347-366

TfL (2007), 'Rolling Stock Information Sheets', Transport for London, London.

Websites

http://en.wikipedia.org/wiki/British_Rail_Class_458 (Visited 28 Nov 2010)

http://en.wikipedia.org/wiki/E231_series (Visited 28 Nov 2010)

http://www.emus.co.uk/sub.htm (Visited 27 Nov 2010)

Chapter 18 Rolling Stock Maintenance

by Piers Connor

18.1 The Need for Reliability

Railways are made up of complex mechanical and electrical systems and there are hundreds of thousands of moving parts. If a railway service is to be reliable, the equipment must be kept in good working order and regular maintenance is essential if this is to be achieved. A railway will not survive for long as a viable operation if it is allowed to deteriorate because of lack of maintenance. Although maintenance is expensive, it will become more expensive to replace the failing equipment early in its life because maintenance has been neglected.

Rolling stock is the most maintenance intensive part of the railway system and is the most vulnerable if maintenance is neglected. A stalled train will block a railway immediately and will reduce a timetable on an intensively used system to an unmanageable shambles for the remainder of the day. Reliability is the key to successful railway operation and maintenance should be the number one priority to ensure reliability is on-going.

18.2 Maintenance Facilities

Trains require special facilities for storage and maintenance. The basic design of these facilities has changed little in the last 100 or more years and, in many cases, the original sites and buildings are still in daily use. Sometimes, these old layouts have made adapting to modern maintenance systems very difficult.

Figure 18.1: *View of the stabling area of the London Underground depot at Stratford showing open stabling sidings and modifications shed. Photo: P. Connor.*

The layout of a maintenance facility or depot will usually consist of a storage yard, a car cleaning area, an inspection and light maintenance shed, a heavy maintenance shop and, possibly, a separate locomotive shop or at least an area for locomotives if EMUs are the main service providers.

18.3 Depot Access

An essential feature of any depot is good access, for both road and rail. Good rail access means that trains can get in and out of the depot without delaying trains on the main line and without upsetting operations within the depot. It is no good if a train coming in has to stop at the entrance while the driver gets instructions from the depot control office and the rear of the train is still standing on the main line. This can remove two or three paths from a timetable. The access track into (and out of) a depot should be long enough to hold a train clear of the main line and the depot fan. If the railway is equipped with ATP (Automatic Train Protection), the changeover between ATP and manual operation will probably have to take place on this track. This must be carefully incorporated into the depot track design.

Road access is equally important. Large items of equipment may be needed to be delivered to the depot (transformers, pre-assembled traction units) and space to allow heavy trucks to get into the depot and turn, unload and exit must be provided. In some cases, it is necessary to provide car delivery access by road. Hard standing areas and unloading facilities like cranes or gantries must be considered when designing such a depot. The hard standing needs to be located over or near a suitable track so that cars being delivered can be craned off the road vehicle and mounted onto their bogies, which have been delivered in advance and are already on the track. The craneage can be hired in if the permanent installation of such equipment is not considered justifiable.

18.4   Cleaning and Stabling

Trains are stabled in depots or sidings when not in use and they need to be cleaned and serviced. Cleaning means a regular exterior water wash and interior sweeping and dusting or vacuuming. At longer intervals, seating upholstery and carpets must be shampooed. Exterior washing is usually means a drive through washing machine that will wash the sides and, perhaps, the roof. Suitable facilities must be provided in the stabling areas where trains are stored. Water, power and toilet cleaning systems need to be provided in such areas, adjacent to each train to be serviced. Access to trains must be designed so that cleaning staff can reach them safely whilst carrying their equipment. This usually means floor height walkways alongside trains, or at least up to the first car of a set if through inter-car connections are available.

The layout of a stabling area is important. Ideally, each road should have an exit route at each end, so that, if one end gets blocked for any reason, trains can still get out the other end. There is no reason why two trains should not be stabled on each road if the length is right, again provided an exit is available at each end so that, if one train fails and is not sent out on time, the other is not blocked in. Of course, site availability is always an issue and compromises are inevitable. It may even be necessary to stable two trains on a single ended track. Even this is viable if management of the fleet is flexible and allows trains due for entry into service to be swapped at short notice. This is one of the essential skills of a good depot supervisor.

Train stabling areas are traditionally outdoors largely because of the expense of constructing large sheds. However, covering the stabling areas with some sort of weather proof structure is always preferable. It protects the trains and the staff working on or around them and reduces contamination by pollutants, frost, snow and wind damage. A covered area will also provide some benefit in hot conditions and could help to reduce the air conditioning costs.

18.5   Toilets

Modern trains that have toilets need to have them serviced regularly. A toilet discharge facility is required in any depot where trains have toilets. The discharge has to be done away from the main buildings and where there is road access for the removal of effluent if it cannot be disposed of down a sewer. Emptying of effluent tanks is normally followed by rinsing and then recharging of the system with flushing water containing formaldehyde to break up the waste matter.

18.6   Train Washing Machines

These work on the same principle as a car wash, except that, usually, the train is driven through the wash and the washer itself stays in one place. Some designs of train washer work like a very long car wash, where the train stands still and the washer moves during the cleaning cycle but these are rare. Normally, water is used for a daily wash, while a chemical wash is used at less frequent intervals—usually several weeks. Many daily washes have a detergent added to assist the process. In referring to a daily wash, this might extend to three days between washes, depending on local practice and degree of pollution and dirt collection.

Figure 18.2: *A view of the approach to a drive-through train washing machine. The car sides are washed as it passes through rotating flails. The car ends and roofs have to be washed by hand. Beyond the washer is an automatic equipment inspection arch. Photo: P. Connor.*

Washing machines require that the track on either side is straight for at least one car's length (Figure 18.2). This is to ensure that the car goes into the wash straight. There will also be a need for proper drainage facilities, complete with waste water management and, for the chemical wash, waste retrieval using a clarifier or separator. It is usual to use recirculating systems nowadays, reusing the water from the final rinse at least, if not the 'ready mixed' water.

Washing machines may need a roof under certain conditions and they must be protected from adverse weather, particularly cold. Freezing temperatures will play havoc with the pipes of a poorly protected machine. Most operators do not wash under freezing weather conditions, so as to avoid ice forming around the doors and other moving parts. Ice will quickly prevent train doors from operating and will render a train useless as a result.

Chemical washes are used for heavy cleaning and the chemicals used will often require the train to stand for some time while the chemical reacts with the dirt on the car body. The standage must be protected against drips and the waste collected. In places where there is space, it is advisable to do the chemical wash where it is protected from the weather. Some form of special ventilation is likely to be required. In some facilities, the chemical and water washes are contained in the same washing machine.

18.7   Wheel Lathe

Train wheels wear just as car tyres do and they need to be checked regularly. When the wear reaches certain limits, the treads either have to be reprofiled to the correct shape or the wheels replaced. Reprofiling wheels is a slow and expensive process but train and wheel design and maintenance has improved considerably over recent years, reducing the periods between visits for reprofiling. Even so, there are still persistent cases of railways running into unforeseen or unusual wheel wear problems and the wheel/rail interface still needs a lot more research before it is fully understood.

Most modern depots are equipped with a wheel profiling facility known as a wheel lathe. These are normally designed so that the wheels can be reprofiled while still on the train. Removing the wheels requires the train to be lifted and this is an expensive business and very time-consuming. To avoid this, the underfloor wheel lathe or 'ground' wheel lathe was developed.

Wheels can be removed from a train by a wheel drop, where the wheelset is lowered underneath the train into a basement below the depot floor. Sometimes, whole tool rooms are provided in such areas but the ground conditions sometimes make such places difficult to keep dry and difficult to conform with modern evacuation requirements.

Modern wheel lathes can also reprofile a wheelset that has been removed from the train. Otherwise a separate wheel turning facility has to be provided in the workshop. Cutting has been the most common method of reprofiling but, recently milling machines, have been making a comeback as they can offer a longer tool life and better tolerance control on diameters.

Wheels on a bogie or wheels on a single vehicle must be reprofiled within limits compared with each other. For example, a standard set for one type of passenger coach says that wheels in the same bogie must not vary in diameter by more than 5 mm. Wheels under the same coach must not vary more than 10 mm on different bogies. The most modern vehicles might require a tolerance as low as 3 mm. When wheels that drive a speedometer are reprofiled, the speedometer will have to be adjusted to compensate for the difference in wheel diameter caused by the reprofiling.

Some modern wheels lathes are designed to turn both wheelsets on a bogie at the same time. These 'double-headed' lathes have developed as a result of electronically controlled AC motors, which require that the motors in the same circuit turn at the same speed so as to match the inverter frequency. This makes it essential that wheel diameters with motors within a traction power circuit are equal.

Although it might seem obvious, the roundness of wheels is important, especially at very high speeds. An eccentric wheel can cause extreme loads on the wheel, axle, bearing and suspension, leading to failures. An 'unround' (out of round) or eccentric wheel is alleged to have led to wheel tyre failure of a German ICE at Eschede in 1998, causing a high-speed crash with heavy loss of life. The wheel is alleged to have had an eccentricity (difference between major and minor axes of the ellipse) of 1.1mm, against a limit of 0.6mm. Wheels are often damaged by skidding during braking. Skidding (called sliding) causes a flat patch (called a flat) to wear on the tyre and, when the wheel begins rolling again after a slide, the familiar "tap, tap, tap..." of the flat will be heard. Overheating during braking can also damage a wheel.

Even if wheels, by some lucky combination of circumstances, do not wear significantly, reprofiling to remove work-hardened metal is likely to be needed at around 1 million km, otherwise Martensite fragments can drop out of the wheel tread, leading to tyre damage. This damage can also be caused by local overheating during skidding and/or braking.

18.8 Inspection Sheds

Special facilities are required to carry out rolling stock inspections. A properly constructed building, capable of accommodating a whole train, should be provided. Access to the underneath of the train is essential

Figure 18.3: *View of the inspection area of the London Underground depot at Stratford showing the posted rails allowing access under cars. Photo: P. Connor.*

and this must be designed to allow reasonable working conditions and safety. There are various ways of doing this. The most common used to be a pit provided between the rails of the maintenance tracks and, sometimes, pits on either side of the track as well, to allow access to the sides of the underframe equipment. A more common approach today is the 'swimming pool' design, where the floor of the shed is sunk and the tracks are mounted on posts (Figure 18.3). This gives better access and improves the light levels under the cars.

18.9   Shore Supplies

Inside train sheds and shops, it is necessary to provide shore supplies for trains and power for tools and maintenance equipment. Where overhead

Figure 18.4: *View of the roof access area of a tram depot. Special arrangements are necessary to ensure the overhead line supply is switched off before access is allowed. Photo: F. Schmid.*

electric traction is used, the overhead wires are usually installed inside inspection sheds but not in shops were vehicles are lifted. If it is necessary to get access to the roofs of trains, the overhead current must be switched off and the switch secured by a lock. Any person working on the roof will have a personal access key for the lock to ensure the current remains off until the work is complete and it is safe for it to be restored. The access stairs to the roof level walkway will also have a locked gate that can only be unlocked if current is off.

In the modern depots built for the Eurostar Channel Tunnel trains in London and Paris, the overhead catenary in the workshops is designed to swing away from the roof when required to allow access to the roof mounted equipment.

Where there is a third rail traction system, for safety reasons, the sheds are not equipped with the third rail, so a supply through a long lead is provided. The lead is plugged into a socket on the side of the train. Various systems are used around the world. It is now usual for the shore supply socket on the car to be switched so as to isolate the current collector shoes from the supply. This is to avoid electric shock risks to persons working on or near the shoes. In older installations, this facility is not provided and a shore supply will energise all electrical equipment on the train, including the shoes. In these situations, special precautions have to be taken to ensure no 'overhead leads' or 'stingers' are inserted on a train being worked on.

For third rail systems, the shore supply cables are usually fed from electrified rails suspended from the shed roof. The cables are hung from trolleys running along the rails so that the supply is available along the whole track.

It is common to use the overhead leads to power the train out of the shed until the leading collector shoes are in contact with the current rails outside the shed. This is sometimes called 'railing'. The train is then stopped and the overhead leads removed. The leading car is then used to drag the rest of the train out of the shed. Care has to be taken to ensure all leads are removed before allowing a train to leave the shed and enter service.

18.10   Lifting

The traditional method for accessing bogies was to lift the car body off the bogies by use of an overhead crane or cranes. Each vehicle to be lifted has to be separated from its fellows in the train and dealt with separately. If one car in a set is defective, it has to be uncoupled and pushed into the shop for lifting. To access the bogies, the overhead crane is used to lift one end while the bogie is rolled clear and then the body is lower onto stands. Then the other end is lifted, the bogie rolled clear there and the body lowered onto two more stands. Motors, wheels and other items can then be worked on or removed from the bogie as necessary. Naturally, this takes up a lot of track space in the shop and requires time spent on separating the vehicle from the train and then from its bogies. For overhauls, the bogie may be removed to a special area where it is placed on stands for stripping and refitting work. A quicker lifting method is to use two cranes that lift both ends of the car body together and free both bogies at the same time. The body can then be removed to another part of the workshop for maintenance.

Jacks are the usual method of lifting nowadays. Vehicles can be lifted individually or, if a fixed formation is used for normal service, more recent practice has been to lift the whole train set. This is done by synchronised jacks. The jacks are linked by control cables and controlled by one person from a control desk. The big advantage of this system is that you don't have to break up the train into individual cars to do the work on one vehicle. The time saved reduces the period the train is out of service.

Figure 18.5: *View of the lifting area of the depot at Stratford, London. The lifting jacks are in place prior to lifting the whole unit. Photo: P. Connor.*

Permanently fitted underfloor jacks are also provided in some locations. Again, the lifting system is synchronised to allow several cars to be lifted at the same time if necessary. This is quicker then uncoupling each vehicle, especially if there is only one requiring attention.

Rolling stock can be lifted on a track where there is no pit, especially if there is a need to exchange a piece of underfloor equipment. A fork lift truck can be used to do this if there is enough room at the sides of the trains for it to manoeuvre. Otherwise a small scissors lift table can be used. In all cases, it is essential to ensure that the floor will take the weight of the train raised on jacks. Most modern rolling stock is designed to be lifted with its bogies still attached so that exchange of one piece of underfloor equipment can be carried out on a lifted train without disturbing any other cars.

Figure 18.6: *Bogie Drop System Provided at Oxley Depot, near Wolverhampton. Photo: P. Connor.*

Another system used in some shops is the bogie drop. The train is run over the lifting road, which has a pit and is positioned so that the bogie to be removed is located over a special section of track. The bogie requiring removal is disconnected from the train, using the pit for access. The car bodies are then lifted, leaving the disconnected bogie on the track. The section of track where the bogie is located can now be lowered into a basement area and the bogie removed and replaced by a fresh one.

A variation of this system has the train lifted by raising the sections of track under the bogies. The car bodies are then supported by stands placed under them and the bogies to be changed are disconnected. Once free, they are lowered to floor level and serviced or exchanged for new bogies. Turntables can be installed to assist in the removal of the bogies to other maintenance areas.

18.11   Maintenance Workshops

It is still common to see workshops for railways provided with tooling and equipment to allow a full range of engineering tasks to be undertaken. This will include milling, boring, grinding, planing and cutting machines as well as part cleaning facilities (including bogie washing and car underframe cleaning or 'blow-out' as it is sometimes called), plus electronic and pneumatic testing shops. Good storage and materials management facilities are also needed. Computerised systems are now widely available.

Not only does the rolling stock require maintenance but also trackwork, traction power equipment, signalling, communications equipment, fare collection systems, electronics of all types and buildings maintenance. The main depot of a railway has to be equipped to handle all these. Works trains will be needed to ferry equipment and staff to work sites along the line and these will be serviced at the depot. Refuelling facilities will be needed for diesel locomotives and DMUs. Storage for hazardous materials and fuel must be in a secure place with proper fire protection facilities. Waste disposal must also be properly managed and waste recovered if possible.

18.12   Maintenance Programmes

Rolling stock maintenance can be programmed in one of three ways; by mileage, by time or by conditioning monitoring. Of these three methods, condition monitoring is the most recent. Traditionally, maintenance was carried out on a time basis, usually related to safety items like braking and wheel condition. Many administrations later adopted a mileage based maintenance system, although this is more difficult to operate as you have to keep records of all vehicle mileages and this is time consuming unless you have a modern train control and data gathering system. There is also the fact that a train will deteriorate just as quickly if it is stored unused somewhere as it would if it was being run in service every day. Only the items that deteriorate will vary.

Modern trains should be able to run for some weeks without a maintenance inspection. One train operating company in the UK wants to get inspection intervals out to 90 days on its new EMUs. Comparing this with the three days between inspections that electric trains got at the beginning of the 20th century and the 7-daily inspections still being carried out in the 1980s on some similar fleets, shows the rapid progress of the last few years. It is impossible to give fixed time or mileage periods here for maintenance as each type of train varies. There are often special rules for high speed trains and for heavy freight. Individual railways have adapted their maintenance to the local conditions and, in many places, certain types of safety inspections are required by law. As an example, the Channel Tunnel Shuttle trains cover about 5,000 kms a week and get an initial inspection every seven days. However, the French high speed trains (TGV) are given a daily visual inspection of the underneath and the pantographs. The toilet system is emptied every three days and the trains return to their base depot every 5-6 days for their 4,500 kms inspection. Examination of equipment such as traction motors and bogies takes place every 18 days.

Condition monitoring is achieved by checking the operation of the equipment and only changing something if it shows signs of wear beyond preset limits. The checking is often done using on-board monitoring and storing the data gathered in a computer for downloading at the maintenance facility. Of course, it is a recent development made available by the introduction of information technology on trains. Such systems are now becoming so sophisticated that it is possible to have failure predictions of some items of equipment. A combination of on-board data gathering and depot maintenance systems have been developed into complete maintenance management systems on lines where modern rolling stock has been introduced.

18.13 Failures

As already mentioned, reliability is the key to running a successful railway. If the equipment, especially the rolling stock, is not reliable, the railway is not workable. A good railway management will keep track of its performance and its failures and, by this means, ensure that problems are eliminated before they become endemic.

A number of methods can be used to monitor performance. The traditional way was to measure on-time performance. The number of minutes late of each delayed train was recorded and collated into daily, weekly, monthly and annual statistics. Usually, the time of arrival at the destination station was the basis but an intermediate delay is often also used to quantify a delay to a service. The cause of each delay is decided - yes, it does require a decision, as we will see later - and the cause investigated. In the case of rolling stock, there is probably a technical reason for the delay and there is usually a check to see if other, similar incidents have taken place. If so, there may be a design fault that needs a modification to the fleet to rectify. Checks are also done on maintenance procedures to ensure that the process is being carried out properly and, if so, whether the system needs to be modified.

Causes of delays are investigated to find out what happened. Imagine the case of a train that comes to a halt in the middle of nowhere. The emergency brake has applied and driver observes he has lost all the brake pipe air. After checking that the conductor has not stopped the train and no passenger alarm valves have been operated, he starts trying to find out the cause. After a while he finds the cause—a burst hose between coaches. Back to get a spare hose but there is no spare hose in the emergency cabinet. He has to isolate the defective portion of the train and limp on to the next station where he can get a hose and repair the train. Delay to his train? 25 minutes actual delay at site plus 17 minutes lost going to next station at reduced speed plus 35 minutes replacing the hose. Total delay 77 minutes. But what was the cause?

Initial observation of this incident would suggest a defective hose. The delay would be allocated to rolling stock and the engineering department would have a few words with the supplier to tell him what happened and discuss possible causes and remedies. However, in our case, an enquiry is held because the conductor on the train says he heard a loud bang under the train just before the emergency stop. The enquiry finds that, upon investigation, a shovel was found by the track in a bent and battered condition. The underneath of the train shows signs that it was hit by something. The damaged hose shows cut marks near the burst. It is concluded that the permanent way workers in the area had left a shovel on the track, it struck the train and damaged the hose. Allocation of delay: Permanent Way department. It wasn't a rolling stock failure at all, although it was aggravated by the lack of a spare hose, which is a rolling stock error. Eventually, as a result of some bargaining, the delay is split between the two departments, both of whose performance is measured on train service reliability.

Such investigations and the subsequent bargaining were traditionally part of the railway culture and have recently become more important since the commercialisation of the business. No one wants to be blamed for delays, since service performance is part of their contract and part of their payment structure.

18.14   Performance Measures

Rolling stock performance in respect of failures can be measured by MTBF (Mean Time Between Failures) or MDBF (Mean Distance Between Failures). It is sometimes measured by numbers of failures per year, month or week but this may not represent an accurate rate consistent with mileage. On the other hand, rolling stock does deteriorate rapidly in storage and this, in itself, produces failures, although these may not be the same failures seen under normal service conditions. Failure rates are sometimes quantified in service performance by availability. The performance is expressed as, for example, 95% availability. In other cases it is quantified as, say, 92% on-time. This is more unreliable as a statistic if the on-time regime is cushioned by huge amounts of 'recovery time', as is often the case today.

Performance monitoring also depends on the real definition of a delay. At one time, the Inter City services in the UK were using 10 minutes as the definition of a delay. This was much derided in Europe, where on-time performance meant just that. If you were not on time, you were late. Perhaps a more equitable way to define a delay is by the loss of a train path. Most main lines will give a three minute headway or 20 trains per hour, assuming equal speeds and performance. A three minute delay will therefore lose a path and, in the commercial structure of a modern railway, deprive the track owner of the sale of a path to another train operating company. In a metro or suburban operation, the path will be two minutes or slightly less, so a two minute delay would be an appropriate measure of performance.

One other point about performance is that time out of service is as important as the frequency or duration of failures. Another measure applied to equipment is the MTTR (Mean Time To Repair). A short delay that requires a train to be taken out of service for repair become more critical is the train takes a week to get back into service. It's not good design if the train owner has to lift the car off its bogies in order to replace a fuse. Short MTTR is another important part of good rolling stock performance.

Chapter 19   The Human Factor

by David Hitchcock

19.1   Introduction

If people are involved, there is a human factor. Systems where people necessarily interact with infrastructure, vehicles or information must give due
consideration to how those interactions will be performed. This is called
'ergonomics' or 'human factors', defined by the International Ergonomics
Association as: "the scientific discipline concerned with the understanding
of interactions among humans and other elements of a system, and the pro-
fession that applies theory, principles, data and methods to design in order
to optimise human well-being and overall system performance."

Ergonomics demands a robust approach to understanding and integrating:

1. The user characteristics

2. Activities and tasks performed

3. The use of equipment

4. The environment or workplace

19.2   User Characteristics

It is pragmatic to consider three categories of user; primary, secondary
and tertiary. Primary users are those who have the most interaction with

the system or equipment. Secondary users may have less exposure, but nevertheless place significant demand on the system. Tertiary users are those who have important but less frequent involvement with the system. Considering the vehicle as an example; the primary user would be the driver who performs most of their duties in the cab. Secondary users would be the passengers - the core component of the railway's purpose. Tertiary users include the maintainers and cleaners who should be accommodated to suitably perform their essential duties.

Beyond this categorisation, it is also key to acknowledge and provide for the wide variability presented by all users. It is rarely adequate to consider only the so-called 'average' (50th percentile) user. Indeed, Bailey (1982) reports a classic experiment, which actually demonstrated that no individual is average. A total of 4063 men were classified according to ten measurements used in clothing design and not one was found to be average in all ten dimensions and less than 4% were average even in the first three. The average size person simply does not exist. Pheasant and Haslegrave (2005) explain the differing sizes of populations and the need to design solutions that accommodate all user sizes between the 5th percentile (smaller) and 95th percentile (larger) users. There is a wealth of 'anthropometry' (body size) data available to help the designer and provider ensure this minimum physical provision.

With more recent increased awareness of those with impairments and disabilities there is, perhaps, a growing expectation to provide 'accessible' design or even to create 'inclusive' products and environments for everyone, regardless of age, gender or circumstance by working with users to remove attitudinal, political, social and technical barriers.

Irrespective of the level of provision and intent, it is also vital to recognise that users of the railway vary in many more ways than their shape and size. Staff and passengers present differing ages, ambitions, desires, emotions, experience, genders, psychological characteristics, roles, skills and so on. All should be considered and accommodated. At the heart of this is consultation with users through the design and implementation processes; an ergonomic railway is not created by designing and providing a system based on tables of data and our own assumptions, but by understand and addressing the range of user characteristics.

19.3 Activities and Tasks

From depot to shopping mall there are numerous activities performed in the use of the railway by the different types of users noted above. Efficiencies will be compromised if passengers cannot easily find their way through the process from identifying which train they want to catch to disembarking at their destination. Risk will be increased if staff workplaces, public facilities and vehicles do not consider human behaviour; including concepts such as foreseeable misuse (the things we shouldn't really do, but do anyway, e.g. prising off the paint tin lid using a screwdriver?). Occupational ill-health will develop if due consideration isn't given to the postures and movements of maintenance staff and drivers. To gain optimum human factors, the detail of these activities needs to be understood and reflected throughout the system.

A common and effective technique to better understand tasks and activities, principally by adopting a technique of progressive re-description, is that of hierarchical task analysis. This method enables tasks to be broken down into bite-size chunks so that specific problems or weaknesses can be identified and targeted improvement measures be implemented to see an overall improvement to the performance of that task. Hierarchical task analysis has five stages, as shown in Figure 19.1.

Describing the actions in 'neutral' terms, that is without specifying particular body parts or techniques allows them to be considered in ways which do not unnecessarily exclude particular people with, for example, specific reduced capabilities. This aids accessible and inclusive design.

19.4 Use of Equipment

Like users and activities, properly understanding the issues of providing fit for purpose equipment is the foundation of a usable and safe rail system. Again, the issues crosses both staff and passenger needs. Control centres are perhaps an obvious starting point given their core role in keeping the system running and responding appropriately to abnormal situations. But the ticket machine that isn't accessible can lead to frustration, delays and have a negative effect on passenger flow. Inappropriate hand-holds or grips on items that have to be moved can lead to injury and ill-health through increased manual handling risk.

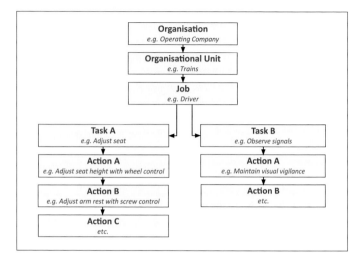

Figure 19.1: *The key stages of hierarchical task analysis. D. Hitchcock.*

In this context, equipment might be described as fit for purpose if it:

- Performs the functions intended by the designer. In other words, its features are realised according to the end-user's needs.

- Performs in the manner expected by the user. In other words, it operates according to the convention known by the user and within their capabilities.

- Is accessible and usable for all its target users.

- Is so designed that its size and shape facilitates good fit and reasonable comfort for the user.

- Presents no undue risk to the user.

- Presents no undue risk to other people who interact with it, including members of staff, members of the public, children, installers and maintainers.

- Allows for reasonably foreseeable misuse.

- Operates satisfactorily throughout its life cycle.

19.5   Environment

In many ways it may be the environment that can cause an otherwise well designed solution to be compromised, or even fail. Passenger information systems that go unnoticed by people on the concourse because of inappropriate placement within the station. Signage that is confused by the amount of 'visual noise' caused by hoardings and advertisements surrounding it. Important displays in the cab, which the driver struggles to read because of glare and reflections can cause distraction, discomfort and error. Ill-fitting Personal Protective Equipment, which must be worn to counter the effects of working outside, may be a source of dissatisfaction and under-performance for staff. Reduced grip caused by unsuitable gloves will increase risk in manipulation tasks. Beyond these physical limitations are the accompanying 'psychosocial' factors - an individual's psychological response to the activities they perform and the environment in which they are performed. They can sometimes appear trivial (e.g. a change of room layout, a different cleaning regime, moved storage facilities etc.) but their impact can be substantial.

19.6   Putting it All Together

It is all well and good being aware of the four factor groups described in the previous sections but the reality is that, for anyone other than the trained ergonomist or human factors practitioner, the vast range of factors can appear overly-confusing, or even too daunting, to tackle. The application can then become little more than best guess with reference to some basic anthropometry data or literature that is tried out on 'a few people in the office'. While this might be considered by some as better than nothing, inevitably the outputs can then be compromised designs that at best work only for some rather than the majority of intended users.

Furthermore, there are often limited opportunities to apply the principles to brand new designs for stations, rolling stock or even job designs. Usually, it is a question of managing existing provision; making the best of what's already in existence and prioritising improvement actions as necessary. What we need is a practical and efficient means of identifying the user needs and attending to any shortfalls within the system. The remainder of this chapter suggests how this might be done.

19.7 Gathering the Information

The nature of the ergonomics discipline is that solutions are derived from known data and information, not from assumptions. It is this that yields effective, safe and usable systems. It is, therefore, important to recognise that the majority of input should be that of gathering sound and robust information rather than heading straight into a process of creative and iterative design. As Gene Krantz (Flight Director) instructs his NASA team in the Apollo 13 movie (1995) when responding to the heavily damaged spacecraft and trying to get the astronauts safely back to earth, "Let's work the problem, people. Let's not make things worse by guessing." To 'work the problem', there are a number of fundamental ways of gathering the required information.

19.8 Walkthrough

Taking the opportunity to make an informal walkthrough an existing facility can help gain an overall understanding or feel for the place or organisation. What is being displayed on notice boards? What are the welfare facilities like? Does there appear to be a strong sense of ownership? Who are the characters? What you sense from this will need validating but a snapshot may help focus the priorities of further investigation. It's quick and it will almost certainly give much greater context than sitting in the design office or a project meeting.

19.9 Use the Available Literature

A good starting point is to review what has been done already in the area of interest. There are general and specific text books, journals, online sources, standards and guidelines that present case studies and applied ergonomics theory, which can save us needing to reinvent the wheel. Along with up-to-date anthropometric data, these can provide a quick route to solutions. A word of caution though. Unless the information can be specifically applied, it is wiser to adopt the principles advocated and involve some user testing rather than just presume that what worked in one context will automatically work in another—humans introduce too much diversity for straightforward transfer.

19.10 Watch

Good ergonomics is founded on an understanding of what people really do, not necessarily on what they are supposed to. To get a meaningful insight into this behaviour requires a combination of observation and consultation. It is possible to use direct observation in actual settings (e.g. the station concourse in question) and comparable settings (e.g. other station concourses). The information can also be gathered by video recording. In addition to the ethical issues, each approach has its relative strengths and weaknesses. Direct observation enables relatively swift capture but can promote changed behaviour from those being observed who may try to exaggerate particular actions either to perform in an untypically optimum manner or to unreasonably highlight issues of concern to them. This can be avoided by the use of video recording, but the angles of view can be limited and the amount of footage can be too excessive to practically analyse. Nevertheless, both methods can be deployed to generate this essential aspect of information.

19.11 Consult

It is unrealistic to capture observation of every important aspect of users' interactions with the system. Therefore, to ensure that all the important information is attained it is also necessary to consult with users. In essence, users will tell us some things that we will not observe and vice-versa; so this two-pronged approach produces a fuller and more reliable picture. The extent of the observation and consultation will vary according to the size and needs of the project.

Three choices of consultation are common. For issues perhaps affecting a relatively small number of people, one-to-one interviews with key users may be sufficient. More widespread consultation can be quickly gained through discussion groups in which a number of representative users can explore the issue together to find matters of agreement and disagreement.

313

An even wider consultation may be achieved through survey; but another warning—surveys can yield a lot of information but it is important to bear in mind that on many projects, relatively short deadlines and other avenues of investigation can mean that too much data actually compromises the final analysis.

Surveys can be conducted face-to-face, on the telephone, online or by the distribution of hard-copy questionnaires. Whichever, it is important to pilot all questionnaires and forms to make sure they can be understood and will collect the information needed. It is also important to make the data collection materials appealing and usable for respondents. For example, using too small a font size can be off-putting; or providing inadequate space for answers can lead to undesirably abbreviated responses.

19.12 Simulate

Simulation, computer or otherwise, can have a part to play. Simulation technology can illustrate environments and solutions to indicate and even test ideas. Some can integrate ergonomics and anthropometry data to demonstrate intended performance and sufficiency of fit. Of course, the accuracy of output is dependent on the information input and the direct involvement of actual or potential users can be limited, so there is always the possibility that impressive visualisations do not tell the whole story and do not consider

Figure 19.2: *Third Age Suit. D. Hitchcock*

psychosocial factors and the like. Unfortunately, perhaps because of the impressive look and feel of the outputs, designs can be signed off as suitable without any further user assessment. It is very important to be aware of the limitations alongside the benefits of this approach.

A second form of simulation is much more basic but seemingly rather helpful. It takes the form of those involved in the design or assessment of solutions 'pretending' to be a different type of user. This can give very useful insight to project team members. The wearing of visual impairment simulation glasses, moving around in a wheelchair or even being encumbered with the unfamiliar manoeuvring of a badly-laden children's pushchair offers designers and assessors a snapshot of just how different physical designs can look and feel from different perspectives.

With rail being a system that carries the gamut of user types, consideration of their needs is imperative. Of course, observation and consultation with real users who have real impairments cannot be substituted, but the experience of simulation offers the benefit of some first-hand experiences that can give otherwise unrecognised focus and priority to the project team. And this does not simply apply to disabilities. For example, we are faced with accommodating an ageing population, who in the main remain fully active, although they do present deteriorating physiology such as reduced joint movement, muscle strength and the ability to control rapid and accurate movements, alongside corresponding reductions in visual and cognitive abilities. Simulation of the physical reductions can be provided by what is known as the 'Third Age Suit' (Hitchcock et al, 2001).

19.13   How Much Information is Necessary?

All of this information gathering might suggest an unrealistic and convoluted process for which projects may have insufficient resources. However, there is only a need to gather enough information to tell the story. If the concern is, for example, risk of musculoskeletal injuries then, once the risk factors are understood, the investigation is complete.

19.14   Validating the Information

Ergonomics is commonly considered a 'soft' science because, in addition to objective data such as anthropometry, it also draws on subjective information in the form of perceptions and opinions. There is also, once again, the additional matter of considering a vast range of human diversity. It is, therefore, especially important to try and validate information to see where the agreements are and where the commonality lies across

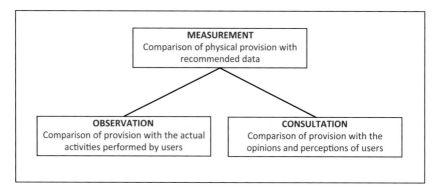

Figure 19.3: *Example Model of Triangulation. D. Hitchcock.*

the needs of the users and the delivery of the system, facility, equipment or environment. This is achieved through 'Triangulation' - the technique of using two or more sources of information and data to validate the findings of investigation. A typical model of triangulation is shown in Figure 19.3.

19.15   Using the Information

Armed with the information, it is time to move forward in the development cycle. In the consideration, appraisal or review of an existing provision, the information should be used to see how effectively (if at all) the provision satisfies the user needs. Where shortfalls are identified, the improvement measures will be driven by the same needs. This is where good ergonomics comes into its own because of its attention to the detail. By pinpointing the specific issues of concern through the investigation, it is a straightforward exercise to target those for improvement and measure the impact of the changes. This enables managed and quantifiable change rather than simply asking users, "Is this better?", "Does this work?", "Do you like it?" or other vague questions that can lead to design approval without addressing some or all of the key issues, or even, more confoundedly, finding user rejection without knowing precisely why.

In the case of designing new provision, the information generated from the investigation can be used to generate an ergonomics specification for the new equipment or facility. All too often tenders, specifications and the like identify the need for ergonomics but give no detail as to what that entails. Safety? Usability? Comfort? Efficiency? The understandable argument from designers, manufacturers and project managers is that the lack of detail leaves too much room for improvisation and even guesswork. Engineering requirements are specified in considerable detail. So should the ergonomics. Without this detail, the designer will tend to rely on what Scott (2005) describes as their intuition, citing Pheasant's (2006) "five fundamental fallacies:

- This design is satisfactory for me; it will, therefore, be satisfactory for everybody else.

- This design is satisfactory for the average person; it will, therefore, be satisfactory for everybody else.

- The variability of human beings is so great that it cannot possibly be catered for in any design; but since people are wonderfully adaptable it doesn't matter anyway.

- Ergonomics is expensive and since products are actually purchased on appearance and styling, ergonomic considerations may conveniently be ignored.

- Ergonomics is an excellent idea. I always design things with ergonomics in mind - but I do it intuitively and rely on my common sense so I don't need tables of data."

19.16   Testing Solutions

Kanis & Wendel (1990) found that "industrial designers rely on literature searches; experimentation with existing products; trials with new designs by the designers; generalised private experiences and presuppositions. None involved testing with users of existing products or of concept mock-ups." This is a fundamental problem and arguably one of the principle reasons that often, designs provide compromised solutions or, even worse, fail. Seemingly good designs that present solutions to a recognised need, offer the right functionality and have undergone rigorous technical evaluation, do not then work in their application.

User testing is an essential component of ergonomics, particularly when considering the multi-user profile of the railway. User trials enable us to evaluate designs to help ensure they are fit for purpose. They allow us to try out designs, hands-on, while conducting or simulating tasks for which they are intended.

19.17   Fitting Trials

Fitting trials use full size, unrefined mock-ups to help determine the position of elements of a design, such as controls, so that the product or equipment will fit the range of users for which it is intended. They are used when there is insufficient anthropometry data available for a particular application and/or to evaluate designs to make sure they will fit in practice.

There are four stages to conducting fitting trials:

1. Select a group of representative participants - a range of sizes of key dimensions is especially important, but also consider gender, age, roles, experience and disabilities.

2. Build a crude mock-up that can be adjusted for each dimension to be determined. Ask the participants to position items within the mock-up to the preferred (optimum) and minimum (e.g. closest) and maximum (e.g. highest) acceptable positions.

3. The protocol for psychophysical experiments such as fitting trials, is that for each of the design elements, each subject is asked to state their positions twice by being tested in both directions (e.g. lowest to the highest, then highest to lowest) because, for example, the optimum is typically higher in the ascending trial.

4. Results are analysed to determine the positions acceptable to all. This is done by plotting all of the positions for each design aspect and finding a dimension that falls between as many 'acceptable' results as possible and, ideally, close to as many 'optimum' results as possible.

In Figure 19.4 fitting trials data has been plotted to determine the height of a control; in this example, no single height is suitable. The data suggests the position needs to be adjustable between 70cm and 90cm.

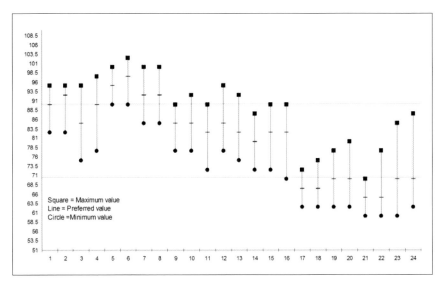

Figure 19.4: *Example Fitting Trial Output. Graphic: D. Hitchcock.*

19.18   User Trials

User trials utilise both unrefined and more sophisticated mock-ups, proto-types or even finished articles to evaluate their suitability for use by their target group. It is usually best to begin with simple card mock-ups to elicit critical feedback before moving on to higher quality ones to validate the original findings.

Figure 19.4 below shows a relatively refined mock-up constructed of MDF and integrating the genuine pedal that was being tested in the evaluation of the acceptability of a new design of Driver's Safety Device (DSD). The MDF is an accurate representation of the cab foot well and the seat is the actual model used and positioned in the real cab. To provide a degree of distractive realism, throughout each trial, the participant watched a film of a train journey with a 'driver's eye view'.

The important thing about user trials is that they assess the relevant criteria. Although this may sound obvious, it is not uncommon for designs and installations to be assessed by asking the 'big', high-level questions of stakeholders listed earlier such as "Do you like it?" These are, of course,

319

Figure 19.5: *Mock-up of train driver's cab for DSD trial. D. Hitchcock.*

likely to be among the ultimate goals but they rarely inform on the relative strengths and weaknesses of a solution, the detail of which will help ensure that the key issues are addressed.

With a discipline that ultimately endeavours to ensure system suitability for everyone (or, at the very least, the majority), it is impossible to accurate specify the precise criteria that must be considered - it is very much a case of needing to project-specific. However, in order to not leave the task too daunting or unwieldy, it is helpful to suggest some common questions that probably need to be addressed, as listed and described below.

Is it accessible?

Can all those users who need to actually benefit from the provision? Is the automatic ticket machine designed so that wheelchair users can get to it, use the controls and read the displays? Can the larger driver attain and maintain a healthy posture in the cab or do they have to squeeze their legs beneath the desk? In simple terms, can the user get to the provision in order to use it?

Does it fit?

A comparison against current and relevant anthropometric data will enable a quick check on whether or not designs will fit their intended users. Applied anthropometry data sources are available for many items from office furniture through depot tools to passenger seating. There are also transport specific guidelines available, such as the UK's Department for Transport publication 'Inclusive Mobility' (2002), which even extend the data from the 5th-95th percentile range to inclusivity.

Is it usable?

ISO 9241-11 defines usability as, "The extent to which a product can be used by specified users to achieve specified goals with effectiveness, efficiency and satisfaction in a specified context of use." Is it possible for a naïve user to navigate the online booking system? Are those in the control centre able to adjust their seats so that they receive postural support without compromising their ability to maintain vigilance? The demand for usability is extensive throughout the rail system.

Is it safe? Again this might seem an obvious factor but, from an ergonomics perspective, it should incorporate the range of interactions that will be encountered by people, so that it encompasses the fitness for purpose concept and human behaviour. Considering three categories of hazard, under both normal and foreseeable conditions, can be particularly helpful here:

- Physical hazards - things of a physical nature such as sharp edges, hot surfaces, trip conditions etc.

- System hazards - things that may cause users to act unsafely, poor task design and so on.

- Design hazards - these can arguably be described as physical or system hazards, but it is useful to specifically consider aspects that, although they may appear appropriate, because of their very design will not work (e.g. poor fit, which forces poor posture).

Is it acceptable?

Acceptability is very important. It can make the difference between an abandoned (rejected) solution and a successful one. A solution may satisfy all of the functional requirements, but if it is unacceptable to users, at best it will be used reluctantly, leading to dissatisfaction. Worse still it will be avoided - say, to choose the bus instead of the train. Unacceptability can occur for many reasons; too expensive, looks ugly, wrong colour, lack of affordance (the design aspect of an object that suggests how the object should be used), awkward to use, wrong size etc. It is a human response to a design, therefore, it should be addressed through user consultation. Beyond the concept of acceptability is the idea of 'desirability'—do users actually strongly want it? Is it attractive to them?

Does it satisfy the stakeholders?

Ergonomics should rightly be at the centre of all human interactions, but it is unrealistic and unnecessary to consider it to be the priority issue for each and every one of those interactions. Sometimes its role will be major, on other occasions less so. What is key is that at the early stages of a project the stakeholders agree the extent of its contribution so that its impact is balanced effectively with the needs of the business and its other active components.

19.19   Is it supported?

Like all good management models, the use of ergonomics should be monitored and improved as necessary in its review and refinement. People

Figure 19.6: *A Practical Approach for Ergonomics. D. Hitchcock.*

need support to understand how to make the best use of a system; initially and also often in the form of reminders. It may sound banal, but do sedentary workers actually know how to adjust their seats and what kind of posture to attain and maintain? The high level of bad backs and other musculoskeletal disorders that are consistently reported suggest perhaps not. Apply similar fundamental issues across the system and there is the potential for much under-performance and many sources of error. While some things will be intuitive, there is a need to spot where all categories of user have an essential need for information and training.

19.20   Finally - A Practical Approach

Drawing all of this together, we can define a fundamental and pragmatic approach to the application of ergonomics. A means of providing for the human factor. In concluding, the model in Figure 19.6 is suggested as a guide to the deployment and application of good ergonomics.

323

References

Bailey, R.W. (1982), 'Human Performance Engineering: A guide for systems designers', New Jersey, Prentice Hall.

Broyles Jr., W and Reinert, A. (1995), 'Apollo 13, Movie Script', available at: http://sfy.ru/?script=apollo13.

Department for Transport (2002). 'Inclusive Mobility - A Guide to Best Practice on Access to Pedestrian and Transport Infrastructure', London, 2002.

Hitchcock, D., Lockyer, S., Cook, S., and Quigley, C. (2001), 'Third Age Usability and Safety - An Ergonomics Contribution to Design', International Journal of Human-Computer Studies, Volume 55, Number 4, Academic Press.

ISO 9241-11:1998, 'Ergonomic requirements for office work with visual display terminals (VDTs), Part 11: Guidance on usability'.

Kanis, H. and Wendel, I. E. M. (1990), 'Redesigned use - A Designer's Dilemma', Ergonomics 33(4), Taylor & Francis.

International Ergonomics Association (2014), available at ttp://www.iea.cc/whats/index.html

Pheasant, S and Haslegrave, C.M (2006) 'Bodyspace: Anthropometry, Ergonomics and the Design of Work', Third Edition, CRC Press.

Scott, A. (2005), 'The Black Art of Ergonomics', in D, chapter 24, QUT School of Design, Brisbane.

Chapter 20 Aesthetics in Railway Infrastructure Design

by M. R. Zolfaghari

20.1 Introduction

The railway is a safety critical system and a significant industry, socially and economically, across the world. The railway industry is diverse and dispersed, with a complex nature. In many locations, these factors have made the railway an extensive system, requiring large numbers of staff with different cultures and backgrounds working in diverse workplaces across the country. For these reasons, the management of staff and the issues involving human factors play an essential role in the success of this industry. Having attended many field trips to different railway stations and workplaces in different countries, the author has been able to observe many human factor issues and, in particular, the effect of aesthetics within the railway infrastructure, passenger perception and the performance and productivity of staff.

Within the scope of railway infrastructure, we can include tunnels, train control centres, platforms, trackside areas, stations and internal offices. The railway environment is a mostly tightly controlled, highly disciplined area with strict regulations and complex technical features. Working and commuting in such an environment without the appropriate aesthetic considerations can affect both passenger perception and railway staff job satisfaction, productivity, health and motivation. As a result of the author's observations, a general problem in rail infrastructure aesthetics has been identified.

It is considered that a combination of art and technology can directly affect railway employees' long term physical and mental health, job satisfaction, productivity and motivation (Kwallek, 1998). These can also profoundly affect passenger perception and therefore station functionality. There have been a number of studies regarding the effects of aesthetics on passenger perception but the author is not aware of a similar study investigating the effects of aesthetics on staff motivation. For instance, the Metro of Napoli in Italy has recently undergone significant artistic and innovative refurbishments (Figure 20.1) but the author was unable to find any study or investigation that had been conducted into the effects of these changes on staff performance and motivation.

Figure 20.1: *An example of an aesthetic feature applied in the Metro of Napoli. Photo: F. Schmid*

In order to test the effects of aesthetics of railway infrastructure on staff motivation, health and job satisfaction, the author conducted a practical survey. In parallel, the affect of design parameters on passengers would be considered. However, this is a complex topic that requires an academic review, an understanding of organisational psychology concepts and a knowledge of different aesthetic features and of survey techniques.

Figure 20.2: *An example of, perhaps excessive, aesthetics for interior decoration in an elaborate classical style at Sao Bento Station, Porto, Portugal. Photo: M. R. Zolfaghari*

The most important aim of this particular study was to find a tangible relationship between workplace aesthetics and staff behaviour. The author believes a good understanding was achieved of what changes can be made within a limited timeframe, budget and official permissions. The activities and studies were focused on study fields at railway stations and internal offices.

20.2 Literature

In order to investigate the effect of aesthetics of railway infrastructure on passengers and railway staff, there are some useful concepts and parameters that need to be considered. There are also some findings from previous researchers active in this field that can help the conduct of a precise practical study in this field. Clegg (2000) presents a socio-technical model that emphasised modern technologies and the industrial segment (Figure 20.3). However, the amount of concentration on the physical design of the workplace is limited in this concept.

Cognitive performance can be considered as another factor in the study of the affect of infrastructure aesthetics on people. Cognitive performance refers to the behaviour of staff, such as short-term and long-term memory and the ability to process information. To survey the effects of the

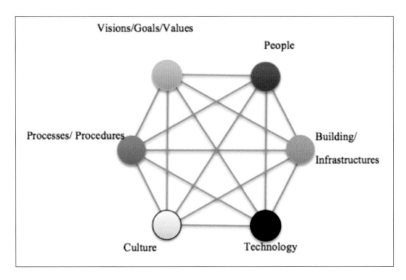

Figure 20.3: *Diagram of socio-technical system, illustrating the Inter-Related nature of an organisational System (Clegg, 2000). Diagram: M. R. Zolfaghari*

aesthetics on people in stations, metros and other railway infrastructure components, cognitive performance should be considered and measured. This concept can play a significant role in the design process of rail stations, control rooms, offices and platforms.

Wickens (2010) presented a diagram (Figure 20.4) that could demonstrate the information process procedure by humans. This diagram illustrates that the physical environment can affect people psychologically. The author applied this concept in the survey to measure the effects of the work environment on the accuracy, performance, quality, productivity and physiological health of railway industry staff. Apparently, these effects can be generalised also to apply to passengers and commuters using railway infrastructure regularly. As an example, the author realised that the perception by a person of the station and platform environment and his/her general perception of the whole journey, can affect the performance and feelings of that person for the rest of the day.

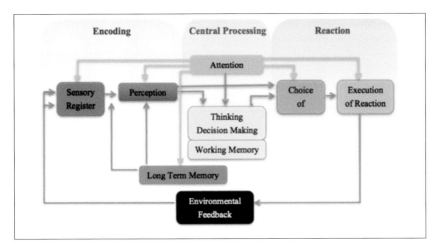

Figure 20.4: *The Procedure of Information Process, (Wickens, 2010).*

20.3   The Effects of Colours in the Workplace

There have been many studies about the effects of colour on the psyche and attitude of humans. During recent decades, the fact that humans must spend much of their lifetime in an enclosed environment, such as an office, has prompted scientists to study better approaches to the design of workspaces, which are more innovative, relaxing and motivating. One of the most important requirements to achieve such an aim is to understand the effects of the workplace environment on employees. In the last two decades some studies have been performed in closed office environments in order to investigate the impact of colour on the health, productivity, job satisfaction and performance quality of staff (Kwallek, 1998, 2002-2005). One of the study topics was which colour or combination of colours increases staff performance quality and health in enclosed offices. Most of the studies were focused on monochromatic, single and bright colours and the subjects had limited interaction with the studied colours. The impact of colours on staff would dramatically vary over a long term examination (Klitzman,1989).

One of the most important debates is on the choice of colour that gives the best moods, productivity and perception. Generally, studies have demonstrated that the colour type and scheme alone does not have an apparent effect on productivity. However, if the personal abilities in screening environmental incentives were considered, the types and scheme of colours show some differences in productivity and efficiency (Kwallek, 2002-2005). The author has applied these concepts and other applicable findings by Itten (1996) in their own survey approach. Each colour has some individual emotional effects.

The exact emotional effect of a certain colour is widely variable based on individual attitudes, mental moods and cultural background. The effect of colours changes with the surrounding colours at the work office. For instance, working in an office surrounded by green colour and light is completely different from having some small pieces of green colour in some parts of the office. The interesting point is that it is difficult for individuals to precisely explain their perception of the emotional effects of a specific colour (Itten, 1996). In the aesthetic design process of this project, the ideas of Johannes Itten, Swiss expressionist painter and designer, and the physiological effect of colours, have been applied.

The author theorised that aesthetic considerations should be taken into account in the rail industry because they have a profound effect on passenger perception and staff motivation. They can also affect health, job satisfaction and productivity. In the study, the author chose to focus on the impact of aesthetics on rail industry staff motivation because it is a relatively new subject. Most of the previous studies were conducted into the subject of passenger perception.

20.4   Definition

One of the most challenging considerations in this study was the definition of 'aesthetics', because it was necessary to define the framework and aspects of the project. The author defines the aesthetic as 'Proper use of available space, equipment and environment to get the best results in terms of visual aspects, interior design and staff perception and consequently more efficiency using a mixed of artistic and psychological and sociological sciences to design a workplace.'

This, obviously, is not a comprehensive definition as this topic is a very complex with many different aspects that cannot be covered in a simple definition. On the other hand, this definition uses the term 'available' for space and some other parameters, because of economic considerations. This definition mostly works for improving existing rail industry infrastructure with minimum costs and design effort. Nevertheless, to achieve better aesthetics, it is apparent that stations, underground areas and other rail industry workplaces should be designed considering the aforementioned mixed of various sciences.

20.5   Research Procedure

Of course it was not feasible to change architectural structure, lighting systems or interior designs for this research but it was possible to create a similar effect by adding some simple aesthetic features such as pre-prepared A0 sized posters — employing knowledge of the effect of colours on staff and the environment of the study site — which were then displayed in certain stations, platforms and control rooms. The chosen sites for this research were in the Birmingham area, UK.

As a first step, a questionnaire was prepared, based on philological and organisational behaviour studies. At each site, interviewees were selected for two interviews. The first was based on the prepared questionnaire. The intention was to design a questionnaire that avoided prejudice and did not influence the interviewees. After the first interview, aesthetic features were applied in some parts of offices, platforms and study sites, encouraging people and employees to participate in the procedure. For approximately five to six days at study sites, investigations were carried out on the reactions of staff and people to the applied changes. After one week, a second interview was conducted with interviewees to investigate the effects of the aesthetic changes on their moods, feelings and motivation and perception. The questionnaire was consistent but the order of the questions was varied depending on the interviewees' moods and the line of discussion. The results were analysed, based on the studies and the information acquired.

The findings from the literature reviews were used to prepare a comprehensive questionnaire involving the majority of people with various characteristics and expectations and containing different aspects of aesthetic considerations. There were some considerations when designing questions. Firstly, the questionnaire should not lead the interviewee. In other words the questionnaire must not be biased. For instance, most

Figure 20.5: *Part of Birmingham New Street Station during refurbishment showing the difficulties in providing a good visual impact in a railway environment. Photo: M. R. Zolfaghari*

staff were not familiar with the effects of aesthetics on their productivity, health and satisfaction, therefore questions must not convey this to the interviewees.

Based on studies seen in the literature review, the author decided to ask the questions in different orders depending on each individual's mood, answers and perception. The author believes that following this approach, better results could be obtained rather than by using a formal interview. It was not practical to make the perception of staff of their workplace environment measurable, however the author decided to ask the interviewees about how much they enjoy working in their workplace using a scale of one to ten. It was initially considered that this might be not be a sufficient measurement; however, during the survey and interviews the author realised that interviewees do think deeply about this question and were careful about marking their satisfaction of the workplace. The author strongly believes that these marks could be considered as a reliable reference.

After this phase, the relevant workplaces for study were chosen. Four rail industry workplaces in the Birmingham area of England were chosen: The

Network Rail central office located in the Mailbox building in Birmingham; the Network Rail executive office in New Street Station; the New Street station area (platforms and control rooms) and finally the Railway Research office of the University of Birmingham.

The New Street Station Office was an old-fashioned and poorly designed office with no natural light, old-fashioned architectural aspects, insufficient artificial lighting, no natural ventilation and some mostly dark areas. Platform offices were in a critical condition. In the author's opinion, dim, old and damp offices can seriously affect staff health and their job satisfaction. It also can affect platform staff attention at work. Simple rectangular corridors, with no harmony with ceilings in terms of colour and design, is one the biggest negative aspects from the architectural perspective. On the other hand, the design had no access to natural light. In recent studies, it is stated that modern architects should try to make optimum use of natural light. This has two main advantages: energy saving and improved perception.

As the author wanted to carry out the research in various railway industry scenarios, a study site was chosen at the Network Rail central office in Birmingham, the nearby Mailbox Building and the Network Rail offices based in New Street station.

The most important consideration for the author was choosing posters that could improve the moods of staff and help them to recognise and think about their workplace environment. As a first step, some staff were chosen for an interview, after which the posters put up on the walls in suitable locations, which are more likely to be seen by staff. For instance in the Network Rail office in the Mailbox, the study looked at a workplace for staff working at computer monitors. Some posters were placed within the sight of staff to test the effect of them on sight accuracy and brain relaxation after looking at monitors for a long time.

The walls of the basement floor of the Network Rail office was covered with industrial paintings related to the rail industry and second reason was that the author wanted to try and examine his theory with pure aesthetic aspects not focusing on a specific branch such as industrial art. The author chose posters giving sense of calm, motivation and relaxation. For instance there is a picture of a family in balloon. The author chose that picture because he believed that this can remind staff of their family and it was interesting that two of staff stated the same after the second interview.

Figure 20.6: *Network Rail Central Office, Birmingham: Applying aesthetic features by use of posters. Photo: M. R. Zolfaghari*

The other study area was New Street station platform control offices. New Street station platforms have some small control rooms with two staff in each one. These rooms are in poor condition and the author believes that they need serious changes and are not suitable to be used as workplaces, especially for such critical jobs. The author tried to put up some posters in some of these rooms. Even though these changes were small, they were said to make staff happier about their workplace. There is no aesthetic consideration in those rooms. Everything is disorganised but, in spite of that, the systematic work proceeds well. However, dirty walls, unorganised wiring, no sunlight and lack of activity space can seriously affect job performance and job satisfaction.

Because of local limitations, it was not possible to apply these aesthetic changes to other parts of the station, but an informal survey was conducted around the station to investigate staff views in various work conditions.

Lack of external windows to admit daylight is an obvious feature of Birmingham New St station (Figure 20.7). In the internal offices, the lack of windows is compensated for by ventilation systems opening into the office areas. Various ducts recirculate air, but these systems are old and on the top floor, there are some fast food restaurants and coffee shops, so the air being blown into the office carries food odours. At lunchtime, when these restaurants are more active, staff prefer to leave their office of because of

Figure 20.7: *Birmingham New Street station concourse area - before refurbishment. Photo: M. R. Zolfaghari*

the food smells. It can be said that even this issue should be categorised as an aesthetic consideration, because it is not a satisfactory use of architecture and design. Thus, the application of good architectural science could avoid such problems in a work place. It is obvious that this problem can affect on staff performance in the long-term it will influences staff and passengers' health and satisfaction.

For the existing design of New Street station, the large concrete columns could be decorated to soften their external image. With the application of suitable architectural design, they could be finished as a rounded shape or circular column. For both staff and passengers, the environment could be improved if these columns were covered by alternative finishes. For instance, if there are eight columns in the station, there could be eight large paintings or posters that could be rotated every three or four days to provide variety and interest.

In addition, the finishes of walls in the station do not have any kind of harmony or aesthetic value. These free spaces are mostly allocated to advertisements. The author believes that station mangers should consider the types of advertisement when they sign contracts. They should oblige companies to apply artistic ideas in their advertising so that, in addition to financial benefits, there can be positive aesthetic benefits. The author believes that changes can profoundly affect station functionality, staff performance and passenger perception.

In designing future workplaces, the author proposes the preparation of a comprehensive handbook, including aesthetic considerations and workspace design in terms of human factor issues. The handbook should be a code of practice to be followed when a new workspace is constructed and used in the rail industry. It must cover all of the aspects of human expectation within a workplace, with regard to temperature, aesthetic requirements, lighting, including the use of natural daylight, sufficient private work stations and noise isolation. Choromatalogy, using proper colors for specific workspaces depends on function of each section of a workplace, compulsory regulations to use visual arts such as paintings, statues and architectural features and other features.

20.6   Office Survey Findings

The study led into some interesting findings. The vast majority of rail industry staff in the UK are technically well-educated. They are interested in and enjoy their jobs, even in difficult circumstances. However, they are not educated on the impact of the work environment and conditions that affect their motivation, job satisfaction, productivity and health. When asked whether they had any suggestions for aesthetically improving their workplace, a surprising response amongst employees was "I have never thought about it before". The author noted that, although many people obsess about diet to keep healthy and in shape, few are concerned about the effect that their workplace environment has on their mental health or the effect that aesthetics - even in technical workplaces - could have on their well-being.

The author found that most of staff naturally appreciated aesthetics in their workplace but, because of everyday priorities and circumstances, financial benefits often replaced inherent expectations and needs. Unfortunately, staff are not aware that by considering their workplace environment they can improve efficiency and well being during working hours.

Figure 20.8: *The train control centre office in Porto, Portugal. The simple poster on the wall offers an example of aesthetics provided for staff. This is a simple and low cost approach, as proposed in this study. Photo: M. R. Zolfaghari*

Furthermore, some managers consciously neglect this concept due to the additional costs that it might entail. Proper education and financial justifications for such considerations should be included in future educational staff programmes.

The reaction of staff to aesthetic changes can be categorised into three groups; those who are enthusiastic to the change, those who are indifferent and those who are reluctant to change. It was observed by the author that after the changes had been made and then discussed, even the staff that were initially reluctant to change became interested in the change and workplace improvements. Of course, there were some employees who were insistent on their opinions but, by comparison, the percentage of staff who adopted a more positive view was considerably higher. Some of the more reluctant staff initially disagreed with the changes but, after the first interview, they specifically chose to participate in applying the changes. This demonstrates that if employees are informed of the reason for the implementation of changes, they are likely to change their minds and try to improve their workplace and consequently productivity will be increased.

Quality performance is very important to the rail industry, which is safety-critical and relies heavily on health and safety processes. Identifying approaches to improve performance can therefore help to assure the safety and performance of the whole system. The author believes that there is a strong justification for the costs of implementing aesthetic changes in the workplace. In addition, if managers can motivate staff to help with the process of improving the workplace, there would be a cost saving for the implementation of changes. Based on the author's experience from this study, staff enjoy participating in the improvement of their workplace.

From the study, the author found that about 65% of staff were open to change. They sometimes stopped to look at the posters and talk to their colleagues about the changes. The author believes that this automatically increased the interaction amongst staff and made their relationships friendlier. If these changes were on a larger scale and the employees were involved in the process it could obviously increase the spirit of cooperation and create a united society of colleagues. At the end of the survey

Figure 20.9: *Arch shaped ceiling in a railway station, Kashan, Iran. This is a complicated and artistic arrangement but the whole concept could be used in the design of new stations and workspaces. Photo: M. R. Zolfaghari*

period, about 60% of staff personally proposed changes to be applied to offices. Some suggested large-scale, industrial, artistic photos; some suggested that each office could have removable frames containing posters that staff could swap to different areas of the office during the month. The use of cheap, coloured wallpaper was another suggestion. Staff believed that these approaches could keep costs low and encourage managers to apply aesthetic changes to rail industry offices. Some 60% of staff offered suggestions for changes that could be applied to offices.

20.7 Aesthetics in Design

In this small survey, the author has shown how improvements in station and office design and decor can improve perceptions of work for staff and of travel for passengers. If tackled at the design stage with an architectural approach, the results can be more cost effective and can cover wider areas. The author visited some aesthetically designed stations and got much inspiration from them. These pictures give some ideas on good concepts and suggestions for the design of new stations and rail industry work places.

Figure 20.10: *Rato Station, Lisbon, Portugal, using simple and low cost visual effects and local lighting, to provide a good platform aspect. Photo: M. R. Zolfaghari*

In one example, we find that in Persian historical and ancient architecture, the use of arched ceilings was very popular because it was believed that the geometrical shape of the arch is attractive to the eye and gives a sense of lightness, relaxation and movement to the person. Figure 20.9 shows a sample of arch ceiling recently built in Iran. It is a mix of ancient and modern Persian architecture. The author strongly believes that the approach can open new horizons to designers. The preparation of such a handbook can be recommended as a future study, especially focusing on architectural issues and interior design for railway premises.

In another example, the use of wall decorations has been integrated into the platform design of Rato Station, Lisbon, Portugal (Figure 20.10). As is clear from the photo, the use of simple and low cost visual effects and sympathetic local lighting has provided a beautiful platform for both passengers and staff. These kinds of aesthetic effects can easily be used in design of new rail offices and stations.

The Prieto Station in Bilbao (Figure 20.11) has a large glazed wall over the entrance between the platforms and the station concourse. This type of decoration demonstrates the investment of the community in public facilities and helps to provide a sense of value and security.

In the case of Bordeaux station, the mixture of classical and modern architectural themes with special lighting has provided a warm, calming and friendly environment that leads to a good perception for passengers and staff working there. The use of simple but artistic features on the ceilings and walls provides a totally different appearance resulting in unexpected visual benefits.

20.8   Conclusions

In this chapter, the author has provided some ideas regarding improvements to workspaces, stations and railway infrastructure generally and the value of applying aesthetic considerations to railway premises. In particular, the author includes the following ideals:

- Continuous education about the impact of station environment and the effects of applying aesthetic considerations should be added to the technical and organisational education system of the rail industry. Managers and governmental bodies must be appraised of the benefits of aesthetics applied in stations. This can reduce the costs of possible human-based faults and the costs resulting from mental and physical damage to staff. The primary cost of this education and the improvement to workspaces, would be compensated by future productivity and the enhanced reputation coming from positive passengers' perception.

- Encouraging staff to participate in improving and refurbishing railway workspaces. This will result in many benefits. First, it can reduce the costs of improved staff performance and second, it can increase the sense of co-operation and friendship amongst staff.

- Railways should engage local artists including interior designers, painters and lighting experts to propose improvements to small stations and railway workplaces. In this way, the costs of designing and implementing refurbishment would be reduced and a better workspace can be constructed. This can help to ensure the productivity, health and job satisfaction of staff.

- For existing infrastructure, ways to provide economic refurbishments include painting walls with water soluble, cheap bright colours, using lighting filters to localise and change lighting level and colour; using big size posters as visual arts in workspaces, using low-cost wallpapers and using low cost carpets for damaged floors. Similar approaches can be applied to workspaces that do not need major refurbishments or workspaces with high risk of damage or pollution, such as train depots. For more important workplaces needing major changes, a total refurbishment is essential. A good example of this kind of place is Birmingham New Street station.

- The author recommends use of arch shaped and high ceilings with carvings or mouldings to make attractive and innovative workspaces. Creating arch shape ceilings gives a sense of being in a different space, which is totally different from being under a simple rectangular ceiling.

The author believes that this study has shown a rational justification for managers and designers of railway industry to consider aesthetic features in their plans. Also the findings of this research can help to encourage the production of a comprehensive handbook for design of future stations and other premises so as to improve passenger perception and staff productivity in the rail industry.

Figure 20.11:
*Prieto Station,
Bilbao, Spain,
showing dec-
orated glazing
over the sta-
tion concourse.
Photo: M. R.
Zolfaghari*

References

Collins, B. (1993). 'Evaluation of Subjective Response to Lighting distri-
butions: A Literature Review'. NISTIR 519. Gaithersburg, MD: National
Institute of Standards and Technology.

Evans, G. W., & Johnson, D. (2000). 'Stress and open office noise'. Journal of Applied Psychology, 85(5), 779-783.

House J. S. (1981), 'Work Stress and Social Support'. Addison-Wesley,
1981.

Klitzman, S. J. M. S. (1989), 'The impact of the physical environment on
the psychological well-being of office workers', Maxwell Pergamon Macmil-
lan Plc: 733-742.

Kupritz, V.W. (2003a). 'Accommodating privacy to facilitate new ways
of working'. Journal of Architectural and Planning Research, 20(2), 122-
135.

Kwallek, N., Lewis, C., & Robbins. A (1998), 'Effects of office interior
colour on workers' mood and productivity'.

Menzies, D., & Bourbeau, J. (1997), 'Building-related illnesses'. New
England Journal of Medicine, 20, 1524-1531.

Rae, M. (Ed.).(2000). IESNA Lighting Handbook, 9th Edition. New York: Illuminating, Engineering Society of North America.

Rashid, M. & Zimring, C., (2008). 'A review of the empirical literature on the relationships between indoor environment and stress in health care and office settings - problems and prospects of sharing evidence'. Environment and Behaviour 40 (2), 151-190.

Schauss, A. (1979). 'Tranquilizing effect of colour reduces aggressive behavior and potential violence'. Journal of Orthomolecular Psychiatry, 8, 218-221.

Witterseh, T., Wyon, D.P., Clausen, G., (2004). 'The effects of moderate heat stress and open-plan office noise distraction on SBS symptoms and on the performance of office work'.

Yudelson, J. (2009). 'Green Building Trends: Europe'. Washington, DC: Island Press.

Zalesny, M.D., & Farace, R.V. (1987). 'Traditional versus open offices: A comparison'.

Bibliography

Building Design. http://www.buildingdesign.co.uk/elec-technical/profile-t1/profile-building-regulations-effect-on-lighting-design.htm.

'Color and Scenic Images in Workspaces', Journal of Environmental Psychology.

Dabholkar, Pratibha A. (1996), 'Consumer evaluation of new technology-based self-service options: An investigation of alternative models of service quality'. International Journal of Research in Marketing, 13 (1), 29-51.

Elsevier, Transportation Research Part A: Policy and Practice, Volume 42, Issue 4, May 2008, Pages 709-717.

Gibson, J.J. (1979). 'The Ecological Approach to Visual Perception'. Boston: Houghton Mifflin.

Heydari, S., (2009). 'Architecture and Lighting'. Tehran University Publication, Tehran.

Kenney, D. J. (1987). 'Crime, Fear, and the New York City Subways: The Role of Citizen Action'. London: Praeger.

Lam, W.C. (1977), 'Lighting and Perception as form givers in architecture'. McGraw-Hill, New York.

Owenz, B., (2000), Daylight in Architecture.

Merleau-Ponty, Maurice (1962/1945) 'Phenomenology of perception'. London & New York: Routledge & K. Paul Humanities Press.

Network Rail, 'The Value of Station Investment, Research on Regenerative Impacts', Report: November 2011.

Ross, J C (2000) 'Railway Stations: Planning, Design and Management', Architectural Press, Oxford (350pp).

Uzzell, D, Brown, J, & Breakwell, G. (2000). 'Public Perceptions and Attitudes Towards Crime, Safety and Security in Three International Railway Stations: Waterloo, La Gare de Lyon and Roma Termini', Report to the International Union of Railways, Paris.

Wickens, C.D. &, Hollands, J.G. (2000).'Engineering Psychology and Human Performance', third ed. Prentice-Hall, Upper Saddle River, NJ, USA.

Chapter 21 Environmental Impact Assessments

by Diana Kabeizi

21.1   Introduction

Environmental Impact Assessment (EIA) is the analysis and evaluation of possible environmental consequences of future decision or activities likely to cause significant effects on the natural environment (land, air, water, plants, animals, etc.) and the manmade environment e.g. buildings, heritage sites, settlements and cultural monuments. EIA is also defined as the systematic identification and evaluation of the potential impacts of proposed projects, plans, programs or legislative actions relative to the physical, chemical, biological, cultural and socio-economic components of the environment. The assessment helps in providing data for informed decision making and measure implementation to alleviate and lessen the likely effects and thus protect the environment.

An EIA is carried out for any project that will have significant environmental effects. These may be classified as short and long term (duration of the effects); positive (increase in economic activities) and negative (resettlement of species and human population); direct (construction and operations activities e.g. resettlement); indirect (transport related like water, air, land pollution); small scale or regional, cross-boundary; cumulative and temporary or permanent (are the effects reversible or irreversible?) effects. In most cases the EIA will have been linked to the Environmental Management System (ISO 14001:2004).

21.2 Statutory Requirements

The Statutory Instrument 1999 No. 293: 'The Town and Country Planning (Environmental Impact Assessment) (England and Wales) Regulations 1999', sets out activities and developments under Schedule One that require a mandatory EIA. It includes railways under, 'Construction of lines for long-distance railway traffic.' Schedule Two mandates an EIA for all other activities and projects that will have significant environmental effects like: "Construction of intermodal transshipment facilities and of intermodal terminals and construction of railways (unless both of these are stated in Schedule One) where the area of development is over 0.5 hectares for the former and one hectare for the latter."

Thus, an EIA should be carried out for projects like urban and rapid transit railways, light railways, metro and tramways because they all involve a substantial investment and they are likely to have significant impacts on the environment. The EIA ought to be undertaken in accordance with the requirements laid down by the Transport and Works (Applications and Objections) Rules 2006 (TWA), which are a means of authorising guided transport schemes such as the construction and operation of railways and tramways.

The TWA order procedures are associated to the European Union Directive (85/33/EEC as amended by 97/11/EC also Article 3 of Directive 2003/35/EC), which requires members to assess the significant environmental effects of public and private projects, and derive mitigation measures through compiling an Environmental Statement (ES). An ES provides the public, project funders, planning authorities and other interested parties all information about the project that might impact the environment and alternatives or measures that will help reduce or minimise the effects. Project funders reserve the judgement on whether an EIA is required or not at the screening and scoping stage, the also require an approved Environmental Statement to consider application for funds.

21.3 The Process

The EIA for a major project like an urban railway should be in agreement with the legal requirements, supplied to planning authorities for consultation and made available to the public thereafter. It should not only focus on the physical environment but also on human, biotic and social environment and their developments. It is vital that the project is clearly described and the environmental factors that will likely be affected by the project. In recent times in Britain, both the Crossrail project in London and the High Speed 2 rail project have been through this process.

A comprehensive EIA should be carried out to:

- envisage environmental impacts of big and critical projects;

- inform decision makers on any environmental aspects pertaining a project;

- involve public participation and therefore reduce unnecessary public unrests and opposition in the course of project implementation;

- help ascertain ways of minimising likely adverse environmental effects;

- enable the process of execution of an environmental cost benefit analysis;

- avoid unnecessary costs and time wastage after early identification of probable environmental effects at the planning stage;

- increase developer and promoter's accountability process that will ensure funding of the project.

21.4   EIA in the International Context

An overview of the environmental issues relating to urban transport in an international context points to a report by the European Federation for Transport and Environment (T&E, 2008), which notes that over a thousand protected nature areas, especially bird species, are under threat from major transport projects. This observation serves to reinforce the argument that, although rail transport has lower carbon emissions than all other forms of transport, it still has effects on the environment. The report calls for the enactment of EU environmental legislation that hinders or blocks the funding of projects with adverse environmental effects.

Although EIA procedures have been widely adopted in the developed as well as developing worlds, various countries signed and committed themselves in the ESPOO (EIA) Convention. The 1991 endorsed convention came into force on 10 September 1997, focussing on those activities and projects with significant adverse environmental impacts across international boundaries. The agreement sets out procedures for members to inform, consult and discuss with each other about projects with significant trans-boundary impacts such as global warming, or any other international community environment threatening impacts. Notable among such projects are:

- nuclear power plants in Finland;

- the undersea pipeline between Croatia and Italy and

- the construction of the Channel Tunnel, the EIA of which was the first in the UK to be undertaken in accordance with the draft EEC directives.

The Channel Tunnel EIAs into air, safety, noise and air pollution did not identify significant impacts for the project. However, environmental objections were raised over the high-speed link to London that was subsequently linked to the Channel Tunnel (HS1).

21.5 Checklists

It is useful to compile a of list all the environmental items, concerns and considerations that will be taken in from the project scoping to every stage of the EIA through to its completion. The checklist should be designed by the project developer in consultation with the project environmental officer and project funders. A simple guideline for the chosen items is given in Table 21.1

21.6 Environmental Impact Assessment Process

Different projects go through different EIA phases but generally the EIA process includes designing the project objectives; identifying the likely environmental aspects and their impacts; laying out the EIS stages; EI consultation; base lining the environmental issues; setting out the requirements, impacts, mitigation procedure, assessment systems, and audits. Consideration for an EIA should start at project's inception stage and

Item	Priority	Importance	Completion
Project objectives Environmental objectives			
Environmental aspects			
Impact assessment methods			
Public consultation			
Alternative options			
Comparison with other projects			
Environmental Statement and Non technical summary			
Mitigation strategies			
Post project monitoring and Audit			

Table 21.1: *A guide checklist for an environmental impact assessment*

proceed through the project implementation phases - it must feature in the whole project life cycle. It is common practice to include information on EIA process in the ES as project environmental information for the public and other interested parties like fund providers.

21.7 Environmental Screening and Appraisal

This is carried out at the project development stage. The Project developers have to assess whether an Environmental Impact Assessment is needed or not by reviewing the project proposal against EIA requirement checklist. They can also request a screening opinion from the relevant Planning Authority with the following information:

Description of the Project
Urban projects objectives more often than not are required to be in line with the environmental issues for example "....the project will develop a safe, efficient and environmentally sustainable urban transport system". The promoters of the project have to make applications to Secretary of State or National Assembly for projects in Wales with sufficient information to enable unified decision making. In addition to the objectives, information is also required on the importance of the project. The requirements have to be fulfilled by the applicants before the projects' implementation can be approved.

Identification and Description of Environmental Aspects
The promoters have to identify any relevant information on environmental

features, natural or man-made, the destruction of which has a significant impact on the environment when the urban railway projected is finally implemented. Several environmental aspects relate to urban transport and these may be classified as physical, ecological and human or economic development.

- Physical; geology, climate, topography, soils, scenery, water bodies, air quality and noise. The physical aspects have to be carefully appraised, especially with the growing concern of the climatic aspects of major projects; the promoters are most likely to face resistance from environmentalist.

- Ecological; flora, fauna, and fisheries although a rare occurrence in urban areas, also need to be considered (where they exist) in plans to develop and manage urban railway systems.

- Human or Economic Development; consideration should be made to population in the urban areas, archaeological sites, land use, economic conditions, cultural and historical sites. Transport projects have on several occasions altered accessibility to such sites hence affected the level of economic activity and corresponding economic growth that they stimulate.

Each of the aspects should be critically examined to identify the likely significant effects the project has on them so that suitable mitigation measures are formulated for the impacts. They should be also assessed on the basis of their classification in terms of duration and whether they are direct or indirect. Environmental aspects ought to be clarified according to the nature of impact and ultimate effects.

Anticipated Environmental Impacts
Likely environmental effects can be assessed at both construction stage of the projects or at the operation stage of the transport projects. Appraisal of likely effects of the project on the environment, the extent and significance, reversibility and irreversibility and the timescale of these effects should be estimated:

- The probable physical impacts of developing, redeveloping and managing urban railways include soil erosion, topography changes, climatic changes, noise pollution, dust from construction, loss of vegetation;

- Emissions to the atmosphere (Nitrogen Oxides, CO_2) toxic, dangerous and hazardous waste spills to land and water bodies, drainage blockage, radioactive and electromagnetic releases. The effects of the pollutant should be estimated by examining the engines, types of vehicles and fuel that will be used in the projects.

- Machine operations that will almost certainly cause noise and vibrations to the surrounding environment and the after effects noise of the vehicles for example wheel screech on rail crossings.

- Resettlement and land acquisitions from residents, business, cultural heritage sites, deposit and soil nuisance to roads and blockage of walkways for example in the Thameslink 2000 project.

Impact Significance

The magnitude of a particular environmental impact can be assessed by experts or by use of qualitative and quantitative methods. Quantitative assessment methods may not always be available for different effects although they give more consistent results. Geographical Information Systems (GIS) that store, manage, analyze and presents geographic data are often used to represent the spatial attributes of railway projects even though they may be limited to just mapping and therefore do not give a comprehensive evaluation and degree of the environmental impacts. However recent developments in GIS have widened their application and use in impact assessment, For example climate change models have been combined with Environmental GIS to test the environmental effects of man-made projects on climate changes. The Esri GIS software measures and assesses the effects of projects on wildlife encroachment, or on water quality, and calculates the degree of changes over time. At this phase the actions for the impacts should be devised and tested.

Mitigation Measures

These are measures to lessen, avoid, minimise and compensate, avert or prevent significant environmental effects of the new railway. Some environmental impacts for a typical railway cannot be avoided so a plan has to be made on either alternatives or mitigation measures. The amended EC Directive on EIA requires other option and reasons why that particular option for main project has been considered. Environmental mitigation measures when suggested early enough at inception stage will reduce projects costs; avert undesirable unrest among the local community and/or action groups. This could also include decision of not developing or going ahead with the proposed project if the impact cannot be mitigated.

351

- For the physical impacts, controlling soil erosion and topographic changes, redesign of culverts and drainage systems, replanting of grass, trees or replace vegetation. Setting up soil and earth barriers will reduce runoffs and refilling areas that have been excavated during the course of construction will help reduce removal of top soils.

- Several measures have been suggested for the mitigation of CO and NOx emissions like planting of greenery at the construction site to reduce their concentration,

- For water quality and sewage management, appropriate means should be devised and water treatment plants should be used where applicable. All harmful and toxic substances should be blocked from entering water systems (surface and ground) at construction stage.

- The project developers need to avoid mixing dangerous construction material like tarmac, concrete (which will produce dust) as far from human settlement as possible. Materials, wastes and soils that are excavated should be disposed in all environmentally practice according to the set legislation.

- Avoidance of carrying out late night construction in areas where there is human settlements to mitigate noise impacts from heavy machinery.

- GIS offers tools for environmental law, ecology, land, habitat, species and pollution management before it occurs by formulating scenarios using a combination of data or even when it has occurred during the course of project implementation by organising cleanup programs.

- Projects that involve resettlement and displacement of people; early consultations with the affected people have to be agreed on with reallocation of land, relocation and compensations. During the construction period there may be an influx of workers that may socially impact the surrounding communities, suitable accommodation should be provided that will not negatively impact on the local people.

- Alternative methods to influence traffic flows like construction bypasses especially for pedestrians and cyclists, construction methods and which materials not to use, indicative routes or sites, relocation of animals or plant species can be acted upon.

- Not to construct, 'Do nothing', 'Zero option' or 'no go-ahead' with the project is the last mitigation measure usually considered when the environment impacts are adverse, irreversible and outweigh the short and long term benefits both during the construction or operation of the railway is with the project.

21.8   Environmental Monitoring and Evaluation

This is carried out during the project implementation. EIA should not stop when the ES has been approved and Environmental Permit (EP) has been awarded but measures should continue to be devised and implemented to avert effects that are likely to occur at project development and implementation phase. Constant reporting to the environmental officer is necessary to ensure that all measures have been followed. EIA should be part of every stage of a project cycle.

21.9   Environmental Audit

Periodic audits have to be undertaken to ascertain that the environmental management and planning system is being followed and that the measure proposed are yielding positive results. Proper feedback procedures after the project completion will provide reference for similar future projects. The environmental audit should reveal how well the mitigation measures were followed and the benefits achieved at the design, construction and operation of the project.

21.10   Case Study

Sheung Shui to Lok Ma Chau, KCRC, HongKong

Description
The Kowlon-Canton Railway Corporation (KCRC) Sheung Shui to Lok Ma Chau Spur Line is a branch of their East Rail route and it serves as the second rail-passenger boundary crossing between Hong Kong and the Chinese mainland. The 7.4 km line runs from the existing Sheung Shui Station of East Rail to a new boundary crossing at Lok Ma Chau

(LMC) whose aim was to relieve the increasing congestion at the original Lo Wu border crossing and to cope with the growth in cross-boundary rail passenger traffic. The project cost about HK\$656.5 million in 2002 prices, and was funded through KCRC's internal sources and external borrowing.

The Spur line was probably one of Hong Kong's most contentious environmental projects because of the nature of the land upon which it was routed and it has turned out to be a reference for all subsequent EIAs carried out for major urban railways. A full EIA for the project was undertaken and the first report was approved by the Environmental Protection Department (EPD) on 11 March 2002 with several Environmental Permits being issued thereafter. The objective of the EIA was to provide information on the nature and extent of environmental impacts arising from the construction and operation of the proposed line and related activities that were taking place concurrently.

Environmental Impacts

At an early stage of the project planning cycle, consultation was started with conservation groups, village representatives and the District Boards such as the Yeun Long Provisional District Board and the San Tin Rural Committee. There was considerable resistance and opposition from action groups but with environmental monitoring and auditing in place and mitigations agreed, the project plans were finally approved after many consultations and modifications. 'Worst case' potential environment effects were identified in the EIA reports, together with a methodology for the appropriate assessment. They included:

1. Changes in topography due to tunnelling;

2. Vehicle and air-conditioning noise due to access road construction;

3. Ecological changes of the long valley agricultural freshwaters wetland and consequent displacement of over 200 bird species and the fish pond habitats in the Lok Ma Chau area;

4. Social impacts to the villagers and local communities through land acquisitions, clearances, resumption, displacement and resettlement.

5. Feng Shui issues;

6. Noise and Water quality impact because of the passenger bridge construction;

7. Diversion of maritime traffic;

8. Blocking of water flow across the Shenzhen River and

9. Displacement of rare bird species like the Black-faced Spoonbill, Black-necked Grebe, Black-winged Stilt and Imperial Eagles

Mitigation Measures

Satisfactory mitigation measures were required before issuing environmental permits and subsequently project approval.

1. An environmental committee was selected to monitor every EI aspect;

2. The area adjacent to the railway was enhanced for commercial fishponds

3. Pollution control measures, such as establishing more vegetation for the areas affects by the construction and operation of the railway;

4. Creation of areas of freshwater wetland;

5. Temporary noise barriers were installed and

6. Water quality treatments to neutralise acid soil.

21.11   Case Study

Thameslink

Description

The Thameslink project, whose objective was "to increase accessibility to, from and through the heart of London by improving and expanding the existing Thameslink service", provides an enhanced north-south rail connection through central London by creating more tracks, upgrading train control, increasing train frequency and rebuilding stations.

The Thamelink project set out its objectives (DfT, 2006), including:

- to reduce overcrowding on existing Thameslink and other London commuter services;

- to reduce overcrowding on the Underground;

- to reduce the need for interchange between national rail and Underground services;

- to provide for the introduction of new cross-London services and

- to facilitate the dispersal of passengers from the St Pancras/King's Cross Channel Tunnel Rail Link(CTRL) Station.

Although no new routes are being built, there is significant new construction with enlargement of trackage, extension of platforms and rebuilt station facilities. There are a number of environmental impacts, such as:

1. Natural resources including ecology, bio-diversity, surface water resources, soil and ground water;

2. Cultural heritage like archaeology; landscape, townscape and built heritage;

3. Amenity and welfare for example air quality including microclimate; noise and vibration, visual amenity; transport and access; local community and socio-economic issues.

Planning

EIA consultation included over 100 organisations and many individuals, residential groups. Over 60 Local Planning Authorities were consulted. Regular meetings were held with statutory bodies and we participated in ministerial briefings, workshops and exhibitions. The principles of the consultation strategy were disclosed and widely discussed with consultees at the outset and formed part of the scoping and methodology report that was issued at an early stage in the EIA process. A number of significant design changes were made in response to concerns raised by consultees. Almost 300 formal legal agreements were entered into with individuals and organisations to protect their interests during the construction and operation of the Thameslink 2000 scheme.

21.12 Stakeholder Checklists

A useful way of ensuring that a project has covered all the required environmental issues is to compile a checklist that covers all stakeholders and includes such items as emissions, noise, road congestion, energy use, climate issues, social improvement, health, heritage and local legal requirements. Construction impact as well as project impact is likely to raise many issues, so the promoter and project management must allow for public information campaigns, local government, inspections, regulation and local campaigns against the project.

Issues will be over natural things such as bats, insects, other wildlife, flora, and water and noise pollution. There will also be costs for moving wildlife systems. There will be a struggle to overcome antipathy by engineers and operators, e.g. where bats are regarded as pests and costs that were not allowed for in the project budget. Post project, it is useful to determine if the environmental systems worked. Was it done properly? What lessons were learned and are there any new approaches to the whole thing.

References

Statutory Instruments 1999, No. 293 'The Town And Country Planning (Environmental Impact Assessment) (England And Wales) Regulations 1999' http://www.england-legislation.hmso.gov.uk/si/si1999/99029305.htm sch1 DfT ,2006).

Bibliography

Canter, L. W. (1996), Environmental Impact Assessment (Second Edition). New York: McGraw-Hill inc.

Environment, Transport and Works Bureau November 2004 [ETWB(T)CR 25/1016/97]

Environmental management systems - Requirements with guidance for use (ISO 14001:2004) a voluntary, global standard for environmental management systems governed by the International Organisation for Standardisation,the British Standards Version.

Environmental Impact Assessment And Management Edited By P. Fouracre, TRL Limited, Crowthorne, Berkshire, UK.

Muthusamy, N. and Dr. M. Ramalingam, 'Environmental Impact Assessment for Urban Planning And Development Using GIS' in Martin J. Bunch, V. Madha Suresh and T.

Statutory Instruments 1999, No. 293 'The Town And Country Planning (Environmental Impact Assessment) (England And Wales) Regulations 1999', http://www.england-legislation.hmso.gov.uk/si/si1999/99029305.htm sch1 DfT 2006).

Vasantha Kumaran, eds., Proceedings of the Third International Conference on Environment and Health, Chennai, India, 15-17 December, 2003. Chennai: Department of Geography, University of Madras and Faculty of Environmental Studies, York University. Pages 290-299.

Transport and Environment, (2008),'Nature sites at risk from EU transport projects', European Federation for Transport and Environment.

Helen Byron & Lucy Arnold, RSPB (2008), 'Trans-European Transport Network (TEN-T) and Natura 2000: the way forward—An assessment of the potential impact of the TEN-T Priority Projects on Natura 2000' http://www.birdlife.org/eu/pdfs/TEN_T_report2008_final.pdf

ESRI UK Application areas http://www.esriuk.com/industries/subindustry.asp?indID=17&SubID=55

LegCo Panel on Transport Subcommittee on matters relating to railways Sheung Shui to Lok Ma Chau Spur Line Essential Public Infrastructure Works Environment, Transport and Works Bureau November 2002

Josh, LAM Kam-Wai and Richard, KWAN Kin-Yan (2008), 'The Art and Science of EIA in Achieving Sustainability In a Hong Kong Transport Development Project', The Art and Science of Impact Assessment, May 2008

KCR East Rail Extensions Sheung Shui to Lok Ma Chau Spur Line, Train Noise Performance Test Report, October 2006

http://www.epd.gov.hk/eia/register/report/eiareport/eia_0712001/Volume1/kcrc-ss-lmc-eia-f-6980-1.htm

Ng Cho Nam (2006), Wetland compensation and EIA lessons learnt from Hong Kong.

KCRC Lok Ma Chau Spurline Mitigation Area

Dr Michael Leve KCRC Lok Ma Chau Spur Line mitigation Area, Asia Ecological consultants.

From Environmental Impact Assessment - Thameslink 2000 - Sep 03-June 04 http://www.templegroup.co.uk/key_projects/44/Environmental_ Impact_Assessment__Thameslink_2000___Sep_03_June_04.html

Chapter 22 The Sustainability of Urban Railways

by Robin Hirsch

22.1 Introduction

Railways of all kinds have always needed to be sustainable in all ways, but primarily in three ways: economically, socially and environmentally. They should be affordable to the society they serve, bring a better quality of life for as many members of that society as possible and minimise environmental damage to that society.

But they can do so much more than this: they are capable of reducing a large amount of the environmental damage that excessive road traffic can cause; they can offer reliable and punctual transfers of both freight and passengers between cities and the countryside around them and provide frequent and predictable journey times to those wanting to get around the city itself; and they can add immensely to the economic well-being of the country and the cities that they serve. No modern city of any size can function productively without an effective metro railway network: as the many city roads clogged up with traffic testify, building more roads merely leads to more traffic jams.

22.2 Environmental Sustainability

The easiest category of sustainability to achieve is environmental. Almost all urban railways run on electricity, which may be much more environ-

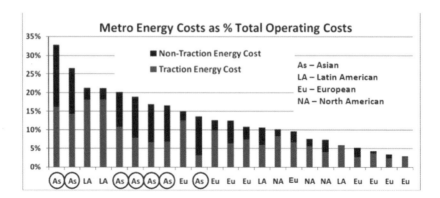

Figure 22.1: *Metro Energy Cost as % of Total Operating Cost. Graphic: R. Hirsch.*

mentally favourable than buses burning diesel fuel. But it is governments, not railways, who decide whether to use the most renewable or the cheapest sources of power generation, or to incentivise power companies to do so. Countries like Canada and Norway find it relatively easy to pursue green power policies because of the ready availability of hydroelectric power there but, in other countries, coal and fossil fuels are the main contributors and their electricity requires the use of more carbon.

This reduces the railway's advantage over road traffic, but that is outside the railway's control. Their management should not be held accountable for such differences but only for the areas they can control, such as their use of energy and especially its waste. As Figure 22.1 shows, energy intensity varies widely, from (allegedly) only 2.5% of total urban railway operating costs to as much as 33%. Even if these figures may not be fully comparable, it is indisputable that some metros have a massive potential for saving energy - especially in Asia and Latin America - by adopting best practice.

When deciding between investment in a new railway or a new motorway, it is worth remembering that railways require a relatively narrow footprint compared with new roads and are therefore less polluting than the roads and all of the motor vehicles likely to use them.

22.3   Social Sustainability

Social sustainability is also relatively simple to achieve. For less advanced and also for very large countries, freight railways are the most cost-efficient means of transporting freight over long distances quickly and easily, enabling country people to market their goods to city dwellers. If rail has a higher modal share of freight, it is also likely to reduce road congestion, which also has social benefits. The same applies to passenger services. For advanced countries with high levels of car ownership, metro and suburban railways are the only way to assure quick and punctual journeys into and around town and if most passengers travel by rail, there will be less traffic jams.

Moreover, rail travel tends to act as a leveller, enabling most passengers travelling at the same time of day to enjoy the same standard of service at a standard fare. In countries and cities that use yield management pricing, off-peak fares are considerably cheaper, thus encouraging the population to use scarce rush-hour capacity only when absolutely necessary. This encourages passengers themselves to behave in a socially and environmentally sustainable way.

22.4   Economic Sustainability - Fundamentals

The form of sustainability that is most challenging is economic sustainability. Railways cost a lot to build, urban railways even more because they must be elevated, underground or displace expensive real estate. In the years up to the early years of the twenty-first century it cost €2 billion to build 18 km of the Athens metro, €1 billion to build the first 7 km of Paris's Line 14, and €5 billion to build the 16 km of the Jubilee Line extension. The 118-km Crossrail is anticipated to cost €19 billion, a far lower cost per kilometre, largely because about half of it will not be in London itself.

These are very substantial sums. But they are by no means the whole cost of the metro. On top of the original building cost, all railways, in particular urban ones, constantly need enhancements. Extra capacity, safety, speed and comfort are among the enhancements demanded by the increasing number of passengers who want to travel on the network. Urban railways are the lifeblood of the city: without them, the city will grind

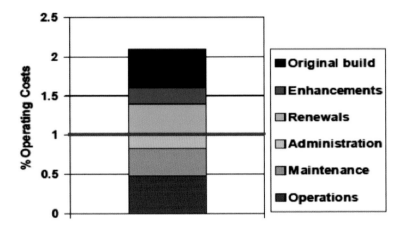

Figure 22.2: *Typical Make-up of Total Operating Cost Over Time. Graphic: R. Hirsch.*

to a halt; but with them, it will continue to grow and with the increase in its population will come a demand both for extra lines and for a more intensive service on the existing ones. As the network ages, renewals will account for an increasing amount of operating cost, even if they are treated, like enhancements, as capital expenditure. Figure 22.2 details the typical makeup of total operating cost.

It is almost always the city, central government, the regional government or all three that provide the initial build cost of urban railways and they normally cover most enhancements and renewals as well. But, with operations cost, maintenance cost and administration expenses, there are wide variations between Europe and North America on the one hand and East and South Asia on the other. In East Asia, most cities or governments expect metros to break even at the operating level or make a small profit. In Europe, with the exception of the UK, there is more emphasis by the political authorities for low fares and thus a decoupling of the profit motive. This means that the metro is constantly dependent on the local city government for an adequate subsidy to fund an acceptable amount of maintenance. This has often meant that the metro is actually under pressure to carry out less maintenance than it ought to.

As Figure 22.3 shows, out of 27 participants in a CoMET study (2010) on a model for metro railway sustainability, only eight (less than 30%)

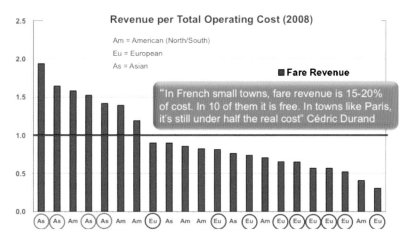

Figure 22.3: *Fare Coverage of Cost in CoMET and NOVA Railways. Graphic: R. Hirsch.*

— all of them Asian or South American — received enough fare revenue to cover their full operating cost (including maintenance and administration). This meant that these metros could therefore take all of their decisions on cost and investment on a commercial basis. All of them run very high frequency services, which are generally considered to provide excellent quality and good value for money. In general, their investment programmes were planned over a longer period of time and in most cases considered using full lifecycle cost including maintenance and future enhancements.

At the opposite end of the spectrum, four railways (15%) ran an operating loss. While in the short to medium term, these losses were in some cases plugged by the issuance of bonds, in the longer term they were totally dependent on their city or regional governments to come up with enough money to cover their deficit. As the quote from Cédric Durand in Figure 22.3 shows, this was fully accepted in many European countries and worked adequately as long as the authority generated enough tax income, but it tends to lead to high unionisation, poor discipline and low labour productivity. Moreover, as soon as that tax funding was endangered or reduced, the shortfall is passed on to the metro.

This certainly happened in New York, London and Berlin: in each case a huge backlog of maintenance built up over time, the quality and reliability of the service suffered severely, crime increased and ridership dropped off. Only after a major refurbishment effort over many years did these metros improve their assets, reliability and security and thus regain their ridership; in the case of London, resulting in a return to an operating profit.

Most railways did not declare losses even if they or their passengers were subsidised in some way or another: often, the railway operating company is paid by the city or regional transport authority to run a particular level of services. The fees are usually calculated on the expected cost to the metro company of operating the service at the target level of frequency. In this way the transport authority takes the risk that there will not be as many fare-paying passengers as expected; the metro operating company is incentivised to reduce cost in the short term to below the fee for running the service.

This is considerably better than the case where the state or city simply covers the cost of any loss, where there is neither any incentive to save money ("Oh, that would merely mean that we got less money from the government" said one manager, rejecting a good way to improve profitability) nor is there much incentive to ensure that the unions moderate their demands.

However, it does not provide any incentive to make major investments to reduce cost in the longer term. Such decisions will still be dependent on the political will of the city or regional government, who will be tempted to micro-manage the metro company, which then leads almost inevitably to a loss of initiative and motivation among metro managers.

22.5 Economic Sustainability - Key Elements in Economic Success

What kinds of metros are economically sustainable and which tend to be at risk? More than anything else, profitability is correlated with a high level of network utilisation. All profitable metros run very frequent trains and have a high modal share, linked to an adequate fare level.

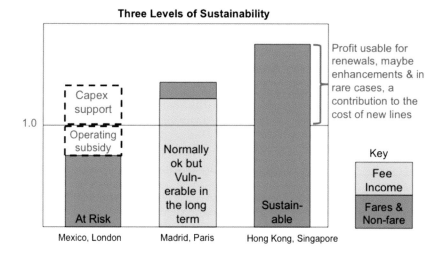

Figure 22.4: *Three Levels of Economic Sustainability. R. Hirsch.*

Up to 95% of a metro railway's cost is fixed - in the sense that the marginal cost of increasing train frequency is very low indeed up to the point when additional trains or an upgrade in signalling systems are needed. In reality, of course, fixed costs such as station lighting or administration are only fixed in the sense that running more trains will not increase them: management can often reduce them by introducing new technologies or increasing productivity.

Metros such as Hong Kong's MTR and Paris's RATP are changing over to LED lighting in stations and trains, cutting energy cost by at least 50%. (MTR's urban trains in Hong Kong cut energy by 52% with LED lighting; in Censier-Daubenton station in Paris the saving reached 65%.) RATP (2012) say that power consumption of transport spaces accounts for about 12% of their overall energy consumption, so by the end of the changeover in 2015, LEDs may reduce RATP's total energy use by 6 percentage points. Similarly, railways can reduce overhead management costs by simplifying their organisation structure and introducing automation and technology. After a benchmarking study on stations in 1998 with other metros in the CoMET group, Hong Kong MTR reduced its station staffing by between 8 and 12% across its network by reducing the number of layers of management and increasing the span of control, together with the introduction of better remote monitoring technology.

Unit costs such as passenger capacity km or car km, which are commonly used to compare the cost of one railway against another, are of course quite variable by volume. Since Unit cost=Total cost/Total Units Operated, every additional train operated within the same operating hours reduces the average cost per train. The nearer to capacity that a railway operates, both in terms of capacity per train and especially train paths per route km, the lower the unit cost and the higher the profitability of the railway (or the lower the subsidy that will be needed.)

Of course, the additional train will not be worth running if it is empty, but a higher train frequency leads to more demand for rail travel. When considering a change in frequency, a railway should analyse whether the marginal revenue (fare plus non-fare revenue) will exceed the additional cost incurred if each additional train is operated. In other words, does that train make a net contribution to fixed cost? If a reduction is considered, will the railway really make a saving greater than the marginal revenue of that train, in spite of probable union objections?

In most cases, the additional cost will consist only of the energy required to run each extra train, plus any possible overtime or productivity bonus that must then be paid to its driver. There may be a very small impact in terms of additional rolling stock maintenance, but it is likely to be negligible. Of course, if the crew schedule is running at maximum utilisation, there may be the need for an additional driver, but this will generally be the exception rather than the rule.

Whether or not there is demand for a high frequency railway will depend on four factors that current railway management cannot influence, namely demographic, competition and design of the network and stations:

1. Do most of the metro lines link densely populated areas of the city?

   - Is the city itself densely populated enough to be able to justify the metro? (Narrow corridors of population also help.)

2. How free are buses and taxis to compete with the metro?

   - How does their journey time and predictability compare with the metro?

- Are their fares regulated? Is that policy integrated and congruent with fare regulation for the metro?

- How congested is traffic on the roads parallel to the metro lines?

3. How wide apart are the metro stations?

- Frequent stations decrease productivity and increase unit cost.

- They improve accessibility to the metro but make it slower - as shown by passengers in London running from station to station to prove they can beat the train!

4. Have the stations been built large enough for long trains and with enough space in and around their access level for retail outlets to earn non-fare revenue?

If the answers to these four questions are favourable, it should be possible to run a high frequency, profitable railway if fares are set adequately high with reference to the elasticity of demand in that city. If not, no metro will be able to run at a profit and it will only be economically sustainable as long as the city is willing and able to provide an adequate subsidy.

22.6 Elements that railway management can influence or control

Asset Utilisation

As mentioned in the previous section, profitability is correlated with a high level of capacity utilisation with very frequent trains and a high modal share.

In 1999, an analysis of CoMET and Nova metros showed that profitability was not correlated with the size of the network - in fact, excessively large and complex networks tended to be less profitable - nor was it correlated with the number of passengers. The correlation of profitability with fuller trains (passenger km/capacity km) was negligible, at $R^2=0.0105$, but much stronger with intensity of operation, measured as car km per total network km, which measured $R^2=0.3356$. When the number of passengers carried was included, measured as passenger-km per route-km, the correlation was $R^2=0.4158$, as shown in Figure 22.5.

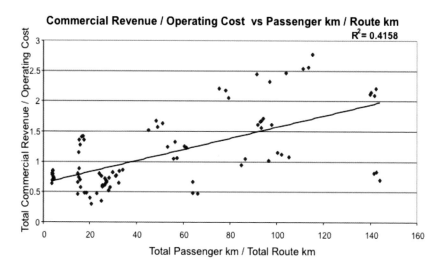

Figure 22.5: *Correlation with the CoMET Normalised Definition of Profitability. Graphic: R. Hirsch.*

The fact that the correlation between the utilisation of operated capacity (passenger km/capacity km) is so low is highly intuitive, when we consider that many metros are extremely crowded. For those metros with less frequent or shorter trains running on the network, not only will the network cost be amortised over less car km, but as the metro provides less capacity, a proportion of the potential demand (and revenue) will be suppressed as passengers choose not to travel on over-crowded trains. It is better always to anticipate the probable increase in demand and to provide enough capacity to prevent over-crowding.

This reminds of the importance of taking a fully system-wide viewpoint when targeting high asset utilisation. Ideally, a metro should aim to use all of its assets to the maximum capacity, not just rolling stock or its operating control centre but the whole of the network. As far as possible given the population density, when building extensions it should also aim to ensure that its stations and its train service are providing similar capacity and running at similar levels of utilisation, so as to avoid bottlenecks due to the inability of stations to handle the volume of passengers alighting from trains.

Fare Setting

Metro fares are a highly sensitive political issue. Virtually no metros are permitted to set fares at a revenue-maximising level and only in very few cases do fares keep pace with local wage levels. This is highly undesirable, both because it creates continually rising demand that threatens to over-take capacity and also because local wage levels drive the metro's labour cost, the most significant element of the total cost of operation.

Metros can and should continually address and attempt to improve labour productivity at least at the same rate and the most effective metros have more or less achieved this, year on year for decades. But they are not capable of keeping pace with the full rise in wages in every year in which there is an increase. Moreover, there must be a limit to which productivity can be improved indefinitely, or at least a point where it becomes more and more difficult to make any further advances.

Unfortunately, it is always politically attractive to voters to attempt to set fares at an unsustainably low level, leading to unprofitability, a decline in service quality and the need to subsidise the metro. In many cities, politicians first prevent rises and then belatedly discover fare levels are unsustainable, at which point they are forced to permit large occasional increases. This makes it very difficult for the metro to plan ahead and to follow a rational, consistent investment policy. Much money is then wasted through such inconsistency of funding and underinvestment almost always results from it.

The solution must therefore be to educate and influence the politicians responsible for regulating fares and preferably, to conclude a binding, on-going agreement with the local authority to take into account movements in the local wage level in setting fares. As an example, Hong Kong's MTR Corporation and their authority adopted the following formula:

Permissible Annual Δ Fare Adjustment $= \Delta$ [Cost Index] - P+K,

where:

[Cost Index] is mainly a function of the unit price of wages and electricity;
P = Productivity Factor is a factor that recognises the need and ability to reduce inputs over time through technology or other means; and
K provides a mechanism to invest in enhancements and capacity. The cost index selected when the fare adjustment was adopted consists of 0.5*CCPI+0.5*Wage Index,

where

CCPI=the Composite Consumer Price Index, made up of food and housing for three different levels of household expenditure.

Not only should metros and their local authorities agree such a mechanism for adapting to wage levels. Any local authority that regulates both rail fares and bus fares should also ensure that they are compatible one with another. It is completely counterproductive to have lower metro fares than bus fares, when the bus service can almost never match the metro in punctuality, reliability, speed and probably comfort, but it probably can outmatch the metro in profitability. This was the situation in Lisbon, where the authority hoped thereby to encourage more passengers to take the train rather than the bus; but generally speaking it is not fare levels that determine train ridership, but rather accessibility of a dense enough local population to the station, a route to where most people want to go and a high enough level of service in terms of punctuality and comfort.

What the metro and the authority needs in such cases is an understanding (and enough research into) the levels of elasticity of demand in the city concerned, both in terms of fares and other relevant decision factors such as service frequency, punctuality and comfort in each of the different public transport modes on offer. It should take into account the different levels of cost of time and generalised cost of travel by the types of passenger that favour each transport mode. If a metro finds that its authority is not taking such Elasticities into account, it should definitely take a lead in introducing such disciplines into the fare-setting process.

Non-Fare Revenues

As Figure 22.6 below makes clear, some metros obtain a significant contribution to their revenue and their cost coverage from non-fare revenues. While in some cities such as Beijing and New York, the political authorities are very reluctant to allow, let alone encourage, non-fare revenue in their metros or subways, in others such as Shanghai, Hong Kong, Singapore and London, a very important contribution can be made from such revenues.

In Hong Kong, the generation of additional potential sources of income has for many years been one of the key performance indicators used to manage the company. Moreover, MTR has developed a highly successful

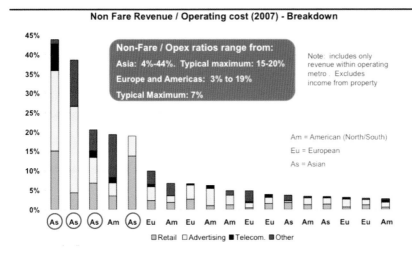

Figure 22.6: *Non-fare revenue by type of revenue. R. Hirsch.*

Rail+Property model, which has enabled MTR to develop or extend many lines with little or no capital subsidy from the state.

In the Rail+Property model, the railway works with developers to build a large city consisting of housing, offices and retail shopping malls and entertainment facilities above and around the stations. MTR has not only carried this out in Hong Kong, but has also successfully developed similar models in other Chinese cities, notably Shenzhen. Since MTR maintains ownership of some of the real estate along the rail route, it then benefits from the appreciation in the value of the land from having the metro close by. It is also able to use that property as collateral to fund loans to construct the next network extensions. In this way a virtuous circle is created.

Non-fare revenue is not, however, a substitute for a good fare policy. It will always only constitute a limited percentage of that fare revenue. Figure 22.6 shows that although some Asian metros have achieved 44% of operating cost, in most cases non-fare revenue is limited to about 20%. The growth of such revenue must never distract from the primary purpose of the metro, which is to provide a good or excellent rail service.

It is notable that only two European metros have a significant amount of such revenue, but both London and Berlin have increased this type of revenue enormously in the last two decades, having seen the successful example set by Chinese metros in particular.

Labour Productivity

As we discussed above in the section on fares, a critically important role of metro management is the progressive improvement of labour productivity, normally measured as labour hours per passenger km and per car km. This can be done in four or five principal ways:

- The substitution of technology for human manual intervention. This includes the automation of operations, from the driving of trains through the use of smartcards rather than the issue of tickets, to remote condition monitoring for assets and passengers and de-skilling of maintenance tasks by the use of augmented reality.

- Business process analysis and redesign, including the simplification of organisation structures and tasks, widening the span of control and the elimination of unnecessary tasks, for example through reliability-centred maintenance, and the elimination of waste through higher quality and reliability operations.

- Growing the size of the network so that any overhead staff can be amortised over a larger number of assets and potential revenue sources.

- Operating longer or more frequent trains, or both, so that all of the fixed infrastructure and the people working to operate and maintain it may be amortised over a larger number of passengers.

- For the same reason, it may be worth considering increasing the number of hours of operation per day or week, but this should be done with care, since it can add complexity and the need for additional staff and make it more difficult to complete track maintenance within the available time.

We indicated earlier that there may be limits to possible improvements in productivity, but in practice we find that even if the speed of improvement slows down over time, it is normally possible to go on squeezing out slightly more improvements in quality, reliability and productivity virtually on an indefinite basis.

Cost Control

As we noted above, greater intensity of operation, better asset utilisation and improvements in quality, reliability and labour productivity will all lead to lower unit costs. But there are many other ways of controlling and reducing cost, such as

- Good asset management, acquiring assets that deliver better reliability, require less maintenance, last longer, are equipped with remote condition monitoring and themselves order any necessary spare parts, but do not contain unnecessary functionality and 'gold plating'.

- Ensuring that assets, services and supplies of energy and consumables are procured at minimum total cost - which should include the cost of operation, maintenance and any risk of malfunction.

- Efficient scheduling of staff and assets, especially rolling stock.

- Appropriate use of outsourcing and subcontracting to maintain an adequate supply of skills at the same time as control over wage rates.

- The use of appropriate technology and methods of operation to minimise the use of energy.

22.7   Conclusions

All metro railways should find it relatively easy to achieve environmental and social sustainability, but few indeed will be able to be fully economically sustainable without the following:

- High enough population density, both in the city as a whole and along the metro lines, especially near the stations, to justify a high frequency train service that will be adequately full.

- Political governance that allows the metro to operate under prudent commercial principles; to set fares on a basis that takes wage rate rises and elasticity of demand into account; and to do all that it can to generate a high level of non-fare income.

- Constant improvement in labour productivity.

- Effective asset management.

- Good customer service, including a high level of punctuality and reliability.

- Tight control over cost.

References

CoMET (2010) Study presented to the World Metro Summit in Shanghai in 2010.

RATP http://www.ratp.fr/en/ratp/r_76407/led-lighting-for-ratp-metro-and-rer-stations/.

Index

379

D

F

N

O

P

389

W

Contributors

John Austin: Austin Analytics.
Carolyn Casey: London Underground.
Piers Connor: University of Birmingham & PRC Rail Consulting Ltd.
Colin Goodman: The University of Birmingham.
Nigel Harris: The Railway Consultancy Ltd.
Sonja Hedgecock: London Underground.
Robin Hirsch: Kingdom Technology Partnership.
Diana Kabeizi: Makerere University, Uganda.
Richard Morris: Positive Impact Management Solutions.
David Oldroyd: The University of Birmingham.
Holly Pike: University of Birmingham.
Felix Schmid: The University of Birmingham.
Mohammad Reza Zolfaghari: The University of Birmingham.